The Separation of Church & Freedom

(A War Manual For Christian Soldiers)

by Kent Kelly

Library of Congress
Catalog Card Number: 80-80341

International Standard Book Number: 0-9604138-0-4

Order from:
Calvary Press
400 South Bennett Street
Southern Pines, N. C. 28387

THE SEPARATION OF CHURCH AND FREEDOM
(A War Manual for Christian Soldiers)

INDEX

DEDICATION

This book is gratefully dedicated to William Bentley Ball. He began as my attorney and became my teacher and friend. He instilled in me an unusual love for the Constitution, the law and the cause of religious liberty. Without his advice and example this volume would never have been written.

SPECIAL ACKNOWLEDGMENT

Every book is the product of the efforts of many dedicated people whose names never appear on the cover. My wife Elizabeth and my children Allen, Kecia, and Kasey have invested untold patience and support in the cause.

The pastors and people of the churches of North Carolina who have stood with us, and, in particular, the men and women of Calvary Memorial Church have provided an inspiring example for me to follow in the cause of religious liberty.

The unsung co-authors of this volume are Sissy King and Scott Norman, my research assistants, and Pastor Dan Carr——all of whom invested many hours in dusty libraries, detailed discussions, and disrupted lives.

The true heroines are my mother Bessie Kelly and my secretaries Sally Davis and Gerri Taylor who were forced to wander through the maze of my manuscript to accomplish the typesetting and typing.

AN IMPORTANT WORD TO THE READER

The subtitle of this book is *A War Manual For Christian Soldiers.* Such terminology is not to be construed as an inflammatory approach to the subject at hand. Ours is a war of ideas. *"The weapons of our warfare are not carnal but mighty through God to the pulling down of strongholds."* The Bible abounds in metaphors directed toward soldiers of the Cross. We are engaged in an idealogical conflict which calls first and foremost for cool heads and burning hearts.

Our enemy is not the government. We are the government. It should be our desire with Lincoln that "government of the people, by the people and for the people should not perish from the earth." Until and unless we participate as we should in that government, our freedoms will continue to dissipate at a rate proportionate to our apathy.

Our greatest enemy is ourselves. We have a Father Who has presented to us *"the glorious liberty of the children of God"* (Romans 8:21). We have a Saviour of Whom it is said, *"If the Son therefore shall make you free ye shall be free indeed"* (John 8:36). We have the Holy Spirit of Whom we read, *"Where the Spirit of the Lord is there is liberty"* (2 Cor. 3:17). We have a Bible which says, *"Stand fast therefore in the liberty wherewith Christ hath made us free and be not entangled again with the yoke of bondage" (Gal. 5:1).* We have a form of government which is the most amenable to freedom of any ever known to human experience.

Our greatest enemy is ourselves because we tend to allow Satan, who is a defeated foe, to proclaim his gospel unchallenged in the halls of government. Satan has preached for decades that "Christians shouldn't get involved in politics," and we have believed him. This book explodes that myth and challenges God's people to stand up and be counted for the cause of Christian liberty.

Christian education is the focal point around which this book is written. Abraham Lincoln said, "The philosophy of the classroom is the philosophy of the government in the next generation." Christian education has become the object of frontal assault by men who believe sincerely in "the other religion," which is Secular Humanism. We have come to realize that the rights of Bible-believing parents to educate their children in a church context, free from state intervention, is the front line issue in our generation.

Fundamentalists MUST see the need to rally behind the Christian school movement. The church school door is the CHURCH door at which bureaucratic control is knocking across America. Some would say, "the school door is only a side door of the church"—a principle with which I violently disagree. But be that as it may, more fortresses have been entered and conquered by avoiding the front door than history could tell.

The author makes no claim to academic credentials or intellectual ability as qualifications for writing this book. This is a burden from the Lord written out of an insatiable compulsion. The research is unimpeachable, the logic is Biblical, and the style is conversational to the greatest degree possible. Literary masterpieces go down in history; only plain talk in plain language can alter the face of history.

This book is composed of three distinct sections:

Volume I — *The Theatre of War*
Volume II — *The Philosophy of War*
Volume III— *The Practice of War*

If you are new to the subject of Church-State conflict you need a warning at the very outset. After long deliberation I chose to begin with the most difficult material in order to preserve the power of logical progression. Please don't let this discourage you from reading the book.

No doubt you will find *Volume III* to be the more relevant of the three sections, since it gets down to the practical implementation of our warfare. However, as you read *"The Practice of War,"* questions will arise in your mind which can only be answered by the previous sections.

This book is designed to take you step by grueling step from the extremely complex issues of law which face us, to the final implementation of what we believe. You may be like the preacher in our state who said, "Brother, I don't know what any of this fight is about, but at least I know whose side I'm on." If things are that simple for you, *Volume III* is the first section of this book you need to read.

On the other hand, be forewarned that in your church, in the media, in the courtroom, in the community at large, you will find people who want answers. "You say you don't believe in taking a license? Why?" "What is the church doing involved in the State's business of education?" "What about Romans 13?"

This book is designed to answer all those questions and more so that you will *"be ready always to give an answer to every man that asketh you a reason of the hope that is in you with meekness and fear." 1 Peter 3:15.*

This is a textbook, a source book, and a legal analysis, as well as a batch of friendly advice; so don't jam your computer at the first sitting. Feel free to skip around from chapter to chapter if the reading gets heavy. Just keep in mind that everything in the book is an absolute necessity if you plan to be on the front lines of this battle for religious liberty.

INTRODUCTION

This book and its purpose may best be understood by identifying the men whose writings appear within its pages. From the vantage points of a pastor, an attorney, and a philosopher, you will find a composite overview of the topic at hand.

Kent Kelly is pastor of Calvary Memorial Church in Southern Pines, North Carolina and administrator of Calvary Christian School. As the author of this book, he brings to the task little more than the fact that he "has been there": Organizing Christian schools statewide; on the witness stand; coordinating nationwide research; publicly debating the issues; lobbying the State legislature and the U. S. Congress; testifying at state and federal hearings; speaking at rallies and seminars in various states; writing extensively for several publications; lobbying the news media; publishing a previous book entitled *State of North Carolina v. Christian Liberty;* overseeing mass mailings to the troops; and just making a general nuisance of himself.

William B. Ball examines the situation as a Constitutional attorney. In addition to holding a J. D. Degree from the Law School of Notre Dame University, Mr. Ball was a professor of Constitutional Law at Villanova University.

He has lectured and debated Constitutional law at the Harvard Graduate School of Education, University of Chicago, University of Minnesota, Amherst College, University of Pennsylvania, and others, as well as testifying as an expert witness before many Congressional hearings.

Mr. Ball has been a member of the Bar of the Supreme Court of the United States for 21 years, and has appeared in 14 cases before that body. He is also a member of the Bars of New York, Pennsylvania, U.S. Court of Appeals (7th Circuit), and U.S. Court of Appeals (3rd Circuit).

William B. Ball is the proverbial "legend in his own time." Mr. Ball has distinguished himself by winning more major First Amendment cases in the field of religious liberty than any attorney in the history of American jurisprudence. To mention only a few, he has won *Wisconsin v. Yoder* and *Lemon v. Kurtzman (Lemon II)* before the U.S. Supreme Court; *Ohio v. Whisner* in the Supreme Court of Ohio; *Vermont v. LeBarge* in the Supreme Court of Vermont; *Grace Brethren Church v. Marshall* in Federal Court in California; *Rudasill v. Kentucky* in the Supreme Court of Kentucky; etc., etc. Altogether he has been involved in cases in 19 states.

Mr. Ball is Chairman of the Committee on Federal Court Relations, former National Chairman of the Committee on Constitutional Law of the Federal Bar Association, Director of the Human Life and Natural Family Planning Foundation, a member of the National Committee for Amish Religious Freedom, serves on the Appellate Court Rules Committee of the Pennsylvania Supreme Court, and is on the National Advisory Board of the Center for Law and Religious Freedom. He is a member of the law firm of Ball and Skelly in Harrisburg, Pennsylvania.

Perhaps most significant of all, Mr. Ball has won a national reputation among the severest critics of all, his peers, as "the expert's expert."

Professor Rousas John Rushdoony presents his views of *The Separation of Church and Freedom* from the perspective of a Christian philosopher. Dr. Rushdoony has served as a pastor, a missionary to Chinese Americans as well as a missionary to the Paiute and Shoshone Indians.

In the academic arena he holds 3 degrees and is a frequent lecturer at colleges and universities across America. As an author he has written 26 books including *The Messianic Character of American Education, Nature of the American System, Institutes of Biblical Law, Politics of Guilt and Pity,* and *Intellectual Schizophrenia.*

Professor Rushdoony has been an expert witness in more than 14 states in litigation involving Christian schools. He has an unusual ability to analyze the all-too-often abstract philosophical thrust of fundamentalism and apply it to the real world.

He has lectured widely, stood for the truth narrowly and contributed immeasurably to the intellectual horizons of present day fundamentalism.

5,000 gather in Raleigh, N. C. for Christian school court hearing.
April 24, 1978—Photo by Steve Murray   xiv

VOLUME I

THE THEATRE OF WAR

PREFACE TO VOLUME I

This section contains chapters by the men mentioned in the introduction.

The Theatre of War in the Church—State conflict must be understood to get a grasp on the issues. Although the war is not new, being as old as God and Satan, wars are fought on different fronts, with each front requiring tactics and information unique to the circumstances.

Each of these three men—--an attorney, a pastor, and a philosopher—- writes from his own perspective and in his own style, to unfold a composite overview of the battlefield.

Chapter 1

REFLECTIONS ON THE FIGHT

William Bentley Ball

Almost three years ago I had the honor to be retained to defend the interests of fundamentalist schools in North Carolina against threatened encroachments by the State. The history of the two ensuing litigations involving schools––the cases known as *State of North Carolina, et al. v. Columbus Christian Academy, et al.* (in which the State sought an injunction to subject the schools to total State control) and *Organized Christian Schools of North Carolina, et al. v. North Carolina State Board, et al.* (in which fundamentalists sought an injunction against the State's imposing of competency testing on private religious schools) has been well related elsewhere. Pastor Kelly, at the time he conceived of this book, asked me if I would prepare a chapter for it, on whatever topic I chose to write. I thought that perhaps I could best respond to his generous invitation, simply by offering some reflections on the North Carolina experience, as I have seen it. These few thoughts, it will be seen, relate to problems of religious liberty, parental rights and American freedoms generally as these come into issue nationally.

I have put these thoughts down at random. I offer them for what they are worth to readers everywhere that this book may catch an eye. I express some concerns, I make some suggestions, and I have also endeavored to express the sense of hopefulness which comes from the knowledge that there are many good people in our country who have great reservoirs of courage and goodness which are still to be tapped. Finally, I have presented these thoughts as the tribute to my North Carolina friends——a loving tribute and a celebration of their marvelous courage and their faithfulness to our beloved Saviour.

RADICALISM

"Radical" is a bad word to many a Christian. It denotes the revolutionist, the hate-maker, the Marxist, the agent of destruction of good things. But the word, itself, derives from the Latin word, *radix,* meaning "root." "Radical," in that sense, means the person who goes to the root of things and who then obeys the principle he there discovers. Now, of course, in our American society not everybody can be a "radical," in that sense, because they have no convictions whatever. Between the opposing pillars of the Christian, on the one hand, and the anti-Christian, on the other, lies a vast, colorless plain of the bland, the neutral, the convictionless. Most Americans are doubtless content with a bland, convictionless life——so long as it is comfortable. But it does not take a Solzhenitsyn to warn us that days of comfort may be numbered in our country. I have lately had the joy of observing the results of Brother Lester Roloff's work in Texas, but the young people whom his work has regenerated have largely been the results of a bland and comfortable society. The life of bland, convictionless comfort is fine until one or more results of it come boomeranging back——in the form of a drug-ridden child, a threatened divorce, loss of a job. Now these personal tragedies are only one sort of tragedy that is brewed by the "bland comfort" way of life. The other kind of tragedy hangs uncomfortably close in the offing——for the

4

American nation as a whole. The national scene is darkening rapidly as we witness: the spectacular growth of violence in our society, the growth of poverty and unemployment, the icecap of statism in the form of rapidly increasing regimentation of our personal lives, the accessions of power passing to a militant and aggressive Communist world, and the growing defenselessness of the United States. I was away from Harrisburg during the Three Mile Island episode but, returning right after it, and observing the nationwide hysteria which attended it (and which was encouraged), I could not but wonder what would happen in our country if the Soviets merely *announced* that they were going to send a nuclear armed submarine toward our territorial waters.

You would think that anyone who claims to be a true believer in Christ would be a "radical," that is, someone who carries out——must carry out——the teachings of Christ in all that he faces in life. Many people who call themselves Christians do try to be faithful to Christ in what they would call their "personal" life. But they appear to distinguish between "personal" matters and "public" matters. As to the latter——even though the "public" matter bears upon the sacred liberties of Christians——they are at best silent and at worst actually aid aggressors against those liberties. Why?

The reasons are various. Some people, where it is government which is the aggressor, are reluctant to act due to a very great respect for government. They feel that government is presumptively right and that the citizens should be very cautious in objecting to actions of government. Others have a sense of their own ignorance and, because of that ignorance, never venture to question government or persons advancing certain issues publicly. Then there are some Christians who have a personal fear of "making waves," "getting involved," being thought to be a "red hot." Some, of course, are in employments, or have business interests, which they feel may be injured by their public action. Finally, there are those——including Christians——who, often due to ignorance, actively support causes which are at core evil, governmental actions which, *apparently* in the public interest, are really harmful to human liberty.

Now, my joy in the North Carolina fundamentalist Christians has been in, among other things, their Christian radicalism. By ways which I will describe a bit later on under the heading "Homework," they managed to define a position which they believed to be *commanded* of them as Christians. Then, with full appreciation that the consequences might be anything from nasty publicity to fines or jail, they went full steam ahead. By "full steam ahead" let me at once say that I do not mean that they acted imprudently or foolishly. Far from it——as my "homework" remarks will indicate. But the point is, that they kept their eye right on Christ and did the then necessary thing. They were *not* deterred by selfish, prideful, human considerations.

Now I must reluctantly contrast this attitude with that of some other religious people whom I have observed over the past two decades. In the face of *direct* governmental assault upon their liberties, some of these "leaders" begin to bite their knuckles and exclaim: "What will our people say?" "What will the media say?" "What will happen to us financially?" "Ought we make waves?" "Won't this bring government retribution on our heads?" I recently observed a striking example of this cowardice and mediocrity in the statement made by an attorney for a particular religious group who said that he could not advise his clients to oppose the recent IRS threats of regulation of religious schools because of his fears with respect to possible IRS retaliation. Here is rank cowardice, a mediocrity of will, the dry rot of resolution——an ultimate betrayal of Christ.

But let me here add a word of severe admonition: not every courageous action is action that should be taken. Unhappily, the converse of the instance of cowardice which I mentioned in the last paragraph, has too often been paralleled by something opposite: rash action based solely on the notion that a combination of indignation and piety will carry the day. I have recently observed the *ruin* of a good Christian cause which was brought about by exactly that mentality. Someone, commenting on the noble goal and the sloppy work, remarked: "God will make up the difference." God did not, and it was presumptuous to expect Him to. The thought is a misapplication of the idea that "Faith Will Carry All." It is a bizarre misunderstanding of the providence of God. As well one might say, when faced with a fire in his home: "I will pray, and God will put it out." What makes it bizarre is that Christ so often admonished us that we must *labor* at what we do in this world. Nothing in His teaching tells us that pious expression, religious enthusiasm, or any degree of religious zeal of and by itself, absolves us *from doing our work.* This brings me to the matter of homework.

HOMEWORK

I mentioned above a ruined cause, caused by a zeal which was unaccompanied by the right kind of work. It's an odd thing: when we come to the field of religious liberty, many a good Christian, buoyed up by his *faith*, conceives that he knows the *law* relating to the protection of faith. And so he barges into legislative hearings, administrative hearings and even into court, more in the

7

role of preacher than man of the law. We ought not deprecate the good will which these efforts manifest, but just as we should demand that anyone who deals with physical ills become equipped by study and experience to medically prescribe, so one should demand that those who deal with public issues, likewise undertake arduous apprenticeships in this work and, little by little, gain competency. One's religious faith itself should make one understand that, particularly when one is dealing with the law relating to religious liberty, one is dealing with a *sacred thing* and that can only properly be dealt with in a manner peculiarly related to the protection of that thing——not through generating religious excitement, not through reckless attacks on others.

There is an old Latin motto, *"Age quod agis."* It means: "Do what you do." That is, don't undertake something and not do it *well*. Scripture contains many admonitions about diligence in work. If I am a construction worker, whose job it is to mix cement, it is my *religious* duty to combine the parts well, to take all the time it is needed to do the job right, and to be the best cement mixer that physically and mentally I can be. If I fulfill that role as a worker, I will be more honored in God's eyes than the doctor, lawyer or CPA who, whatever his fame or affluence, is less than diligent in his work. God is not honored by our enthusiasm——which is the fun of the thing——but by our diligence——which usually is tedious. For a lawyer, better an unsung, publicly ignored effort to research a particular application of the Anti Injunction Act than applause resulting from the headline "Attorney Blasts Secular Humanism."

The North Carolina fundamentalist Christians are specialists in homework. They do things "by the numbers," and they are a special joy to an attorney for that reason. In the *Columbus Academy* case, the first great job was to arrive at a policy which the attorney was then to try to defend. The schools were faced by a scheme of comprehensive regulation which vested in the State a total control of religious schools. The first step in the process of defense was, of course, an analysis by counsel of the statutes and regulations in question, so that the clients (the pastors and school administrators) would know, and not have to guess at, what these laws actually imported. (Further on in this chapter I refer to the very important step in this process under the heading "Gradually Discovering the Constitutional Problem"). Once the attorney had explained the actual legal implications of the statute and regulations, then it was up to the clients to inform the attorney of their policy position with respect to each point which he raised. There is a very important point involved here. The clients may feel that a given set of State regulations are somehow offensive to their religious liberty. Indeed they may be. But the point is to identify exactly *how*. In a recent case, I had occasion to review a set of regulations of which Christian schools were complaining, and indeed they were bad. One of the pastors said: "These regulations impose secular humanism on our schools." Indeed they did. The pastor was then ready to go on the witness stand and make a statement to that effect. Caution! Stop! The regulations did not say a word about "secular humanism." Had the pastor been asked by the State's attorney to point out just where the regulations talked about "secular humanism," the pastor would have been stumped––would have looked like an ignoramus, would appear he had gone off half cocked. In fact, the regulations did impose secular humanism but not in a way that he understood them to. They did so in one way only––by a very adroitly worded passage, the effect of which would have been that the State would have to approve any textbook used in the Christian school. Here

9

again, without deeper preparation, the pastor could have been jackknifed on the witness stand by the prosecutor. Because, if the pastor had responded to the question by saying "This gives the State control of what we read," the charge of "secular humanism" would still remain unanswered. The pastor would have to go a *further* step and say that he understood the law of the land to be that the State is forbidden to lend its endorsement to any religious book; therefore, a textbook designed for use in a Christian school could not be on the State's list of approved textbooks. You see that the matter is not simple and how great the need is for homework and an intimate, probing and deliberative relationship between counsel and client in these religious liberty matters.

It was in this kind of process that the North Carolinians have excelled. It takes a fourfold combination of faith, intelligence, courage and humility. The last mentioned quality is a special safeguard against the kinds of rash moves which ultimately result in getting damaged on the witness stand or by the media. My North Carolina Christian friends were, throughout the litigations, humble, indeed, in their willingness to hear one another out, to sincerely disagree, to take on really difficult research jobs——in other words to think down and down into a problem until finally a luminous certainty of position was achieved. Then they were able to take their position and to answer for it. They, by that process, had gained a *depth* of understanding of the problem and of their position. That meant that, when they would take the witness stand, they would not be found contradicting themselves, speaking foolishly, being embarrassed, being without answer. Rather, under the most aggressive questioning, it would be often *they* who wound up in control of the dialogue with prosecuting counsel, rather than vice versa. His questions would then be opportunities for advancing the cause, rather than causes for defensiveness.

10

Of course, no amount of diligent homework will be of value unless the great ingredient of Christian radicalism is present. I have known myself, in handling of ever so many religious liberty cases, that it is my own sense of the importance of the case that drives me to continually seek to look deeper in order to find solutions.

GRADUALLY DISCOVERING THE CONSTITUTIONAL PROBLEM

In four cases involving plenary State regulation of Christian schools which have gone to State Supreme Courts* an interesting situation has appeared. All four cases involved efforts of the State to impose a form of licensing on Christian schools, and in each case the State uncovered evidence that some Christian schools had previously accepted that licensing or applied for it. Naturally, the State attorneys sought to take fullest advantage of this in two ways: first, they used this in order to try to show that the religious beliefs which the pastors had asserted (beliefs opposed to licensing of the schools as a religious mission) were not really sincere; second, they used it in order to show that the regulations were really acceptable. On the face of it, these arguments of the State were embarrassing. Here the pastors were in court flatly condemning the licensing power of the State and saying that their belief was based upon Scripture. Then the State was producing evidence that some among these very pastors had previously sought or accepted licensing.

---

*State of Vermont v. LaBarge, State of Ohio v. Whisner, State of North Carolina v. Columbus Christian Academy, and Rudasill v. Kentucky State Board of Education

In North Carolina, one of the great benefits of Operation Homework was the soul-searching and Scripture-searching which, for awhile, became the very core of the pastors' deliberations. True Christian humility eventually pointed the way out of the apparent dilemma. Pastor Daniel Carr expressed it on the witness stand in the *Columbus Academy* case in the following thoughts which I here paraphrase:

> *"It is true that some of our schools at one time——some even recently——accepted a license or applied for a license. But that was before we had given sufficient prayerful reflection upon the implications of licensing. We want to be good citizens. We desire public order. We approve of good government. We are not 'anti-government.' We carefully observe the first wing of Christ's command 'to render unto Caesar.' We DO have duties to the State. We ARE citizens.*

> *"But, after licensing began to be required, and after some of our schools were into licensing, we began to ponder the next words of Christ's command: 'the things that are God's.' Today we realize that our schools are not Caesar's, that they belong to God, that parents have rights prior to any interest of the State, that the schools are a religious mission and would not exist if they were not.*

> *"And thus we must confess that some of us have been guilty of wrong-doing——based simply on our failure to have appreciated sufficiently the Lord's Commandment."*

I find that humble answer completely reasonable. It expresses, after all, a truth. I have used it to illustrate, however, the problem which recurs in religious liberty cases——that religious people have sometimes not *thought through* the religious liberty problem which is presented to them. Only a crisis of some kind may impel them to engage in that thinking through.

The foregoing is an example of one kind of situation which crops up in religious liberty cases——the initial failure to have realized the implications of Christ's teachings toward a particular governmental policy. A parallel situation is illustrated by the following: A fundamentalist preacher was on the witness stand and was taken under very heavy questioning by the State's attorney on cross-examination, who asked him to point out those particular sections of a licensing statute to which he objected on religious grounds. The witness was put in a difficult position, because he could not articulate, as a legal matter, just what it was about the statute that bothered him. His attorney was able to point out to the court that a statute may indeed be offensive, on religious grounds, to a believer for reasons that are purely legal. Suppose, for example, the statute reads: "This section is subject to the provisions contained in Section 87701.2(b)(26)." Only if we understand the legal effect of those words, can we know whether or not a religious liberty problem is posed by the statute. Not being a lawyer, it was not possible for the pastor to articulate his objection to the statute. That objection has to be articulated through a person knowledgable in the law. In the case to which I refer, the State's attorney was making much out of the fact that the clergyman in question could not actually "point out" what language in the statute was objectionable. It was then the attorney's job to explain the impact of the language in question and then to ask the clergyman how this related to his religious rights.

I think a good analogy to this situation is found in everyday medical practice. A person comes to a doctor after having felt some kind of pain in an area of his body for perhaps a year. Finally the intensity of the pain drives him to seek medical assistance. In no way is he able to identify, in medical language, the nature of his ailment. Indeed, he may well not be able to even say what organ is affected and may merely have to content himself by telling the doctor, "It seems to be here," pointing to the place. Does this mean he has no ailment? The fact that he cannot articulate it medically does not mean that at all. So it is often times with provisions of statutes or regulations.

ACKNOWLEDGING THE COMMON GOOD

The North Carolina fundamentalists resisted the State in the courts and won a national "first" in the legislature. The new legislation, which grew out of the above-mentioned Christian radicalism of the fundamentalists in North Carolina and their ability to cooperate with one another, is a Magna Carta for religious education in the United States. I mean, that it is a model statute for protecting religious liberty in education. But a significant feature of the statute is its recognition of certain obligations which religious schools have to the State. I mention this, because I feel that some comment is useful on why it is that any fundamentalist school, whose charter is really from God, should be bound in any way to the State.

In the past few years a confusion has arisen in the ranks of fundamentalists with respect to the role of the State. It has been said that, since the fundamentalist school is ordained by God and is responsible solely to the Lord, it must therefore never submit to any sort of regulation by the State in respect to anything and, further, need never report to the State concerning anything. This is a very great misconception.

The Preamble to the Constitution of the United States begins with the words, "We the people . . . " "We the people" it says, in essence, create our Constitution and, through it, our government, in order to provide for a number of things which we need in order to live together as a society. You will note that there is a very important double concept of "we" in those words. First, it is "we"—not "they"—who make the government. Government is "us" in the American concept. If some people in government today, particularly in the administrative branches begin to forget that, it is of course our job to bring them down to reality and to let them know that they work for us. Second, "we" recognizes the fact of society. Our constitution does not consider mankind to be atomized, but rather that we are all God's creations and that we have important relationships and obligations one to another. Laws, therefore, do not serve merely individual goals, but also the *common good.*

In the name of the common good, we do many things together. Consider only such a matter as the national defense (which none of us could provide for alone) or the common traffic light at the intersection. If I am a clergyman, driving my automobile on the way to my church and am faced with a red light at that intersection, I may not drive through it, though I am proceeding to the Lord's work. Indeed, although I am a clergyman, I must bear a driver's license, and the law says that I may not drive *at all* without that license. Does that law interfere with the work of the Lord? May a servant of the Lord be

15

licensed in order to get about in his automobile carrying out the work of the Lord? The answer is that he may. In other words, *we* may impose certain restrictions on *ourselves* which are necessary in order that *we* may enjoy safety, health and order in our lives. It is precisely for this reason that a Christian school is properly subject to *reasonable* fire, safety, building and health requirements. Obviously, not everything that can be dreamt of in the areas of health or safety, for example, would be reasonable. Where the requirement begins to impose a significant burden on the *religious mission* of the school, either in terms of undue expense, undue reporting, needless inspections, or other significant interference, we begin to become alarmed. And where those burdens cannot be justified in terms of *simple common sense,* they are to be rejected. To mention a case in point: Some years ago I represented a fundamentalist school which was located in a lovely old New England church, a white wooden structure which housed eighteen pupils in a pair of very nice classrooms. The State ordered the school shut down because of certain fire standards which had recently been adopted by the State. The imposition of these standards would have cost the congregation an exorbitant amount of money; further, the church would have had to be in large part rebuilt in order to accommodate the changes sought by the State. This cost and dislocation interfered materially with the carrying out of the religious mission of the school. The congregation had limited financial means, and there would have been a prolonged suspension of classes had the alterations to the building have been made.

According to whose judgment were the new requirements necessary? I noted that the State regulations in question were, word for word, the same as those promulgated by a national safety organization. Further

16

investigation showed that that organization designed these regulations for *industrial* structures and they represented the judgments of a remote body of "experts"—none of whom were available for testimony. The whole thing was ridiculous in terms of the little church building in which the school was housed. So what we obtained was the testimony of some local firemen, local contractors and other people of ordinary common sense and good experience. They were able to testify that there was utterly no need to impose the regulations on this little school, that the children were very safe in the building as it was. This is an example of the employment of common sense judgment in determining where the common good lies.

A question often arising in religious school cases relates to whether the state may license the school, require state accreditation of its teachers or prescribe its textbooks. Very clearly, the answer to all these questions is: No. The decisions of three state supreme courts now back up that conclusion. How about curriculum? There I believe that "we, the people" may make a legitimate demand that a child be taught the language of his country, its geography, history and form of government, and how to compute. Beyond this narrow range of subject matter, there is no agreement as to what is essential; but those subjects themselves appear plainly basic to citizenship—*i.e.*, for the person to be able to communicate with others and to be aware of the basic features of the nation of which he is a part.

What about quality? One must ask: would it not be a great advance in our country if every public school child were competent in the above "basics"? Quality control need not be by state edict. The public schools are totally state-controlled, but today are being subject to competence testing programs in view of the public outcry against the declining quality of public education. What has appeared in, for example, North Carolina is the irrefutable answer to state hysteria over supposed dangers of "uncontrolled" private schools: the formidable parent market. Parents who, in these hard days of inflation and rising taxation, nevertheless support private education for their children, *demand* that the quality be there. And I have found that most of them have a very clear idea of what "quality" consists of.

We also have laws, of course, against fraud which will protect the public against false representations of educational quality by private schools.

Finally, many fundamentalist schools have been more than willing to show interested members of the public the results the pupils achieve on nationally standardized basic skills tests——tests from which the public schools these days interestingly shy away.

The North Carolina fundamentalists, in their protracted struggle for educational freedom, were put to exploring the serious issue of the common good. They have made a great advance for the common good in their work.

THE COURTS

We must not hope for victories in courts. We can try for them. We can pray for them. But we must not expect them. In this age it will probably prove true, when the story of our jurisprudence is told, that its level will be no higher than the moral and spiritual level of our society. We are painting only fantasies if we expect our society——pagan and secularist——to produce the opposite in court decisions.

18

I sometimes marvel, in cases I handle, at the confident expectations of good-willed, Christian clients that surely "the courts will uphold our rights." One should not disparage this as simple credulity. It is based on a good civic sense, on patriotism, on an optimism about the American society, and on a stern, expectant demand that judges do good and avoid evil. Sometimes this demand is expressed in terms of "American traditions," denoting times past when supposedly judges behaved as Christians should. I do not disparage this appeal to American traditions (or to the Founding Fathers, for that matter): one can point to many things in our older jurisprudence which reflected Christian values. And what is wrong, anyhow, if we are deceived as to the high moral character of some of our predecessors and if we think that they were mostly just, honorable and noble men? Does it matter that we take possible imaginary figures as our models if the images as handed down are good?

Having said these things, I have these thoughts about our courts at the present time:

First, we should be very grateful for the American judicial system in spite of the gross imperfections of many judges. There are still great possibilities for justice within the system. That is because the very structure of the system––the having of a Constitution, of courts, of the adversary system, of rules of evidence, of appellate courts, of formality in our courts, the still prevalent respect for law, the tenacious hold of judicial precedent. These are things to be treasured, and they are things utterly absent in many nations today.

Second, there *are* still good judges on the bench. Occasionally one encounters a delightful surprise in finding an intelligent, high-minded individual on the bench who has keen sensitivity towards constitutional liberties and justice.

But thirdly, we must not pin any ultimate hopes on our courts (including the Supreme Court). What America is, is bound to express itself in what its judges are. If America continues its trend toward man-centeredness, we are bound to experience a decline in true justice in our courts. If materialism, hedonism, dishonesty and violence grow in American society, the judges we get will come out of that culture and will not, for the most part, be superior to it. If, on the other hand, forces for Christian good begin to make headway in our society, and their influence increases in our cities, our schools, our neighborhoods, our culture, we will be able to expect judges who reflect that.

Fourth, we must never suppose that judges are not subject to the influences of elites and special pressures. I believe that the tragic abortion decisions of the Supreme Court may be attributed to a carefully developed literature and a well orchestrated propaganda movement aimed precisely at bringing about that decision. But give this credit to those enemies of civilization who did that promoting: they *worked* for their result. They were generous toward their beliefs. They were courageous in terms of giving up their own time and in pressing their point of view. One of the major causes of evils that we have experienced through bad judicial decisions has been expert briefing by lawyers who have promoted the wrong side in test cases. All of these things should be a lesson to Christians to "try harder." They have the better case to sell.

Chapter 2

THE SEPARATION OF CHURCH AND FREEDOM

"It should be observed that, if a systematic religion is true at all, intrusion on its part into politics is not only legitimate, but is the very work it comes into the world to do. Being by hypothesis, enlightened supernaturally, it is able to survey the conditions and consequences of any kind of action much better than the wisest legislator . . . so that the spheres of systematic religion and politics—far from being independent—are in principle identical."

George Santayana
Dominations and Powers

The winter of 1620 anticipated far more than the coming of spring. A small company of pilgrims had "undertaken a voyage for the glory of God and the advancement of the Christian faith," as they later said in *The Mayflower Compact.*

To deny that the roots of this nation are firmly implanted in the solid Rock of Holy Scripture and the Rock of our salvation, the Lord Jesus Christ, is to deny the most obvious facts of history.

At the Constitutional Convention in Philadelphia, Benjamin Franklin addressed the founding fathers:

"I have lived, sir, a long time, and the longer I live, the more convincing proofs I see of this truth—–that God governs in the affairs of men. And, if a sparrow cannot fall to the ground without His notice, is it probable that an empire can rise without His aid? We have been assured, sir, in the sacred writings, that 'except the Lord build the house, they labor in vain that build it.' I firmly believe this, and I also believe that without His concurring aid we shall succeed in this political building no better than the builders of Babel... I, therefore, beg leave to move that henceforth, prayer imploring the assistance of Heaven, and its blessings on our deliberations, be held in the assembly every morning before we proceed to do business, and that one or more of the clergy in this city be requested to officiate at that service."

From that day to this the U.S. Congress and the legislatures of most states have had a chaplain and opened each session with prayer. These early lawmakers saw a relationship between the law of the land and the Law of the Lord. Without law we are a nation in anarchy. Without God's law as a basis for the law of the land we are in confusion, which is where we find ourselves in this hour.

"The Separation of Church and Freedom" is a complex journey through history which will require patience and careful attention on the part of the reader. First we will deal with a brief synopsis of theory and then move into a more lengthy discussion of fact.

America is unique in all the history of planet Earth. No nation has ever enjoyed the blessings of God poured out upon us. Even the nation of Israel, a theocracy for a time, failed to be used of God to the salvation of millions, as well as the attendant blessings of prosperity, health and military might in any measure comparable to the United States of America.

No legitimate question may be raised as to the ideal form of government. Theocracy, with rule by God, as will be experienced in the coming kingdom of Christ on earth, is the ideal. Deductive reasoning is not the cause of that conclusion, but rather direct statements from the Word of God, expounding the ultimate failure of all human government.

In the meantime God gave us second best——"One nation, under God, with liberty and justice for all"——a republic fashioned from the ideological rubble of world empires, dictatorships, monarchies, and kingdoms of various sorts; a nation where men could be free. Not free FROM God, but free to obey and worship God according to the precepts of His Word.

Herein lies the problem: Our nation was formed by a majority who had no desire to be free to deny the God of the Bible. They perceived such a course to be national suicide. *"Blessed is the nation whose God is the Lord,"* and He promises destruction to any other type of nation. Had we held to this once dominant wisdom, there would be no *Separation of Church and Freedom* today.

Theoretically we support a theocracy. Not having such government until the Lord Jesus comes to set up His kingdom, we seek the will of God for the present.

Theoretically we support a republic, defined as "one nation under God, with liberty and justice for all." Again, we have no such government, speaking factually.

23

From its inception, our nation has moved swiftly and inexorably away from the Bible-based purpose of its founding until today, when we fight—not for domination— but for the very freedom to exist.

We are, indeed, at war. *The Theatre of War* has shifted from the hills and dales of virgin America, where gun and cannon held sway. No longer is it possible to simply "keep the powder dry" and warn that "the Redcoats are coming," as a means to victory. Christians across the land find themselves on a new battlefield. The enemy is still Satan, seeking to keep God's people from their liberty. But the weapons are now laws and regulations and courts—a war of ideas and ideologies, where our only defense is the wisdom which God alone can give.

Our subject at the moment is theory. Theoretically God could have sent an angel to defeat the British—but He did not. Theoretically our founding fathers could have submitted totally to England and prayed and expected deliverance - –but they did not. God honored the men and women who did, indeed, pray and expect deliverance, yet, at the same time, went into battle with muskets blazing. God honored those who loved liberty more than life and gave them the greatest nation the world has ever known.

James Madison is dead. Patrick Henry is dead. The war has moved out of the countryside into the classroom. This is a new generation with new soldiers, new champions of liberty, and a new *Theatre of War.* We are the soldiers who must fill the shoes of patriots long departed and prepare for the conflict. To fail to pray is disaster. To fail to believe that the battle is the Lord's is to be defeated. Beyond that, we have a responsibility before the God Who gave us this nation to learn who is fighting and why, and join in the war.

"Shall your brethren go to war and ye sit here?" If so, *"be sure your sin will find you out!"* Deut. 32:6 & 23.

The time has come for God's people to remember the admonition of the Lord Jesus Christ, to occupy until He comes. We are the salt of the earth, to hold back corruption——*"and if the salt has lost its savour it is thenceforth good for nothing but to be cast out and trodden under the foot of men."* Matthew 5:13.

The Lord Jesus may come today. If He does not, and we find our freedom to preach the Gospel and train our children trodden under the feet of government oppression, it will be for one reason only——we are "good for nothing!" We have failed in our obedience to the plain command to be the salt of the earth and the light of the world until Jesus comes.

So much for the theory. We are not a theocracy. We are not a "Christian nation." We have no more reason to expect angelic intervention, to keep our nation, than those who may have looked for it to found our nation. We have no Biblical justification to shirk our Christian duty, based on our eschatology. Now the facts.

THE DECLARATION OF INDEPENDENCE

"We hold these truths to be self evident, that all men are created equal, that they are endowed by their Creator with certain unalienable rights, that among these are life, liberty, and the pursuit of happiness. That to secure these rights, governments are instituted among men, deriving their just powers from the consent of the

> *governed, that whenever any form of*
> *government becomes destructive of these*
> *ends, it is the right of the people to alter or*
> *to abolish it . . . "*
>
> *Declaration of Independence*
> *1776*

The *Declaration of Independence,* while not an instrument of government per se, was a statement of purpose which explains the philosophy of government extant in early America. No Union existed when these words were penned. Only a meeting of the minds among leaders of self-governing states——leaders who held a belief in "certain unalienable rights" granted by God, made this document possible.

To exclude the *Declaration of Independence* from history, is to exclude the General from the Army, or the light from the fire. The Revolutionary War was kindled by a mutual desire to defend "self evident" truth, long rejected by the British Government. It WAS religious truth, and no amount of Humanist hocus-pocus in modern analyses of history may change that fact.

Abraham Lincoln viewed the *Declaration of Independence* as a statement of principle, and the *U.S. Constitution* as the embodiment of that principle. He, far better than modern historians, is in a position to speak authoritatively on the marriage between the two documents:

> *"All this is not the result of accident. It has*
> *a philosophical cause. Without the*
> *Constitution and the Union, we could not*
> *have attained the result; but even these are*

26

*not the primary cause of our great
prosperity. There is something back of
these, entwining itself more closely about
the human heart. That something is the
principle of "Liberty to All.' The
expression of that principle in our
Declaration of Independence, was most
happy and fortunate. Without this, as well
as with it, we could have declared our
independence of Great Britain; but without
it, we could not, I think, have secured our
free government, and consequent
prosperity. No oppressed people will fight
and endure, as our Fathers did, without the
promise of something better than a mere
change of masters. The assertion of that
principle, at that time, was the 'word fitly
spoken' which has proved an 'apple of
gold' to us. The Union and the
Constitution, are the 'picture of silver,'
subsequently framed around it."*
    Fragment on the Constitution and Union
       Abraham Lincoln——1860

From these words there can be no doubt that
Lincoln perceived the *U.S. Constitution* to be the
mechanical expression of the most decidedly religious
philosophy embodied in the *Declaration of Independence.*

All this is necessary to grasp the thesis of this
book. Admittedly, I view the scene of history from the eye
of a Fundamentalist. However, that view is not arbitrary,
though it may be replete with scriptural biases. Facts are
facts, and the fact remains that this nation was born out of
a theological approach to freedom and government.

From the *Declaration of Independence* to the drafting of the *Constitution,* a growing consensus was apparent in the minds of state leaders, that a national government was a necessity. The people of Massachusetts echoed the heart-cry of the newborn nation when they spoke of "a government of laws and not of men."

While the states had no intention of giving up their various powers, they saw a need for national cohesion; the instrument to accomplish this was the U.S. Constitution. How that document has affected history is our next consideration.

THE AMERICAN CAESAR

Ours is a nation under God. Beyond that assumption we must proceed to the fact of visible human government. To inquire into the history of America is a rather poor substitute for empirical reality. *The Separation of Church and Freedom* has come about for the simple reason that, to a great degree, "government of the people, by the people and for the people" HAS perished from the earth. By apathy and indifference---through lack of involvement in the political process, our government has fallen into the hands of men who no longer represent the will of the people. Decry this circumstance as we please–the system is not to blame.

"We, the people of the United States, in order to form a more perfect union . . . " These are the opening words of the *Constitution of the United States.* The voice of the people became one with the voice of the *U.S. Constitution* to establish a national government, which would finally prove to be acceptable to all the states. Speaking idealistically, the states envisioned no conflict between local government and national government. Little did they perceive our day when the long arm of Washington reaches almost overwhelmingly into the politics of every state in the nation.

Perhaps we could argue convincingly that "the people" are the ultimate government of America. Another case could be made for the *Declaration of Independence* as the highest authority. My thesis is that "the people" vested their authority in a *Constitution* embodying the philosophy of the *Declaration of Independence,* to obtain a government——"A government of laws, and not of men."

Under the *U.S. Constitution,* by mutual consent, every state in the nation joined hands to establish a national authority. Some may argue that states' rights are the ultimate authority; logic, as well as history, prove otherwise. By ratifying the *Constitution,* the states gave up certain powers in exchange for national goals. Never again could a state lawfully raise an army, or coin its own currency, for example. As many subsequent amendments have demonstrated, the states surrendered their rights in any area which the national body agrees upon.

The *War Between the States* was a war fought, not over slavery, but over states' rights——and it was lost to the Union. If a sufficient number of states approve an Equal Rights Amendment or an abolition of the Religion Clauses of the First Amendment, the altered version of the *U.S. Constitution* will be the binding law, enforceable in every state in this nation. There can be no doubt that "We, the people of the United States, in order to form a more perfect union" have made the *U.S. Constitution* the ultimate governmental authority in America——"A government of laws and not of men."

How all this relates to the Bible is of paramount

importance. In Luke 20:25 the Lord Jesus Christ said: *"Render therefore unto Caesar the things which be Caesar's, and unto God the things which be God's."* Any Bible student knows the Word of God is replete with instructions covering every facet of life. This means we need not assume that a scriptural admonition to *"go up to Jerusalem,"* is a Biblical command for every Christian to purchase tickets for a Holy Land tour. When the Bible commands slaves to be subject to their masters, we need not seek out some country practicing such things, and sell ourselves into slavery.

In dealing with government, the Bible sets forth Christian conduct for those who have a king over them, those who live under a military dictatorship (such as Rome), those who live in a theocracy, those who are slaves, etc., etc. It may seem shocking to our freedom-loving sensibilities that not only does the Lord permit slavery at times in history, He forbids slaves from seeking to escape. All these things are true because bondage, and captivity, and types of government, are tools of the Lord to judge nations.

Christian responsibility to government is totally predicated on the TYPE of government in the country in which one is born. First century Rome is not our model—no military power occupies this country. We have no king to whom to bow. We have no Pharaoh who is our taskmaster. As we use the analogy of "Caesar" we must remember that it is only an analogy. "Caesar" in New Testament times was a man—the highest form of governmental authority. One of the wonderful facts about America is that, in our nation, the highest form of governmental authority is not a man, it is a document—*The Constitution of the United States. The United States Constitution* is "the American Caesar."

History is replete with evidence that a central purpose in the founding of this nation was to insure that its people would never have a king. Nothing could be more antithetical to Americanism than a military occupation such as Rome's, or a Pharoah, or a prince. The *U.S. Constitution* was purposely drafted to insure that no human authority of any kind would ever supersede its power. The President of the United States is not the "king" of Bible reckoning. The "State," with its senators and representatives, is not "Caesar" by definition of the Word of God. These men are servants of the people under our form of government, "instituted among men, deriving their just powers from the consent of the governed, that whenever any form of government becomes destructive of these ends, it is the right of the people to alter or abolish it."

"The American Caesar" is not any man or group of men—it is the *Constitution of the United States*. All officials, from the President, to the Congress, to governors, are subject to "the American Caesar" in the same manner, and to the same degree, as any other citizen. When we, as citizens, challenge any law, regulation, or government official on a constitutional question, we simply follow in the scriptural course of Paul in Acts 25:11 when he said, *"I appeal unto Caesar."*

If we, as Christians, are to *"render unto Caesar the things which be Caesar's and unto God the things that be God's,"* we need two prerequisites to obey that command of the Lord Jesus:

First, we must know what "Caesar" requires- -every Christian should be well versed in the *Constitution of the United States.*

31

Second, we must know what God requires——that means a good working knowledge of the Bible.

I Peter 2:13 sheds light on the key to proper reasoning. *"Submit yourselves to every ordinance (law) of man for the Lord's sake."* God has commanded Christians to recognize human government as a way of life. Born again believers should be the most law abiding people on earth. Notice the verse does not say: "Submit yourselves to every ordinance of God"; it says: *"Submit yourselves to every ordinance (law) of 'man' for the Lord's sake."* Obedience to "Caesar" is not something to be taken lightly and altered at the whim of personal preference. We assume first that law is valid until and unless we have a direct command from God which we know to take precedence over the law of man.

As we engage in the warfare which now faces us, it is imperative that we perceive "Caesar" to be *"the minister of God . . . for good."* "The American Caesar" is not our enemy, it is our friend. *The U.S. Constitution* is the earthly means of our protection from the enemies of liberty.

At this point we may summarize as follows:

1. The U.S. Constitution, founded upon the Declaration of Independence, is the basis for our nation.
2. The U.S. Constitution is the basis for our law.
3. The U.S. Constitution is the basis for our government.
4. The U.S. Constitution is the basis for our Biblical mandate to "render unto Caesar."
5. The U.S. Constitution is the basis for our religious liberty.

Most assuredly this book will not restructure the world's thinking and obliterate the well established view that the "state" or "government" is the "Caesar" to which we relate as a political entity. We cannot deal, in daily life, with the abstract when the concrete hauls us into court.

The Constitution is law, and government officials, sworn to uphold the Constitution, have frequently ignored or misunderstood that document as they legislate, regulate and vacillate.

Ultimately the purpose of my expounding this subject is to call to the readers' attention the fact that the U. S. Constitution is a unique document. Even as an expression of law, it may not be compared to any other system of law ever known to man, in the sense that it is of, by and for the people——"A government of laws and not of men."

The Constitution demands that the state, with its lawmakers, officers and representatives who are the visible expression of "Caesar," must all of necessity be subject to the Constitution as absolute. When the framers of the Massachusetts Bill of Rights envisioned "A government of laws and not of men" they implied two logical necessities:

1. Law is to supersede our public servants.
2. Public servants must administer the law.

To state that in another fashion, the governing force of this nation is to be law, even though the governing agents are men. The thrust of my reasoning concerning "The American Caesar" follows this path of logic. Law, whether it be the laws of a state or the mutually accepted laws of the Constitution, comes from the people. Law is "an ordinance of reason, ordained for the common good, and promulgated." As such it can neither replace the state nor God in our thinking on this subject.

What must be realized is that in America the state was never intended to obtain the absolute, dictatorial Lordship of the "Caesar" of Bible reckoning. Our first allegiance is to the "higher law" of God, as an expression of His Will and Wisdom. Our second allegiance is to constitutional law, as an expression of the will and wisdom of the people of this nation.

When I characterize the Constitution as "The American Caesar," I do so realizing full well that the Constitution is not a functioning agency of government to which practical ministrations may be rendered. At the same time, I challenge the reader to consider that no "divine right of kings" belongs to the governmental entity in the state capital, or in Washington. The "Caesar" of Bible reckoning was a theological force in the nation, as much as a political force. Never may we properly ascribe such a position to human government in the American system.

Any seat of government in our nation is analogous to "Caesar" only in the sense that its occupants function as servants of the people——servants as subject to the law of the land as any common citizen. Dean Clarence Manion, for many years Professor of Constitutional Law at Notre Dame University, in his book *Lessons in Liberty,* illustrated this line of reasoning to perfection with these words:

> *"Let us assume that you see a truck traveling north along a main highway. A hitch-hiker is perched upon the tail-gate.*

When the truck passes a certain crossroad, the passenger jumps off and walks east on the crossroad. Now, let us suppose that you are later called into court and asked to tell what you saw of this hitch-hiker. Would you be telling the 'whole truth' if you merely said that he dismounted from the truck? Would you not think it important to state the fact that he dismounted at the CROSSROAD? And, would you have told the whole story, if you refrained from stating that he immediately went east on the crossroad, while the truck continued north upon the main highway? These additional facts are important because they indicate the REASON WHY the man left the truck. He was not tired of his ride. He merely wanted to go in another direction. It is clear that if the truck had turned to the right (east) at that crossroad, the man would have remained on board. Walking is slower and more tiring than riding, but it is certainly more sensible to walk toward a point we are determined to reach than to take a ride in the opposite direction.

When the American colonies declared their independence in July of 1776, they not only dismounted from the British Government, but they started to travel in a new and different direction.

In what direction was the British Government proceeding when it lost its American passenger? At that time the British Government was traveling the old *road of dictatorship. On that road there was no such thing as the recognition of the God-given liberty and equality of mankind. On that road government steered its course by the compass of the old pagan principle of the all-powerful state.*

The new road was entirely untraveled at that time. No government had ever deliberately turned in that direction before. On the contrary, the old road of state absolutism——the old road of the PAGAN ALL-POWERFUL STATE——was well-known because it had been used for centuries by all the governments of the world. The Americans, however, were convinced that the new road was right, and that the old road was wrong."

No clearer illustration could be drawn to expound the absolute departure of the American way from any other concept of government ever known to man. Dean Manion then summarized *The Purpose of American Government* with these words:

"From a practical standpoint, the next principle of American Government is the most important principle of all. Up to this point, we have seen that American governmental principle embraces the existence of God, human equality, and the recognition of the unalienable God-given rights of the individual man. Next in order, in the Declaration of Independence, comes this declaration: 'To secure these

36

(unalienable) rights, governments are instituted among men.' This statement describes the very heart of our American governmental system. It says, in effect, that government is a servant whose job it is to preserve and protect in each individual the rights that God gave him. This principle makes government a strictly PROTECTIVE agency.

Before the Declaration of Independence, governmental authority was generally recognized to be supreme and unlimited. Government was the master; the citizen or subject was merely the servant. Government gave the orders and the subject-citizen carried the orders into execution. Up to the time of the Declaration of Independence, government told the subject-citizen what his rights and privileges were, and those rights and privileges could be changed by government at any time. The consent of the subject-citizen to these changes was not necessary. This had been the relationship of the subject-citizen to his government in all parts of the world for untold centuries. Imagine, therefore, how revolutionary and startling this principle of the Declaration sounded to the Governors of England, and to the rulers of the rest of the world in 1776. The former master had become the servant, and the former servant became the master."

I would suggest, in view of this line of reasoning, that the *"things that be Caesar's"* spoken of by the Lord Jesus Christ are entirely different under the American system. As Dean Manion stated above, our relationship to government is the exact opposite of any citizen-government relationship the world has ever known before. He said again in his book, *Lessons in Liberty:*

> *"The fact that Constitutional provisions drawn in 1787 are still competently serving as the 'supreme law' of this strange land is little short of miraculous. The United States is one of the youngest children in the world's family of nations, and yet our Federal Constitution is the oldest instrument of government in existence."*

The U.S. Constitution is an "instrument of government," though not the government itself. The U.S. Constitution is "the supreme law of the land," though not the supreme law of the universe. The word of "Caesar" in Bible times was the "instrument of government," though not the government itself. The edicts of "Caesar" in Bible times were "the supreme law of the land," though not the supreme law of the universe. In this sense only, I designate the U.S. Constitution as the American Caesar.

To draw these analogies and make these comparisons is to realize the dangerous psychological concessions we make when we ascribe to the "state" the position and authority of the Biblical "Caesar." Our forefathers came to America as "hitch-hikers" on the "truck" of British rule. The very purpose of "jumping off" and formulating a Declaration of Independence and a Constitution as the instrument of government was to insure forever that no man or men, individually or collectively, would become the "Caesar" of America.

Having said that, I repeat the opening statement of this section. Most assuredly this book will not restructure the world's thinking, and obliterate the well-established view that the "state" or "government" is the "Caesar" to which we relate as a political entity. My only hope is that in ascribing that terminology to the *machinery* of government we will not deny our history. As Dean Manion has said: "The most important principle of all" in American government includes the conclusion that "the former master had become the servant, and the former servant became the master." The state may and does sit in the seat of the Biblical "Caesar." When we *"render unto Caesar"* we render unto the state. But there is a world of difference between sitting in the seat as a representative of the "supreme law of the land" and actually BEING the "supreme law of the land!"

THE KEY AMENDMENTS

> *"Congress shall make no law respecting an establishment of religion, or prohibiting the free exercise thereof, or abridging the freedom of speech, or of the press; or the right of the people peaceably to assemble, and to petition the government for a redress of grievances."*
>
> First Amendment to the U.S. Constitution

> *"All persons born or naturalized in the United States and subject to the jurisdiction thereof, are citizens of the United States and of the state wherein they reside. No state shall make or enforce any law which shall abridge the privileges or immunities of the citizens of the United States; nor shall any state deprive any*

person of life, liberty, or property, without due process of law; nor deny to any person within its jurisdiction the equal protection of the laws."

Fourteenth Amendment to the U.S. Constitution

The ultimate statement of the law of the land, the highest form of authority, is "the American Caesar," the *Constitution of the United States."* To administer this law we have a judicial system composed of judges, both state and federal, both elected and appointed, holding court in various jurisdictions throughout the fifty states.

The 1802 *Marbury v. Madison, (1 Cranch 137),* decision settled once and for all the ultimate authority of the U. S. Supreme Court to interpret the Constitution. This was one of the most far-reaching decisions ever rendered, and said, in effect: "The Constitution is what the U.S. Supreme Court says it is."

The Court took upon itself, at least in theory, the authority to negate or circumscribe any decision by Congress, by the President and his Cabinet, or by any other court in the land. Such was the beginning of *The Separation of Church and Freedom.* Given the assumed validity of our system of justice, religious liberty came to rest in the hands of nine men——the Chief Justice and eight other justices of the U.S. Supreme Court.

As with all other encroachments of control in American history, the seed was planted long before the tree came to fruition. For many decades after the completion of the Constitution, the U.S. Supreme Court refused to get involved in State questions of personal freedom granted by the Bill of Rights. As late as 1873, seventy years after the *Marbury v. Madison* decision, this principle of non-intervention was restated clearly in the famous *Louisiana Slaughterhouse Cases. (16 Wallace 36) (1873).*

The U.S. Supreme Court ruled that, even under the Fourteenth Amendment ratified in 1868, no basis could be found for intervention in state questions of individual rights. Again in 1899, in *Brown v. New Jersey (175 U.S. 172),* this position was reaffirmed. But with *Marbury v. Madison (1 Cranch 137)* the stage was set. To this day——"The Constitution is what the Supreme Court says it is."

The Separation of Church and Freedom began slowly, as the U.S. Supreme Court took it upon themselves to ignore the foundational nature of the religious connotations of the *Declaration of Independence,* and interpret the First Amendment as suggesting freedom FROM God and His Word. States began to follow the precedents, and the rest is history.

Abraham Lincoln, in his *First Inaugural Address,* spoke prophetically of our present dilemma. He said

> *"I do not forget the position assumed by some, that constitutional questions are to be decided by the Supreme Court . . . At the same time, the candid citizen must confess that if the policy of the government upon vital questions affecting the whole people is to be irrevocably fixed by decisions of the Supreme Court the instant they are made . . . The people will have ceased to be their own rulers,*

*having to that extent practically resigned
their government into the hands of that
eminent tribunal."*

This background is vital to an understanding of the
interpretation of *The Key Amendments.*

1925 marked another turning point, which further
narrowed the path of liberty, and further advanced the
power of the U.S. Supreme Court. In this year the "Judges
Bill" was enacted which sealed forever the power of the
Court. Under this bill a "Writ of Certiorari" became the
means of reaching the High Court. In effect this is a
"granting of permission" for a case to be heard. Only upon
consent of four justices, may an issue be deemed worthy
of examination by the Court. Some may counter that a
"Writ of Appeal" protects a challenge where basic rights
are concerned, but the Court must find the question to be
of "substantial federal nature." Again the trend was
toward unlimited power.

It goes without saying that any Supreme Court
decision deals with an individual case and not the nation.
However, it also goes without saying that, given the cost of
litigation, for all practical purposes, their decisions become
the law of the land.

Of course, the logical question at this point would
be——"What do you recommend as superior to the present
system?" My answer——"Nothing!" As previously stated,
we may not lay the blame at the feet of the system. The
system is as close to perfect as human government can be.
Although the U.S. Supreme Court has claimed for itself
the theoretical authority to overrule any branch of
government, or any lesser court, they also profess
themselves to be subservient to "the American Caesar,"
the Constitution.

42

Should we ever awaken to the fact that we have, by default, given our government to the Humanists, we may recover. A Constitutional amendment in favor of religious liberty, requires no more states to ratify it than the Equal Rights Amendment. The U.S. Supreme Court would, undoubtedly, honor such an amendment and tailor future decisions accordingly.

THE FOURTEENTH AMENDMENT AND THE DOCTRINE OF INCORPORATION

1925 was also famous in legal history for a decision entitled *Gitlow v. New York, (268 U.S. 652). Gitlow* embodied the first official application of what has come to be known as "The Doctrine of Incorporation."

The First Amendment says: "Congress shall make no law respecting an establishment of religion, etc." Notice the word "Congress." This is the United States Congress. This is the FEDERAL Constitution. Up to this time, as stated previously, the Court had refused to use its authority to define and apply the personal liberty aspects of the Bill of Rights, leaving this power to the States.

Though the *Gitlow* "incorporation" was a statement of "dictum," (appended comment not dealing with the merits of the case), this marked a major turning point in Constitutional law. For the first time a provision of the Bill of Rights was said to be "protected by the due process clause of the Fourteenth Amendment from impairment by the States."

We tend to think in terms of First Amendment rights, not realizing that without the Fourteenth Amendment we have no First Amendment guarantees from the U.S. Supreme Court. Only since 1925 has the Bill of Rights begun to be "incorporated" into the U.S. Supreme Court jurisdiction and, even today, on a limited basis.

In spite of the sweeping potential of *Marbury v. Madison,* a fact of law is that states reserve to themselves jurisdiction over the broad expanse of judicial actions. U.S. Supreme Court jurisdiction is limited, by choice, to fundamental Constitutional questions and, even then, under the "Judges Bill," only those which they wish to hear. Until and unless a particular Constitutional question recognized by the Court is raised, no case may be appealed to the highest court in the land, and therefore, is not protectable by the U.S. Constitution.

Since the *Gitlow* decision, freedom of speech, freedom of the press, right to counsel, freedom of assembly, right to petition, and others, have been "incorporated" while some have not. Of specific interest to us is the "incorporation" of First Amendment religious liberties. The Free Exercise clause was "incorporated" in 1934 in *Hamilton v. Regents of the University of California (293 U.S. 245).* The "Establishment Clause" was "incorporated," either in 1943 in *Murdock v. Pennsylvania (319 U.S. 105),* or in 1947 in *Everson v. Board of Education (330 U.S. 1),* depending on which Constitutional expert you believe.

While in one sense, we may herald "The Doctrine of Incorporation" as good news, with the poor treatment we are receiving today in some individual states—the other side of the coin is that it was the final stroke to insure that both good and bad decisions by the High Court would be binding on the states. The good news is that we have a hope of maintaining religious liberty beyond state edict. The bad news is that U.S. Supreme Court decisions on religious liberty often have the effect of nullifying any attempts by particular states to extend the bounds of religious liberty beyond the final opinion of a majority of the nine men in power.

THE FIRST AMENDMENT

After giving our attention to the Fourteenth Amendment, we see why it must come first. Any grievances we may have against "STATE" laws could not be taken to the U.S. Supreme Court were it not for "The Doctrine of Incorporation" and our pipeline to the First Amendment through the Fourteenth Amendment.

Based on the foregoing premises we may now, in effect, rewrite the opening words of the First Amendment to say:

> *"Congress (and subsequently the states) shall make no law respecting an establishment of religion or prohibiting the free exercise thereof."*

On this basis we have a right to take our cases to the U.S. Supreme Court provided, of course, that they grant a "Writ of Certiorari" as discussed previously.

The First Amendment, as it pertains to our subject, is commonly discussed using two phrases which we will follow throughout. The First Amendment has an "Establishment Clause" and a "Free Exercise Clause." To divide them properly we would say:

ESTABLISHMENT CLAUSE

> *"Congress shall make no law respecting an establishment of religion."*

FREE EXERCISE CLAUSE

*"Congress   shall   make   no
law . . . . prohibiting   the   free   exercise
thereof."*

Each of these is a world in itself, as you will see in future sections. For the moment our only purpose is to familiarize you with the First Amendment as it relates to our cause.

The U.S. Constitution, "The American Caesar," is brief and to the point on the subject of religious freedom. Aside from prohibiting a religious test for holding public office, the First Amendment contains the only reference to God or religion. Such is the case for two reasons:

1. A consensus among the Christian framers that religious liberty was so basic as to need little elaboration to insure protection.
2. A consensus among the Secular Humanist framers that religion had no place in government.

Both were totally erroneous views. Shocking as it may seem, the sum total of our right to religious liberty in America boils down to sixteen words and how those words are interpreted by the U.S. Supreme Court. *The Separation of Church and Freedom* is a result of an assault on those words over a period of many decades, in which not a letter of the original statement has been changed.

THE ESTABLISHMENT CLAUSE

"Congress (and subsequently the states) shall make no law respecting an establishment of religion." These words have provoked more controversy than tongue or pen have been able to tell. When you hear someone speak of "the separation of church and state" in connection with the U.S. Constitution, they refer to the "Establishment Clause." Indeed, many books on Constitutional law divide religious liberty into two fields called "separation of church and state" and "free exercise." They do this legitimately on only one premise: The U.S. Supreme Court has adopted this approach and rendered many decisions accordingly.

In reality the "Establishment Clause" was never intended to be used in such an anti-Christian fashion. At such a late date in history that statement will be established as fact only in the minds of those who take their research back beyond the biased tirades of present-day Secular Humanist historians and authors. Almost without exception you will find contemporary "experts" expounding a slightly distorted and embellished story which goes like this:

"The Founding Fathers had come from a land (England) where a State Church existed and, knowing the evils of such a system, wanted a "wall of separation between Church and State." They intended to keep the church out of politics and thus said: "Congress shall make no law respecting the establishment of religion' to prevent any religion from becoming the established church in America."

Such a confusing mixture of truth and error usually causes the natural man to take the error and run with it.

My research, which predates modern textbooks, paints a different picture. Those who wrote the Constitution had not come across the Mayflower gangplank to sit down under a tree with pen in hand. Americans had lived in this country with religious liberty for more than 150 years when the Constitution was written. The Church of England was replaced by Episcopalians, Presbyterians, Baptists, Congregationalists and non-sectarian groups, as a diverse majority, by the time decisions were made concerning the First Amendment. Obviously they wanted no Federal control of churches, but that was as far as it went.

As noted above, modern thinkers often misquote the First Amendment to say "Congress shall make no law respecting THE establishment of religion" instead of its proper wording "Congress shall make no law respecting AN establishment of religion." The misquote is indicative of a personal bias rather than an attempt to deceive. They simply believe what they learned in college——specifically, that Americans in that day were against any form of religion being THE religion of America. History——true history—teaches otherwise.

By saying "Congress shall make no law respecting AN establishment of religion," the framers were saying: "We have religious establishments already set up in the individual states and, for that reason, we want no laws from Congress to interfere with an establishment of religion.

Of the thirteen original states ratifying the Constitution, six——North Carolina, South Carolina, New Jersey, Georgia, Connecticut and New Hampshire——had clearly delineated "Establishments." Delaware and Maryland insisted on Christianity. Pennsylvania required belief in the inspiration of the Bible, as well as belief in Heaven and Hell. Massachusetts called for "Christian Protestantism." Thus, ten of the thirteen states approving

48

the Constitution had some form of "establishment of religion" into which they wanted no Federal meddling. Maryland had a strong Roman Catholic population which later became intermingled with Anglicanism, and various states had Jewish and Quaker minorities at the time of the break with England. These latter groups were a departure from the heavily Protestant norm so, with human nature being as the Bible specifies, there was some persecution.

My argument here is not intended to uphold injustice. Persecution is wrong in any society and not sanctioned by those who believe the Word of God. Where establishments were overbearing in certain states and communities, there was religious compulsion in terms of church attendance, taxes levied for support of church and clergy, imposition of required professions of beliefs, etc.

However, it is not true that the Establishment Clause was constructed to prevent such practices, unscriptural and reprehensible as they are. The Establishment Clause had absolutely nothing to do with proscribing states' rights. As previously demonstrated, the Establishment Clause existed for 156 years before it was first applied to the states by the conduit of the Fourteenth Amendment.

The Establishment Clause was penned——1. To insure that CONGRESS would effect no national religion and 2. To insure that states' rights would be preserved to continue their already existing "religious establishments" if they so desired.

We must distinguish clearly in our minds between the way things were and the way things are. Thomas Jefferson, the outspoken advocate of a "wall of separation between church and state" had never imagined, in his wildest dreams, that a day would come when the Establishment Clause would be used by the U.S. Supreme Court to dictate religious policy in the several states. The following reasons prove this:

1. Jefferson was noted for his opposition to expansion of Supreme Court power.

2. The school which he founded, the University of Virginia, was a State school which trained preachers and required compulsory chapel attendance under Jefferson's direction at State expense.

3. The context of the Jeffersonian letter, containing the famous "wall of separation" statement, clearly refers to the legislature of "the whole American people," namely the U.S. Congress.

4. To say that a rabid proponent of states' rights such as Jefferson, (as documented in hundreds of pages of his own writings), would want Federal Courts defining and enforcing civil liberties in the states, is like history someday showing that Martin Luther King, Jr. was a champion of segregation.

Supreme Court decisions of the past 30 years take Jefferson and the Establishment Clause totally out of the context of history to justify the nationalization of the "wall of separation between church and state."

THE WALL OF SEPARATION

> *"Believing that religion is a matter which lies solely between man and his God, that he owes account to none other for his faith or his worship, that the legislative powers*

of government reach actions only, and not opinions, I contemplate with sovereign reverence that act of the whole American people which declared that their legislature should 'make no law respecting an establishment of religion, or prohibiting the free exercise thereof,' thus building a wall of separation between church and state."

Thomas Jefferson
Letter to Danbury Association of Baptists in Connecticut, 1802

Since the "Establishment Clause" and "the separation of church and state" are synonymous in the minds of many today, we need to examine the origins of this phenomenon. Apart from the Bible, no single quotation from a leader on the face of history has ever been more used and abused than "the separation of church and state." At the very heart of the commonly accepted view of American beginnings mentioned previously, stands this bastion of Secular Humanism. That's right folks, we quote it like the Gospel and the U. S. Supreme Court quotes it like the hope of the nation; but no purer statement of Secular Humanist thought has ever been uttered.

In a later chapter we will take a closer look at Jefferson and see that while he was a champion of states' rights and individual liberty, he also espoused almost every dangerous tenet of Secular Humanist thought we fear at the present hour.

The "wall of separation" is our present subject and the "wall" has contributed immeasurably to *The Separation of Church and Freedom.* Jefferson wrote to a Connecticut group called the Danbury Association of Baptists, in 1802, in the words quoted at the beginning of this section. From that passing comment on the First Amendment, in an obscure letter, "the wall of separation between church and state" has come to be known by almost every church member, politician, school child, and citizen at large in America; not only known, but advocated as truth and justice. Please read carefully the following words:

> *"It should be observed that, if a systematic religion is true at all, intrusion on its part into politics is not only legitimate but is the very work it comes into the world to do. Being by hypothesis, enlightened supernaturally, it is able to survey the conditions and consequences of any kind of action much better than the wisest legislator ... so that the spheres of systematic religion and politics——far from being independent——are in principle identical."*
>
> *George Santayana*
> *Dominations and Powers*

America was founded by men and women who believed the Word of God. They sought no society which shuts the church away into a mental monastery, as was the philosophy of Jefferson. He said on more than one occasion:

> *"I inquire after no man's religion, and trouble none with mine: nor is it given us in this life to know whether yours or mine, our friends' or our foes', is exactly the right."*
>
> *Letter to Miles King in 1814*

52

Jefferson was a great statesman and a classic politician. He was not, however, a man who believed in the Bible as the foundation of absolute truth, or Christianity as the only acceptable religion. *The Jeffersonian Cyclopedia* is a monumental work, available at most large libraries, and catalogues thousands of statements on every subject to which he wrote. Never would he acknowledge the God of the Bible as the One True and Living God. In accordance with his wishes, we will leave his eternal destiny between him and his maker. The fact remains that he did not believe *"Blessed is the nation whose God is the Lord"* and fought during his entire career to produce a secular government for this nation and for his own state of Virginia.

Thomas Jefferson was not in the majority, but he was in a position to become famous for formulating a philosophy which was music to the ear of the natural man. Why not exclude religion from government in totality? Then those troublesome ideals of God's Word would place no bridle on Secular Humanist goals. Some able and contemporary associates of the day did oppose Jefferson and his attempt to prevent the Christian religion from prevailing. These men go almost unnoticed on the face of history since Secular Humanists usually write the textbooks.

John Quincy Adams had a cousin named Jasper Adams. Jasper Adams was a professor of mathematics and natural history at Brown University, a professor of moral philosophy at West Point and a president of the College of Charleston in South Carolina. He was an academic, an ardent researcher and philosopher, not given to the fiery, but often unsubstantiated rhetoric of Jefferson. In a published work entitled *The Relation of Christianity to Civil Government in the United States,"* he said:

"A question of great interest comes up for discussion. In thus discontinuing the connection between church and state, did these states intend to renounce all connection with the Christian religion? Or rather did they intend to disclaim all preference of one group of Christians over another as far as civil government was concerned; while they still retained the Christian religion as the foundation-stone of all their social, civil, and political institutions?

"In perusing the 24 constitutions of the United States, we find them all recognizing Christianity as the well-known and well-established religion of the communities. It never came into the minds of the framers to suppose that the existence of Christianity as "THE" religion of their communities would ever admit to a question. It is the duty of the Congress, then, to permit the Christian religion to remain in the same state in which it was at the time the Constitution was adopted. My conclusion is sustained by the documents which gave rise to our colonial settlements, by the records of our colonial history, by our Constitutions of Government made during and since the Revolution, by the laws of the respective states, and finally by the uniform practice which has existed under them."

By the way, Jasper Adams was also a preacher of the Gospel and one-time chaplain at West Point, who was bound by the Word of God to tell the truth.

Much less complexity surrounds the "Free Exercise Clause" of the First Amendment. No "wall of separation" clouds the issue, with this exception: There can be no doubt that our free exercise of religion is hindered, if not totally negated, by attempts to keep religion out of government. True free exercise should also include the right to have our politics and law, as well as our education, dominated by the Bible as the foundation of all truth. Be that as it may, we need to think of the Free Exercise Clause itself.

> *"Congress (and subsequently the states) shall make no law . . . prohibiting the free exercise thereof."*

As we have seen, the "Free Exercise Clause" was "incorporated" as protectable through the Fourteenth Amendment in 1934. The case was *Hamilton v. Regents of the University of California (293 U.S. 245)* and dealt with a conscientious objection on the part of students, to take required courses in military science at a state university. Prior to that time, however, free exercise questions reached the Court on other grounds.

The most famous Free Exercise decision was in 1878. The first Mormon case, *Reynolds v. United States (293 U.S. 245),* dealt with the rights of Mormons to practice polygamy as a free exercise of their religion. The Court said:

> *"Laws are made for the government of actions, and while they cannot interfere with mere religious belief and opinion, they may with practices." (at 166)*

55

As examples the Court cited such practices as human sacrifice and self-immolation, as beliefs which government may prevent in practice. In the case of the latter, however, they made no suggestion as to how you effectively stop someone who decides to pour gasoline over his head and strike a match. As demonstrated by the suicides of Guyana and subsequent discussions among government "experts," it is a logical absurdity to legislate in an attempt to prevent some types of "Free Exercise of religion," no matter how destructive.

In any event, *Reynolds v. United States (293 U.S. 245)* established once and for all that Free Exercise is not absolute. Government in this country may prevent the practice of beliefs with Supreme Court sanction. How far this will be taken remains to be seen. The following quote highlights the danger:

> *"The state has a perfect right to prohibit polygamy, and ALL OTHER open offences AGAINST THE ENLIGHTENED SENTIMENT OF MANKIND, notwithstanding the PRETENSE of religious conviction by which they may be advocated and practiced."*
>
> *Late corporation of*
> *The Church of Jesus Christ of*
> *Latter Day Saints v. United States*
> *(136 U.S. 1) (at 50)*

As the foregoing examples make clear, the Free Exercise Clause, as interpreted by the Court, deals with "beliefs" and "practices" as opposed to the Establishment Clause, which deals with "the separation of church and state."

Without going into detail, I would raise another issue to which you should give serious thought at your leisure. The First Amendment also speaks to freedom of speech, freedom of the press, right of assembly, and right of petition, all of which may be involved in the free exercise of religion, and without which there could be no tangible expression of religious beliefs. The relationship here is of the utmost importance, but goes beyond the immediate attention of this book.

Perhaps the clearest statement available to elucidate where we stand on the current view of the Free Exercise Clause comes from *Cantwell v. Connecticut (310 U.S. 296):*

> *"(The Free Exercise Clause) embraces two concepts, freedom to believe and freedom to act. The first is absolute but, in the nature of things, the second cannot be. Conduct remains subject to regulation for the protection of society. The freedom to act must have appropriate definition to preserve the enforcement of that protection. In every case the power to regulate must be so exercised as not, in attaining a permissible end, unduly to infringe the protected freedom."*
>
> *(at 303 and 304)*

CIVIL RELIGION

At this point we should interject a factor necessary to understanding the total picture. There is a phenomenon inherent in America which some have called "civil religion." It is the outgrowth of our Christian heritage and involves the recognition of "God" in the general sense.

Prayers to open Congress and state legislatures, as well as the Supreme Court; "In God We Trust" on money, various references to a "Creator" or "Supreme Being" or "God" in the speeches of politicians and the documents of the nation——these are all rather passive acknowledgments of "Civil Religion." While we may appreciate these symbols of acquiescence to custom, a clear distinction must be drawn between "Civil Religion" and the "Christian Religion" of the Bible.

The religion of this nation, which gave it founding impetus and made it great, is not "Civil Religion." The religion which saves the soul is not "Civil Religion." "Civil Religion" is nothing more than a healthy branch of the tree of Secular Humanism. The word "secular," to the Bible-believing Christian, may not be defined simply as "without God." There is only one True and Living God and He is the God revealed in the Bible—— AS revealed in the Bible. To us, the word "secular" may only be properly defined as "without the God of the Bible." "Humanism," to quote Huxley, means in essence, "Man is the measure of all things." A fundamentalist definition of a Secular Humanist then becomes "one who believes that without the God of the Bible, man is the measure of all things."

To believe in some sort of personal definition of a vague deity does not preclude the label "Secular Humanist." Anything not sacred is secular, and the only sacred God is the God of the Bible. All others, whether they be the tree of the pantheist, the stone image of the Peruvian native, the ego of the atheist, or the "maker" of a Thomas Jefferson, appeal to "Civil Religion." Each is a product of Secular Humanism——specifically the view that "without the God of the Bible, man is the measure of all things——even the definition of his deity." (See chapter 5 entitled *The Classic Secular Humanist.*

These thoughts are vital to an understanding of "the separation of church and state" which has led to *The Separation of Church and Freedom.* America was founded as a Christian nation. Its people, by and large, were Bible believing Christians whose only God was the God of Bible revelation, whose only source of infallible truth was the Bible, whose only Saviour was God the Son, the Lord Jesus Christ, and whose lives, in every part, must be governed and influenced by the Word of God.

SOME CHRISTIAN HISTORY

As previously mentioned, the First Amendment was never intended to provide freedom "FROM" God. A majority of the founding fathers, representing the will of the people, sought to establish a nation where the God of the Bible could be obeyed and worshipped according to the dictates of conscience.

We must not forget that America has a history which explains the philosophy of the settlers of this land, predating the Constitution by almost two centuries. The oldest English colony in America had a document, written in 1606, called *The First Charter of Virginia.* "Virginia," at that time, was the name given to all of North America claimed by Great Britain. *The First Charter of Virginia* authorized their coming to this country "for the furtherance of so noble a work, which may, by the providence of Almighty God, hereafter tend to the glory of His Divine Majesty, in propagating of Christian religion to such people as yet live in darkness and miserable ignorance of the true knowledge and worship of God." *The Mayflower Compact,* already cited, written in 1620, said their voyage was "undertaken for the glory of God and advancement of the Christian faith."

59

The Fundamental Orders of Connecticut, written in 1639, is called by Harvard historians, "the first written constitution, in the modern sense of the term . . . . and certainly the first American constitution of government to embody the democratic idea." In its preamble, before any elaboration of government was undertaken, these telling words were penned:

> *"Well knowing where a people are gathered together the Word of God requires that to maintain the peace and union of such a people, there should be an orderly and decent government established according to God, to order and dispose of the affairs of the people . . . we do therefore associate ourselves . . . to maintain and preserve the liberty and purity of the Gospel of our Lord Jesus which we now profess, and also the discipline of the churches, which according to the truth of the said Gospel is now practiced among us."*

In this same document the oath of the Governor, who was to carry out the Constitution, said in part:

> *"I, being now chosen to be Governor within this jurisdiction . . . do swear by the great and dreadful name of the Everlasting God, to promote the public good and peace of the same, according to the best of my skill . . . and will further the execution of justice according to the rule of God's Word; so help me God, in the Name of the Lord Jesus Christ."*

These are words from the first written American Constitution. To finalize this thesis we should consider another document entitled *The Body of Liberties,* written in 1641. This was the first code of laws established in America. Four brief statutes tell the story:

> *No. 65. "No custom or prescription shall ever prevail among us in any moral cause or maintain anything that can be proved to be morally sinful by the Word of God."*

> *No. 94. "If any man after legal conviction shall have or worship any other god, but the Lord God, he shall be put to death."*

> *No. 95. (2) "Every church hath full liberty to exercise all the ordinances of God according to the rules of scripture."*

> *No. 95. (5) "No injunctions are to be put upon any church, church officers, or members in point of doctrine, worship or discipline whether for substance or circumstance besides the institutions of the Lord."*

This, the first code of laws established in America, footnoted 18 passages of Scripture as authority for its contents. What greater authorities could be called to testify than the first written American Constitution and the first Code of Laws established in America? The intent of the framers of the later *U.S. Constitution* is unequivocally foreshadowed in these documents. They intended to perpetuate American ideals, not destroy them.

> *"Such as profess faith in God by Jesus Christ, though differing in judgment from the doctrine, worship or discipline publicly held forth, shall not be restrained from but shall be protected in, the profession of the faith and exercise of their religion; so as they abuse not this liberty to the civil injury of others and to the actual disturbance of the public peace on their parts ... "*

> *"That to the public profession held forth none shall be compelled by penalties or otherwise; but that endeavours be used to win them by sound doctrine and the example of a good conversation."*
> *The Instrument of Government——1635*

These classic words, though coming from Cromwell's England, crystallize the thinking of great and godly men on the subject of religious liberty. In the previously quoted words of Jasper Adams, the founding fathers intended "to disclaim all preference of one group of Christians over another, as far as civil government was concerned; while they still retained the Christian religion as the foundation stone of all their social, civil and political institutions."

While we must face reality, and "the separation of church and state" doctrine is a reality, I must also put in my two cents worth on the other side. A growing number of God's people theorize that "the wall of separation between church and state" is better than a State religion, so the case is closed. Never forget that Satan's masterpiece is always a reasonable alternative to the truth. A "conservative" may be nothing more than a Secular Humanist with a better idea. The choice is not between a "State Church" and "a wall of separation." Between the two is a position both tenable and Biblical. Christians were here first, and to acquiesce to the religion of the Humanists is to enlarge the gap in *The Separation of Church and Freedom.*

For 80 years after the U.S. Congress was established, they used public money to support missions. While this is, perhaps, going too far, it is still indicative of the fact that no "absolute wall of separation" was intended by the Americans who founded this nation.

The Court did not go too far and, at the same time, confirmed the origins of America, in reaffirming the ban on polygamy in *The Late Corp. of the Church of Jesus Christ of Latter Day Saints v. United States (136 U.S. 1).* That case was decided on the court's views that polygamy "is contrary to the spirit of Christianity," and that "Christianity has produced (the civilization in) the western world."

It is, indeed, possible to have "the Christian religion as the foundation stone of all (our) social, civil and political institutions," as Jasper Adams suggested. It is equally possible to interpret the First Amendment "to disclaim all preference of one group of Christians over another, as far as civil government is concerned" while not rejecting the One True and Living God and His infallible Word as the hope of the nation. If the Humanists want a nation based on their religion, which is where we stand today through their efforts, they need to go somewhere and start one——not attempt to force our nation to adopt that philosophy.

"Blessed is the nation whose God is the Lord," and by direct implication, "Cursed is the nation whose God is NOT the Lord." Perhaps a more applicable scripture would be: *"The wicked shall be turned into hell and all nations that FORGET God."* Through the absurd idea, even among Christians, that we may forget the God of the Bible, who made this nation great, and turn to a neutral society, America is crumbling. There is no neutrality. The Lord Jesus said: *"He that is not with me is against me."* Any government which is not *"the minister of God for good"* (Romans 13) has no right to exist, by God's standards. When it becomes "the minister of the religion of Secular Humanism to maintain an absolute wall of separation between church and state" the curse of God is upon it.

This is not to say that we should advocate a return to Old Testament law and a theocratic society without God on the mountain. I would not want a human jury to have me stoned for picking up sticks on Saturday, or deciding when a disobedient child is disobedient enough to be stoned. Neither is it God's will, in this age, to put to death those who do not profess faith in Him as the first code of laws in America provided. Excesses are possible. Temporary problems are probable. However, we have less hope at the mercy of a Secular Humanist government than at the hands of one seeking to do the will of God.

We could, and should, have a government which honors God and the Bible, and follows this quotation from *The Instrument of Government* in its approach to religious liberty:

> *"Such as profess faith in God by Jesus Christ, though differing in judgment from the doctrine, worship or discipline publicly*

held forth, shall not be restrained from but shall be protected in, the profession of the faith and exercise of their religion; so as they abuse not this liberty to the civil injury of others and to the actual disturbance of the public peace on their parts . . . "

"That to the public profession held forth none shall be compelled by penalties or otherwise, but that endeavours be used to win them by sound doctrine and the example of a good conversation."
The Instrument of Government——1635

SUMMARY

Up to this point we have attempted to lay the groundwork to give a bird's-eye view of the past, as it relates to *The Separation of Church and Freedom.* I have attempted to intermingle the basic principles to keep them before you constantly. To jog the memory, please give special attention to the following synopsis:

America began as a Christian nation:
——The Mayflower Compact
——The First National Charter
——The first written Constitution
——The first code of laws
——The Declaration of Independence
——80 years of Congress supporting missions with public money
——Religious Establishments to be untouched by the Constitution
——Supreme Court decisions using Christian ethics

——All these and more substantiate the Christian foundations of America.

America developed the American Caesar:
——The U.S. Constitution embodied the will of the people and Declaration of Independence
——The Bill of Rights
——The Key Amendments (First and Fourteenth)
——The Establishment Clause
——The Free Exercise Clause
——All serve as the foundation stones for liberty, with the *U.S. Constitution,* which is a "living document," assuming the position of the "Caesar" of other cultures——"a government of laws and not of men."

Vital to a working knowledge of First Amendment Constitutional law are these factors:
——*Marbury v. Madison (1 Cranch 137)*
——Judges Bill
——Doctrine of Incorporation
——Jeffersonian theory of the wall of separation between church and state
——Civil Religion
——All of which have contributed heavily, in one way or another, to Christianity being lowered to the level of "just another religion," hence, the further *Separation of Church and Freedom.*

As we proceed to the subject of education in particular, seemingly innocuous events, such as the rise of Civil Religion, the ever increasing power of the Supreme Court, and the effect of the "wall of separation" letter written by Jefferson will loom larger in the total picture.

My thesis is relatively simple. From the strong foundation of a God-blessed America we:

——Lost our leadership to religious humanists

——Lost our states' rights to the intimidation of U.S. Supreme Court precedents

——Lost our national religion to neutrality

——Lost our militant citizenship to apathy

——We stand in danger of losing the minds of our children which, unchecked, will be the final blow in *The Separation of Church and Freedom.*

Chapter 3

PRECEDENT LAW

Adjudication: "The application of precedent law in reaching a just decision."

From the inception of legal systems as we know them, beginning with England and spreading to America, judges have relied heavily on precedent law; the idea being that preceding cases and their opinions form a basis from which to decide future cases.

A "landmark" decision is one considered significant enough to make it an outstanding precedent for future decisions.

Obviously there are benefits from precedent law. A system of consistent reasoning on any given issue begins to emerge with the passage of years, and a continuity develops. Any decision which ventures from precedent to any great degree is immediately suspect, so that wild interpretations do no damage to the Constitution.

The practice of law is a mysterious combination of art and science——art in the sense that an attorney has free course to articulate logic which is persuasive, and becomes the basis for precedent; science in the sense that a true definition of science is a "study of observable facts." From the years of precedent, a lawyer has building materials which may be fashioned into almost-concrete arguments, acceptable to the mind of a Supreme Court Justice. The benefits of precedent law are apparent.

Equally observable are the dangers of precedent law. Once a philosophy of law gets a few years under its belt, with attendant supportive reasoning, a bad precedent often carries as much weight as a good precedent. As you will see in the ensuing section, faulty logic is often enforced and re-enforced with the same zeal as a proper interpretation. While it is true that the Court has been known to overturn a decision on occasion, conservative as well as liberal courts lean heavily toward upholding their precedents.

Precedent law is important to us as Christians for this reason: We must "render unto Caesar the things which be Caesar's." "The American Caesar" is the Constitution of the United States. Since *Marbury v. Madison, (1 Cranch 137),* "the Constitution is what the Supreme Court says it is." All these factors bring us to an undeniable impasse.

THE PRECEDENT DECISIONS OF THE U.S. SUPREME COURT TAKE ON THE FORCE OF BIBLICAL AUTHORITY because they are the final word from the powers that be, which are ordained of God. Unless these decisions contradict a plain statement of Scripture, we must obey them. Even then, should we choose to disobey them for conscience sake, the only choice is to be imprisoned for the faith. We can go no higher in our appeal than the U.S. Supreme Court. The United States Supreme Court will seldom venture far from precedent law. Of course, we can appeal to the court of public opinion——or higher still, to the Court of Heaven. But in this country, these last two appeals will be made from a jail cell, if we choose to disobey the U.S. Supreme Court.

What may not be denied is the fact that, in America, neither Satan, nor Secular Humanism, nor State, nor society in general may take away our liberty, without the law to uphold its efforts. When the validity of all law is decided by the U. S. Supreme Court, then the power of that Court and the posture of that Court become paramount.

For this reason we must waste little time discussing the current drift of society, or the attempts by specific men and agencies, to take away religious liberty. Instead, we go directly to the basis for all law——the precedent decisions of the U. S. Supreme Court which interpret the U. S. Constitution.

Chapter 4

SEPARATION THROUGH EDUCATION

"You say——'There are persons who lack education'——and you turn to the law. But the law is not, in itself, a torch of learning which shines its light abroad. In this matter of education, the law has only two alternatives: It can permit this transaction of teaching—and—learning to operate freely and without the use of force, or it can force human wills in the matter."

Frederic Bastiat
The Law

From this point we will focus our attention on a particular aspect of Constitutional Law which ties together the theses of this book.

Education is paramount. Education, in a nation fully given to compulsory attendance laws, is, in essence, the right to the minds of our children. Should we ever lose the right to educate our children, we will have lost the final great battle in *The Separation of Church and Freedom.*

As stated previously, we are bound by precedent law. The U.S. Supreme Court is, for all practical purposes, the determining factor in our struggle for the right to the minds of our children. Perhaps some will say, quite correctly, that God is the determining factor. The fact remains that God has permitted U.S. Supreme Court decisions to be made and upheld by the legal system of this nation for several generations. He may intervene and abolish the U.S. Supreme Court, but until He does, they decide under what conditions a church may have a school, and when a school will be dissolved because its administration is put in jail for violating their edicts. We will be free to do what God has commanded only so long as the High Court allows us to be free. With that in mind we may proceed to examine their reasoning up to this point in history.

Over a period of fifty-seven years, in thirty-four cases, the U.S. Supreme Court has been involved in questions related to church schools, and the more general question of the relationship of religion to education. Out of these cases has come a framework which we must use in defense of liberty. Most effective is a defense which utilizes arguments consistent with precedent decisions; one which takes the High Court's own doctrines and philosophies and applies them to our case in a persuasive manner. This is not compromise—this is common sense. We must learn the language, as well as the philosophy, of First Amendment Constitutional Law.

To evangelize a foreign culture is impossible without first learning the language and the customs. To insult the people, or to be unable to converse in familiar terms, is to preclude any possibility of getting our message across. All the sincerity, all the Bible knowledge, all the conviction in the world is no substitute for doing your homework before you enter a foreign land. The courtroom is a foreign land, but a careful study of the following pages will stand you in good stead when the philosophy of the U.S. Supreme Court on religious education is the topic of discussion.

We will note the evolution of their philsosphy by considering the cases, and the key precedents, established or reconfirmed.

The court steered clear of the religion-education field from its beginning, in 1789, until *Meyer v. Nebraska (262 U.S. 390)* in 1923. *Meyer* involved a Lutheran school in the State of Nebraska, in which the teacher taught German in violation of a state statute against using a foreign language in the education of children. The U.S. Supreme Court, in the *Meyer* case, upheld, at least in principle, the right of a church school to determine curriculum by acknowledging their authority to teach the German language. The court upheld the right of the teacher to teach in a private church school, as well as the right of the parents to hire him.

They also spoke favorably of a parent's right to control the education of his children and, at the same time, they confirmed the validity of the compulsory attendance laws then present in many states. At once we have both a conflict of fact and a conflict of logic. It is impossible to reconcile compulsory attendance laws and the rights of parents to control the education of their children. If compulsory attendance laws are valid, then a parent has a very limited choice should he feel that a certain public school is teaching immorality, or values contrary to what he believes concerning religious education of children.

In this particular case, without citing a single precedent, (because there were none) the U.S. Supreme Court arbitrarily, in an offhanded comment, acknowledged that many states enforced the obligation of parents to give their child an education, by means of compulsory laws.

If we are to begin at the beginning of *The Separation of Church and Freedom*, there is no better point than here at *Meyer v. Nebraska, (262 U.S. 390)*. Satisfying compulsory attendance laws is a root of contention when the subject under consideration is the education of children in religious values.

Acknowledging the "police power" of the State as the mechanism, the U.S. Supreme Court upheld the authority of the State to make parents subject to prosecution, should they fail to have their children attend "a school"—this without definition of a school—apparently leaving such definition to the similarly arbitrary decision of the State.

At this point it would be well to consider a primary factor in the discussion to follow:

The U.S. Supreme Court operates by means of "precedent law," as discussed in the previous section. From this "precedent law" they develop what they describe as "Doctrines," or "Theories," or "Tests," which come out of the various precedents established. We know about "Doctrine" in terms of our Bible study. Our "Doctrine" is based upon the precepts and precedents of the Word of God. The U.S. Supreme Court has their "Doctrine" built upon the precedent of previous decisions and established over a period of years; and these "Doctrines" are followed consistently as you will see as we continue.

In 1925 a landmark case was decided by the U.S. Supreme Court and is cited in almost every religion-education case which follows. *Pierce v. Society of Sisters, (268 U.S. 510)* involved the Roman Catholic Church, as well as a private military school, which were facing a challenge from the State of Oregon of their right to educate their children in a religious context. In *Pierce,* the Court reaffirmed, from the precedent in *Meyer,* the right of parents to control the education of their child. They also reaffirmed the validity of compulsory attendance laws. The Court established in *Pierce* the right to attend church schools but, most important to *The Separation of Church and Freedom,* they also established the power of the State to reasonably regulate all schools and to inspect, supervise, and examine teachers and pupils.

This is a natural outgrowth of compulsory attendance laws, since such laws would have no meaning unless the State had the authority to determine what constitutes a school. In retrospect, these were extremely open-ended principles enunciated in *Pierce.* The circumstances in 1925 were quite limited in terms of the availability of education. Such is not the case today.

One key factor in considering *The Separation of Church and Freedom* in the religious education realm, is to see the unwarranted expansion of these precedents with the passage of time——expansion not only in the scope of the school systems of America, but expansion in the thinking of Supreme Court Justices who often fail to take into consideration the historic context in which some of these early precedent statements were made.

In 1930 in *Cochran v. Louisiana, (281 U.S. 370)* the State of Louisiana passed a statute providing free textbooks to children in all schools, including church schools. From *Cochran v. Louisiana* came what is known today as the "Child Benefit Doctrine" of the U.S. Supreme Court. The reasoning is that the provision of textbooks did not benefit the school or religion; it was done simply for the "child's benefit" and, therefore, was constitutionally permissible.

The "Child Benefit Theory" was more clearly enunciated in a 1947 case entitled *Everson v. Board of Education, (330 U.S. 1).* This was the famous *New Jersey Bus Case,* in which the issue was the power of the State to provide bus transportation for the benefit of children in all schools and, again, including church schools. The U.S. Supreme Court in *Everson* reaffirmed the "Doctrine of Incorporation" discussed in a previous section, and here "incorporated" the Establishment Clause in its application to the states through the Fourteenth Amendment.

The *Everson* Court mandated State "neutrality" toward religion. which was to develop into a "Doctrine of Neutrality" as future opinions were written. This "neutrality" was to be maintained because of the famous "wall of separation between church and state." *Everson* was the first case which clearly discussed in detail the "wall of separation" and the application of that wall to church-religion-school issues.

The Court in *Everson* also upheld State power to impose "secular educational requirements" without noting what those "secular educational requirements" might be, or without giving their definition to the word "secular." *Everson* was, indeed, a landmark case because it firmly established the "Child Benefit Doctrine" and the "Doctrine of Neutrality" and defined the relationship of church schools and government by defending the "wall of separation." *Everson* saw a strongly divided Court in which the dissenting opinions spoke emphatically to the illogical approach of expounding, at length, on the "wall of separation" and then breaching that wall by providing bus transportation to religious schools in the case at bar.

In 1948 a case reached the Court entitled *McCollum v. Board of Education, (333 U.S. 203).* Again in

McCollum, the Court reaffirmed the application of the Establishment Clause of the First Amendment to the states through the Fourteenth Amendment by the "Doctrine of Incorporation." They again reaffirmed the "wall of separation between church and state" discussed in *Everson,* and struck down religious "released time" instruction in public schools. (Public school children were being released from class to attend religion-oriented gatherings conducted by ministers of various faiths.) The Court held that religious instruction, because it was carried out on the premises of public schools, violated the "wall of separation."

In *McCollum* the Court stated emphatically that public education must be "secular" education. We find, today, much publicity given to Madalyn Murray O'Hair and the *Prayer and Bible Reading Case* of 1963, but here in 1948 the die was cast and a clear precedent established; public education MUST be "secular" education.

In 1952, in *Doremus v. Board of Education, (342 U.S. 429),* the Court refused to hear a case which challenged daily Bible reading in the public schools. By allowing the lower court decision to stand, the Court obviously placed its stamp of passive approval upon daily Bible reading in the schools; yet, less than ten years later, the temperament was to strike down Bible reading AND prayer and further extend their decision in *McCollum,* that public education must be secular education.

In 1952, in *Zorach v. Clauson, (343 U.S. 306),* the Court upheld a "released time" program for public school students which was conducted "off" campus. In *McCollum* they had refused to allow "released time" religious instruction "on" campus, but here in *Zorach,* made clear that it would be possible for students to leave school, when necessary, to attend religious services.

In the *Zorach* case the Court again reaffirmed the "Neutrality Doctrine" which was established in *Everson,* but this time added a new dimension, which we call the "Doctrine of Accommodation." The reasoning was that even though Church and State must be separate, this does not preclude the State "accommodating" the religious beliefs of parents and students by allowing them to leave public school to attend religious meetings or to observe religious holidays.

While stating clearly that government is not to be hostile to religion, they again, in *Zorach,* reaffirmed the "wall of separation between church and state."

Ten years later, in 1962, the next religion-education case came before the Court. Entitled *Engel v. Vitale, (370 U.S. 421),* this case involved mandatory prayer in public school. It is quite interesting that prayer had been removed from public schools before Madalyn Murray O'Hair ever came on the scene. That fact received no publicity, but the deed had been done.

Engel is the *Regents Prayer Case* out of the State of New York, in which the Board of Regents had authorized a mandatory prayer to be used for daily devotions in the public schools. The Court not only struck down the prayer, but reaffirmed the "Doctrine of State Neutrality" in matters of religion, and reaffirmed the "wall of separation between church and state."

The following year, in 1963, two cases were heard by the Court simultaneously——*Abington v. Schempp* and *Murray v. Curlett, (374 U.S. 203).* These cases were the famous *Prayer and Bible Reading Cases* featuring Madalyn Murray O'Hair. William Murray, III was her son, the appellant in the *Murray v. Curlett* case just mentioned. The Court here struck down required prayer and Bible reading programs, and again reaffirmed the "Neutrality Doctrine," and reaffirmed the "wall of separation between church and state."

In 1967 a case reached the U.S. Supreme Court which was allowed to stand without written opinion by the Court. This case involved Amish parents in the State of Kansas, *Garber v. Kansas (389 U.S. 51)*. The Supreme Court of Kansas had denied the rights of Amish parents to provide their children home instruction or attendance at an Amish school without "qualified" teachers. There was no definition of "qualified," but the subtle implication of this case did mark a trend of the Court against the possibility of home instruction fulfilling compulsory attendance laws.

A major case against our cause was decided in 1968. *Board of Education v. Allen, (392 U.S. 326). Allen* was another case challenging the power of the State to lend textbooks to children in church schools. The Court again upheld that practice here, as they had in *Cochran v. Louisiana (281 U.S. 370) (1930),* and reaffirmed the "Neutrality Doctrine," "the wall of separation," and compulsory attendance laws.

In these points they followed past precedents but further expanded, in the opinion, some principles which were not so well established. The Court said in *Allen* that the State has the power to require minimum hours of instruction, specify teacher training, prescribe subjects——without designating what those subjects might be. They interpreted *Pierce* as requiring attendance at schools meeting State-imposed requirements as to the quality and nature of curriculum——again without saying how far this may go.

In *Allen* they clearly affirmed the *Garber* implication of rejection of home instruction as satisfying compulsory attendance laws, and stated that the State has proper interest in how schools perform their "secular" educational function——again without defining the word "secular." They did say, however, in a passing comment, that the Court does not agree, based on the evidence before them, that all teaching in church schools is religious.

Allen was, by far, the most damaging case, in terms of precedent law, up to this particular point in time. You can see how a very limited context in *Pierce* was expanded to reach farther and farther into the rights of church-related schools.

In *Epperson v. Arkansas, (393 U.S. 97) (1968),* the Court struck down an "Anti-Evolution Statute," in the State of Arkansas, which prohibited the teaching of evolution in public schools. They further reaffirmed the "Neutrality Doctrine," stating again that the State must be neutral in matters pertaining to church and state.

In the year 1971, in *Lemon v. Kurtzman, (403 U.S. 602),* we find another far reaching decision with regard to church schools. This case is often referred to by the Court as *Lemon I,* because of another case by the same name which came out of it in 1973, to finally resolve some of the financial issues in question.

In *Lemon I,* the State had attempted to supplement teacher salaries and to reimburse schools for textbooks and instructional materials. The *Lemon* case was decided with a companion case entitled *Earley v. DiCenso, (403 U.S. 602)*. These two cases were out of the states of Pennsylvania and Rhode Island respectively, and involved similar issues which the Court decided simultaneously. A major factor in the *Lemon I* case was that the Court took occasion to apply a previous tax case precedent to education.

In *Walz v. Tax Commission, (397 U.S. 664)*, the Court had established some guidelines for determining an impermissible crossing of "the wall of separation." For some time, concern had been growing in the Court over the realization, on the part of numerous justices, that there could be no absolute "wall of separation between church and state." With the passage of time, in numerous dissenting opinions, they had reached the conclusion that some involvement between church and government was necessary, but were unable to state clearly how this should be done.

In *Lemon I* the Court spoke of a "three-fold test" which had evolved over a period of years and was as follows:

1. *A questioned statute must have a "secular legislative purpose."*
2. *The "primary effect" must neither advance nor inhibit religion.*
3. *It must not foster "excessive government entanglement" with religion.*

This "three-fold test" was to be applied time and time again in the cases to follow, and stands today as the primary means of determining whether a particular issue has impermissibly crossed the line of the "wall of separation between church and state." *Lemon I* reaffirmed State power to maintain minimum standards in church schools and reaffirmed compulsory attendance laws. It spoke again to the confusion surrounding the "wall of separation," if that were to be maintained as absolute. From this point forward the Court has used the "three-fold test" in determining how the "wall of separation" must be modified.

Lemon I was also important because it established two other tests or doctrines which are growing in importance. The first of these tests was that of "Pervasive Sectarianism." The Court in *Lemon I* found the Catholic schools involved to have a "pervasive religious nature" and determined that a breach of the "wall of separation" should, in some cases, be determined by the extent to which religion "permeates" the religious school in question. In later cases the Court was to find that some church schools were not "pervasively sectarian" and, therefore, amenable to more help than others.

A second "test" or "doctrine" growing out of the "Entanglement Doctrine," mentioned as the third of the "three-part test" above, was that of "Divisive Political Potential." The Court found that one aspect of "Entanglement," which could make a particular statute unconstitutional, was its tendency to divide the people of this nation along political lines, over religious questions. It remains to be seen how far the Court will allow this to develop, but it could obviously work to our benefit, as more and more cases, which involve the question of religious education, go to court.

A 1971 case entitled *Tilton v. Richardson, (403 U.S. 672),* dealt with church related colleges and universities. The Court upheld Federal construction grants for buildings, to be used for secular purposes, in church-related schools of higher education. In *Tilton* they again applied the "three-fold test" of *Lemon I:*

1. "Secular legislative purpose"
2. "Primary effect"
3. "Entanglement"

and reaffirmed the test of "Pervasive Sectarianism" just mentioned. *Tilton* is a good example of the meaning of "Pervasive Sectarianism." The Court found that the church colleges in this case were not "pervasively" religious. Although carrying the name, they did not, in practice, have a school which was permeated by their religious beliefs. The Court further held in *Tilton* that elementary and secondary church schools are more likely to have a "pervasive" religious nature than schools of higher learning. Also in *Tilton* the Court reaffirmed the test of "Political Divisiveness" in the area of competition for funds, which they established in *Lemon I.*

An interesting case was appealed to the U.S. Supreme Court in 1972. The Court affirmed, without written opinion, a case in which parents made a charge that their Free Exercise of religion rights were violated by the State of Missouri. These parents said they were financially unable to send their children to a church school and, therefore, the State was violating their Free Exercise rights by funding a free public school system and refusing to equally fund church schools.

The Court obviously ruled against them but the challenge was interesting.

Wisconsin v. Yoder, (406 U.S. 205), reached the U.S. Supreme Court in 1972.This case involved an Amish school in Wisconsin and was, without question, the most important case ever adjudicated by the U.S. Supreme Court on the question of religious educational liberty.

The *Yoder* case reaffirmed the power of the State to impose reasonable regulations. It reaffirmed parents' rights to provide equivalent education in a private school——although this was the first time the word "equivalent" was used and, here, without definition. However, the Court spoke to many things which had not yet been resolved, and some of them were resolved to our benefit.

The Court said, for example, that State interest in a matter is not totally free from a balancing process when it impinges other rights guaranteed by the Constitution. The Court said that there must be a State interest of sufficient magnitude to override religious interests and then, going further, said that only State interests of the highest order, not otherwise served, may override the Free Exercise of religion.

In *Yoder* they said the State's interest in compulsory education is by no means absolute. They said also that a person's belief and manner of life must be inseparable in order to be protectable; which is another way of stating that the Court will protect only "convictions" and not "preferences."

One very dangerous comment, yet one which we must face in numerous areas, was a statement by the Court that religious activities are often subject to State regulation to promote health, safety and general welfare.

The Court also reaffirmed, or perhaps better––stated clearly––that the primary role of parents in the upbringing of their children is beyond debate.

One addition to previous holdings by the Court, on the validity of compulsory attendance laws, was to state that these laws are valid in order to provide an informed electorate and a self-reliant citizenry.

Another comment worth contemplating was the Court's declaration that an apparently neutral regulation is not neutral if it unduly burdens the Free Exercise of religion.

In 1972 another case was decided entitled *Essex v. Wolman, (409 U.S. 808).* The Court here reaffirmed the "Doctrine of Entanglement" and established that parents of children in church schools may not receive tuition reimbursement from the State. This case was affirmed without written opinion.

In 1973 the Court heard a case entitled *Norwood v. Harrison, (413 U.S. 455).* This case dealt with a Mississippi law under which children in church schools were provided textbooks by the State of Mississippi. The Court reaffirmed its position, under the "Child Benefit Theory," that this was permissible.

The Court reaffirmed, under *Pierce* and *Yoder,* that the State's role in the education of its citizens must yield to the rights of parents to provide equivalent education in private schools of the parents' choice. As in *Yoder,* they used the word "equivalent" without defining it.

The primary challenge of this case was to the racially discriminatory policies of certain schools, and the Court held that the State could not provide assistance to schools which violated the civil rights of citizens of the United States. They did, however, say that the Constitution may compel toleration of private discrimination in some schools. Also in *Norwood,* the Court reaffirmed that religious schools pursue two goals——religious instruction and secular education.

In 1973, in *Commission for Public Education v. Nyquist, (413 U.S. 756),* the Court again reaffirmed the "three-fold test" of *Lemon I:*

1. "Secular legislative purpose"
2. "Primary effect"
3. "Entanglement"

They also reaffirmed the need for a modified "wall of separation" under this "three-fold test."

In *Nyquist* the Court reaffirmed that church schools perform secular educational functions, and established again that state laws, interfering with parents' rights to have their children in church schools, violates the Free Exercise Clause.

In *Nyquist* the Court held that state grants to repair and maintain church facilities for the health and safety of children were unconstitutional. Obviously this was an attempt to provide grants to the church schools under the "Child Benefit Doctrine," but it failed as being an impermissible "Entanglement" and having the "Primary Effect" of advancing religion.

The Court in *Nyquist* also held that tuition reimbursements to low income families from State funds are unconstitutional. The Court further held that tax benefits to parents of children in church schools are unconstitutional.

1973 was obviously a banner year for church-state cases, with the next being *Levitt v. Committee for Public Education, (413 U.S. 476)*. The Court again reaffirmed the reasoning of *Lemon I* and, in particular, the "Primary Effect Test" so often cited. In *Levitt* the Court held that State reimbursement to church schools for the cost of mandated testing and record-keeping was unconstitutional.

Again in 1973, in *Hunt v. McNair, (413 U.S. 734)*, the issue of construction grants for religious colleges was raised. The previous case cited, *Tilton v. Richardson, (403 U.S. 672)*, involved "Federal" grants to church colleges, while the case here involves "State" grants for construction of buildings used for secular purposes. The Court again reaffirmed the "three-fold test" of *Lemon I:*

1. "Secular legislative purpose"
2. "Primary effect"
3. "Entanglement"

and reaffirmed the "Doctrine of Pervasive Sectarianism" which examines the extent to which religion permeates a school.

Again in 1973, in *Sloan v. Lemon (413 U.S. 825)*, the U. S. Supreme Court held tuition reimbursement, to parents of children in church schools, to be unconstitutional and reaffirmed the reasoning of *Lemon I*.

Marburger v. Public Funds (417 U.S. 961) reached the Court in 1974. The Court, without opinion, upheld a lower court finding based on "Entanglement," that the State could not reimburse to parents the cost of secular textbooks or instructional materials and supplies. In previous cases, such as *Levitt* and *Essex*, the Court had upheld the unconstitutional nature of the State giving money either directly to schools or to parents for any purpose; they had allowed only state provision of textbooks and bus transportation to children under the "Child Benefit Doctrine."

In 1975, in a case entitled *Meek v. Pittenger (421 U.S. 349),* the Court reestablished this position. They held that the State may not provide auxiliary services to children in church schools by means of financial assistance to the schools. The services which may not be financed include counseling, testing and psychological services, speech and hearing therapy, teaching for handicapped, remedial, or disadvantaged students.

In *Meek* the Court reaffirmed the "Child Benefit Doctrine" to allow the State to provide secular textbooks, but held that the direct loan of instructional material and equipment produced an unconstitutional "Entanglement."

The Court, again in *Meek*, reaffirmed the "three-fold test" of *Lemon I:*

1. "Secular Legislative purpose"
2. "Primary effect"
3. "Entanglement"

Another religious college case reached the Court in 1976, entitled *Roemer v. Maryland (426 U.S. 736).* They again reaffirmed the "three-fold test" of *Lemon I:*

1. "Secular legislative purpose"
2. "Primary effect"
3. "Entanglement"

The Court upheld an annual subsidy grant to church colleges if the funds are used for secular purposes. An interesting statement coming out of the *Roemer* decision was that State effort to supervise and control teaching of religion in supposedly secular classes would create an "Entanglement" violation. The Court here also reaffirmed the "Divisive Political Potential Doctrine," which is an expansion of "Entanglement," and reaffirmed the test of "Pervasive Sectarianism."

Wolman v. Walter (76 U.S. 496), in 1977, was the most dangerous recent case and perhaps the most dangerous ever decided. They began by reaffirming the "three-fold test" of *Lemon I:*

1. "Secular legislative purpose"
2. "Primary effect"
3. "Entanglement"

The Court reaffirmed that the State may provide secular textbooks to children in church schools under the "Child Benefit Doctrine." They also reaffirmed that, under compulsory attendance requirements, a state may assure adequate secular education; again, without defining what a secular education entails.

The great point of distinction in this case is that apparently, also under the "Doctrine of Child Benefit," the Court made some striking concessions. As mentioned previously, they refused to allow auxiliary services which involved financial assistance to the schools on a direct basis, but here in the *Wolman* case the Court upheld the constitutionality of a law which provided similar services by means of the State itself making the provision, rather than channeling the money through the school. The Court held that the State may provide testing mandated to examine children in secular subjects. They held that the State may provide health services to all children in church schools, to include doctors, nursing, dental, optometric, as well as diagnostic speech and hearing services. Also under health services they held that the State has authority to provide objective psychological testing to detect students in need of treatment. The Court further held that children in church schools, found to have need, may be given therapeutic services, guidance services and remedial services by employees of the Board of Education or Board of Health, but these services must be administered off the premises of the church school.

From these findings of the Court you will no doubt clearly observe the danger involved. The primary focus of the Court, in all recent cases, has been the financial considerations and the "Entanglement" of state funds with church funds. Clearly more dangerous is the "Philosophical Entanglement" and the "Ideological Entanglement" inherent in the type of treatment authorized by the *Wolman* case.

Under this decision the State clearly has the authority to come into a church school and test the children with state employed psychologists. If they find those children to be in need of help because of any mental aberrations caused by their fundamentalist training, they also have the authority to take those children off the school premises and administer therapeutic services and guidance services to get their minds back in order as Secular Humanist psychologists would define normality.

It should be apparent, beyond controversy, that we are in serious danger of losing our liberty and our children with the sanction, rather than the protection, of the U.S. Supreme Court.

The Separation of Church and Freedom will ultimately be accomplished by the separation of children from parents, under the guise of children's rights and State responsibility, unless something is done. What you can do is get informed and get involved, and the remainder of this book explains how this may be accomplished.

As the previous chapters indicate, the "Separation of Church and State" principle has become the vehicle for *The Separation of Church and Freedom.* Jefferson and others feared too much religion in government and suggested a "wall of separation." The end result has been a swing of the pendulum to the other extreme, bringing us too much government in religion.

The Lord Jesus Christ taught that there is no "neutrality." He said: *"He that is not with me is against me." "Blessed is the nation whose God is the Lord,"* and, conversely, a nation whose God is not the Lord is against the Lord.

There can be no doubt that in a quest to rid America of an established religion of Christianity, the net effect has been to establish the religion of Secular Humanism in its place. There is no "neutrality." So where do we go from here? The question has two answers.

THE LEGAL SOLUTION

The legal solution is to argue for the "wall of separation" between church and state. Sound contradictory? Not at all. To enter a pistol duel with boxing gloves is absurd. To enter a nuclear war with guerilla warfare tactics means disaster. The United States Supreme Court has chosen the weapons and it is not our prerogative to change them. We must fight legal battles within the framework of "precedent law," deviating only where prudent analysis suggests a possible victory.

Ours is not a Christian nation—it is a Secular Humanist nation. Perhaps our great grandfathers could have been successful in challenging the Court to return to Christian principles in First Amendment law. Today it is too late. No longer are we a Christian majority in a Christian nation seeking to retain our Christian heritage in government. We are now a Christian minority in a Secular Humanist nation, seeking to preserve the right to practice our beliefs. Using the philosophy of religion evolved by the U.S. Supreme Court as a definition is the key to understanding.

We desperately need a "wall of separation" between church and state today. This is true because "church" to the U.S. Supreme Court is not at all a church upholding the God of the Bible and Biblical morality. Secular Humanism is a religion by their definition. *Torcaso v. Watkins (376 U.S 488, dictum).*

A summation of the Supreme Court's present philosophy on religion was well stated in the words of Justice Harlan in *Welsh v. United States, (389 U.S. 333, 351) (1950)*. This case dealt with defining the grounds for religious exemption from draft laws, and Harlan elaborated thus:

> *"The prevailing opinion today, has performed a lobotomy and completely transformed the statute by reading out of it*

94

any distinction between religiously acquired beliefs and and those deriving from essentially political, sociological, or philosophical views for a merely personal moral code."

With that type of construction on the meaning of "religion" in the First Amendment, our major legal thrust should be an attempt to show the religious nature of Secular Humanism and insist that it must not play a part in government regulation of our schools and churches. We need a "wall of separation" between church and state until the U.S. Supreme Court learns what "church" and "religion" mean by God's definition.

THE POLITICAL SOLUTION

As we continue the warfare in the courts, using their own terms and precedents against the established religion of Secular Humanism, we must fight on another front simultaneously. In the political theatre of war, we are not bound by legal precedent. A "wall of separation" is neither necessary nor desirable as we seek to reclaim public sentiment, as well as seats in the legislatures and Congress of this nation.

> *"Sovereignty itself is, of course, not subject to law, for it is the author and source of law; . . . Sovereignty itself remains with the people, by whom and for whom all government exists and acts. And the law is the definition and limitation of power."*
> *Yick Wo v. Hopkins, (118 U.S. 356, 370) (1885)*

As Mr. Ball has so often stated: "There is in this nation a tribunal higher than the Supreme Court——it is the court of public opinion."

While we fight a defensive holding action in the courts, there are major victories to be won for liberty by arousing the people to rise up in ballot-box rebellion against the advocates of keeping God out of government. Only with conservative office-holders may we stem the tide of encroachment and see positive laws enacted to change the status quo. For the mechanics of this action see Volume III of this book, *The Practice of War.*

Chapter 5

WE ARE AT WAR
Rousas John Rushdoony

Although done without publicity and fanfare, a war against Biblical faith is under way all over the world, in varying degrees. The civil governments are in the main in the hands of humanists, whose passionate hatred of Christianity is intense.

This, however, is a disguised war. The Soviet Union, as a leader in the humanist vanguard, began its history with a brutal and open assault on Christianity. Later, for strategic reasons, this gave way to another approach, attack by indirection, a method adopted from Nazi and Swedish practices. The Soviet Constitution guaranteed freedom of religion to allay fears and criticisms, but it made this "freedom" totally subject to licensure, permits, regulations, controls, etc. In other words, the state supposedly granted a right while at the same time ensuring that it would be nonexistent. In practice thus, there is no freedom of religion in the U.S.S.R.

In the U.S., there is a concerted effort to accomplish the same goal by the same means. The First Amendment guarantees freedom of religion. While the U.S. has no church establishment, Christianity has been from the earliest days the religious establishment, i.e., the determiner of law and morality in the U.S. But, as John W. Whitehead points out in *The Separation Illusion, A Lawyer*

Examines the First Amendment the U.S. Supreme Court decided by 1952 that "God was dead, and His church was dead." The remaining task was to dismantle the church and Christianity and to make way for the new established religion, humanism. Now that war against Biblical faith, designed to control, dismantle, and eliminate it, is under way.

It is a well-planned war. When virtually all 50 states embark on a common program, in unison, and appear with federal directives in hand, it is no accident. Of course, they declare themselves innocent of any attempt to control a Christian school, church, missions agency, or organization, but this is the practical result of their requirements. These efforts are directed at present mainly against the small or independent groups, those least able to defend themselves. Meanwhile, major church groups are not disturbed or upset. Legal precedent established against these smaller groups can later be applied against all others.

These demands take a multitude of forms: attempts to control church nurseries, the various religious uses of church buildings, zoning regulations, etc. Christian Schools are told that they must pay unemployment compensation, seek accreditation by the state, use state textbooks, teach humanism, and so on. Catholic orders and Protestant missionary agencies are told that they must pay unemployment compensation also. The National Labor Relations Board seeks to unionize parochial and Christian School teachers, and so on and on. Now too there is a demand that Christian Schools be integrated at a percentage set by the Internal Revenue Service, this despite the fact that such schools have not been involved in segregation. In another case, a church is being taken to court for firing a homosexual organist. In one way or another, all are being told they must wear the mark of the beast. (Rev.13:16-18)

Fighting this battle is not easy nor cheap. The great pioneer and leader, whose victories in the *Yoder* and *Whisner* cases represent legal landmarks, has been and is Attorney William B. Ball, of Ball and Skelly, Harrisburg, Penn. Mr. Ball is active in a number of cases currently, and during the summer of 1978, for example, was involved in cases in Kentucky and North Carolina. Attorney David Gibbs has formed the Christian Law Association and is also actively involved in cases in many states. But all these men cannot continue without support. They are working long hours, and often sacrificially. Numerous new cases are arising weekly. Attorney John Whitehead estimates that in a very few years, perhaps two or three, $500,000 monthly will be required to fight these cases!

The price of resistance is high, not only in money, effort, and abuse, but in many other ways. One pastor, facing the possibility of jail, spoke of the very real threat of gang rape by homosexual prisoners who looked forward to assaulting a preacher. It also means the animosity of the compromising churchmen whose conscience disturbs them and who therefore lash out against the courageous men who make a stand. I know that, when I support any who resist, I am usually given "friendly" warnings by these compromisers that it would be inadvisable for a man of my stature to associate with such men, and I have no doubt that these resisting Christians are warned against associating with the likes of R. J. Rushdoony!

But "the battle is the LORD'S" (1 Sam. 17:47), and those who are the Lord's will fight in His camp: they will not seek terms with His enemies.

One reason for the intensity of the battle is this: the growth of the Christian School movement is far greater than most people realize. If it continues at its present rate, the humanists fear that, by the end of this century, (not too far away), the U.S. will have a radically different population, one made up of faithful and zealous Christians. Humanism will then perish. Moreover, the birthrate for humanists has been low for some years now, and the birthrate for various minority groups, even with the "benefits" of welfarism, is beginning to drop markedly from its earlier high ratio. But the people involved in the Christian School movement have a high birthrate. The Christian Schools are producing the better scholars, who are going to be the leaders twenty and forty years from now. This is for them a threat, and a crisis situation.

But this is not all. Humanism is failing all over the world. The politics of humanism is the politics of disaster. Because humanism is failing, it is all the more ready to attack and suppress every threat to its power. The issue is clear enough; humanism and Christianity cannot co-exist. Theirs is a life and death struggle. Unfortunately, too few churchmen will even admit the fact of battle.

The battle is more than political or legal: it is theological. The issue is lordship: Who is the Lord, Christ or the state, Christ or Caesar? It is thus a repetition of an age-old battle which began, in the Christian era, between the church and Rome. *Lord* means sovereign, God, absolute property owner. For us, *"Jesus Christ is Lord"* (Phil. 2:11): this was the original confession of faith and the baptismal confession of the Christian Church. Now, too often the confession, whatever its wording, seems to be a pledge of allegiance to a church or denomination, not to the Sovereign Lord, Jesus Christ. Thus, our great need is to confess Jesus Christ as Lord, our Lord and Savior, Lord over the church, state, school, family, the arts and sciences, and all things else. If we deny Him as Lord, He

100

will deny us. *"Whosoever therefore shall confess me before men, him will I confess also before my Father which is in heaven. But whosoever shall deny me before men, him will I also deny before my Father which is in heaven"* (Matt. *10:32-33*). To confess means to acknowledge and to be in covenant with, to stand for in a position of testing or trial. The question thus is, Will the church of the 20th century confess Jeus Christ? Will it be His church, or the state's church? And whom will you and I confess?

The issue is lordship. Because we are not our own, but have been bought with the price of Christ's blood, we must serve, obey, and glorify God in all our being and our actions (1 Cor. 6:20). We cannot live for ourselves: we are God's property, and we must be used by Him and for His Kingdom. All too many churchmen are like the likeable and earnest young man, very active in a sound church, who insisted that he was "entitled" to enjoy life. A power-boat and water-skiing were his goals, and, in view of his support of, and faithfulness to the church, he felt "entitled" to enjoy these in due time without having his conscience troubled by the Christian School battles, and tales of persecutions at home and abroad. In brief, he wanted Christ as Saviour but not as Lord. He wanted Christ to provide fire and life insurance, so that he could live his life in peace. But if Jesus is not our Lord, He is not our Saviour. If we are not His property and possession, He is not our Shield and Defender (Ps. 5:12; 59:9, 16; etc.).

The Philosopher Hegel, the spiritual father of Marx, John Dewey, and almost all modern humanists, saw the state as god walking on earth. The humanist is a very dedicated and religious man: he cannot be countered by lukewarmness. (Our Lord's indictment of the lukewarm is especially severe in Rev. 3:14-16.) The humanist's church, his lord and saviour, is the state. The salvation of man requires that all things be brought under the lordship of the state. Hence, the current moves against churches, Christian schools, and Christian organizations is a religious move, designed to further the humanistic salvation of man and society.

Because these attacks on Christianity are religiously motivated and are religiously grounded, they cannot be met by merely defensive action, or simply by legal action, although defensive legal action is urgently necessary. Our Lord is greater than Caesar: He is King of Kings, Lord of Lords (Rev. 19:16), and the Creator and Governor of all things visible and invisible (Col. 1:16). We must take the offensive as His ambassadors, His army, and His bringers of great and glorious tidings of salvation, to bring every area of life and thought into captivity to Christ the Lord. Of Christ's victory, and of the defeat of His enemies, there can be no question. What is at issue is which camp we will be in.

We are at war, and there are no neutrals in this struggle. The roots of humanism are in the tempter's program of Gen. 3:1-5, man as his own god, knowing or determining good and evil for himself. Those who claim, in the name of a false and neoplatonic spirituality, that they want to rise "above" the battle, are also trying to rise above Christ and the meaning of His incarnation. To stand for the Lord is somehow unspiritual and unloving in their eyes. They are like the 14th century monks of Athos, who "rose above" the problems of their day and found spiritual ecstasy and visions of God in contemplating their navels. When Barlaam condemned this practice, these loving, spiritual, navel-watchers arose in a fury (of love, no doubt), called a Synod, and cited and condemned Barlaam and his party as heretics! So much for being loving and spiritual! We still have, in other forms, our navel-contemplators all around us, very much around us, but not with us. All well and good: let us donate them to the enemy. *"If God be for us, who can be against us?"* *(Rom. 8:31.)*

View from Court House steps as 5,000 rally in defense of Christian liberty. April 24, 1978—Photo by Cooper Francis

VOLUME II

THE PHILOSOPHY OF WAR

PREFACE TO VOLUME II

This section, entitled *The Philosophy of War* speaks to the reasoning behind the conflict. That a conflict exists means nothing. Men have fought and died, facing prison and suffering, for foolish reasons totally void of logic. We dare not pound the pulpit, and rally, and stir up the people of God, without sound Biblical convictions as our motivation. This means coming to grips with our own personal beliefs as an expression of reason. Walking by faith is, indeed, unnatural but it is not unreasonable.

It was reasonable for Moses to believe that God had the power to part the Red Sea. It was reasonable for Daniel to expect God to vindicate his stand against the edicts of the king.

This section on *The Philosophy of War* is not an attempt to intellectualize faith. It is an attempt to give Biblical justification to those principles for which we stand. In the face of much controversy——the press, the legislature, and many of our brethren who think we have zeal without knowledge, do indeed have a right to demand that we, *"be ready always to give an answer to every man that asketh us a reason of the hope that is in us, with meekness and fear."* I Peter 3:15

Chapter 6

THE PHILOSOPHY OF POLICE POWER

"The law is the substitution of a common force for individual forces. And this common force is to do only what the individual forces have a natural and lawful right to do: To protect persons, liberties, and properties; to maintain the right of each, and to cause justice to reign over all of us."

> Frederic Bastiat
> The Law

Taken in summary, the Bible sets forth only two types of authority––legitimate authority and illegitimate authority. God is legitimate authority––Satan is illegitimate authority. It is, however, possible for authority to be sanctioned by God and corrupted by Satan. For instance, parental authority is God-given, but parental authority may be used to lock a child in a basement and torture him to the point of insanity. Should such an instance arise, governmental authority overrules parental authority by a means described as "the police power of the state."

Romans 13, and various other passages, place legitimate authority in the hands of human government to deal with abuses of divine law. Our system of justice in America speaks of the scope of this "police power" as preservation of the public health, public safety, and public order. Literally thousands of court cases, at all levels, have upheld the police power of the State, and those who believe the Bible have no basis for objection to placing such authority in the hands of human government. Admittedly there may be differences over the extent and scope of the terms, but the principle remains.

At this point our subject is the legitimate authority of "police power." Do you agree with a state-administered system of justice? Should bank robbers be arrested by a police department? Should drug pushers be stopped by narcotics agents? Should health officers be allowed to stop the sale of diseased animals to butchers? Any Christian, holding a Biblical view of human government, would agree with these activities of legitimate authority.

Having accepted "police power" as legitimate authority, we must apply that principle to the church. Is it right for the state to stop sex orgies in the sanctuary of Glide Memorial Methodist Church in California——even though they call it a worship service? Indeed, that is legitimate Biblical authority. Is it right for the state to allow only licensed drivers to operate church vehicles on the public highways? Again, we would have difficulty defining such a practice as illegitimate authority.

The government is faced with exercising its "police power" over the broad spectrum of religious activities: cults meeting in buildings which are fire traps and inviting the public to attend; licensing buses and other vehicles used by a church; licensing insurance companies and credit unions owned by denominations, which may or may not be unscrupulous; licensing hospitals owned by religious groups; etc. When any religious group operates a public facility, some public interests will be served by government agencies, either with or without our cooperation.

For an answer to the dilemma of distinguishing between legitimate and illegitimate "police power" we must turn to the Bible. "Conviction" is a Biblical concept. Valid convictions are Bible convictions based on authority given by God. I Peter 2:13-18 is the most direct passage on Christian responsibility toward human government.

> *v.13 – – "Submit yourselves to every ordinance of man for the Lord's sake: whether it be to the king, as supreme;*
>
> *v.14 – "Or unto governors, as unto them that are sent by Him for the punishment of evildoers, and for the praise of them that do well.*
>
> *v.15 – – "For so is the will of God, that with well doing ye may put to silence the ignorance of foolish men:*
>
> *v.16 – – "As free, and not using your liberty for a cloak of maliciousness, but as the servants of God.*
>
> *v.17 – – "Honor all men. Love the brotherhood. Fear God. Honor the King.*
>
> *v.18 – – "Servants be subject to your masters with all fear; not only to the good and gentle but also to the froward." (crooked)*

Notice an unmistakable message in Vs. 13-15. It is "the will" of God for us to submit ourselves to "every" ordinance (law) of man and to every government official, whether it be the supreme official himself or his delegated agent. *V. 18—Not only the good and gentle people in authority but also the crooked (froward).* God says in effect—don't hide behind your freedom as a coverup for a malicious attitude toward legitimate authority.

In the war you will encounter two types of individuals who will destroy the ranks of God's people—those who think I Peter 2 is the only passage in the Bible on this subject, and others who are unimpressed by its unmistakable message.

Some take the position that we should resist every action of government related to church ministries: "If it's not specified in the Book we don't buy it"—type of attitude. What they fail to admit is that "the Book" specifies that we submit to "every" ordinance of "man," as well as every ordinance of God. We already have a direct command from God to obey every rule and regulation made by human government, whether it be the supreme official, or his delegated agent. Romans 13 does not speak to specific rules and regulations, as does the passage here—it speaks to legitimate or illegitimate authority. Once government has the legitimate authority, we are to submit to every man-made ordinance unless such an ordinance exceeds the bounds of God-given power. Herein lies the distinction:

In a question of health, the state may regulate health conditions in a church under "police power." According to I Peter 2:13 and 14:

> *"Submit yourselves to every ordinance of man for the Lord's sake: whether it be to the king as supreme; or unto governors, as unto them that are sent by him for the*

110

*punishment of evildoers, and for the praise
of them that do well."*

Such regulation may be carried out by the
governor of the state, the legislature, or anyone designated
by them—such as a State Board of Health or County
Health Department. However, should they contend that
"health" includes "mental health" and our teaching is
harmful to the minds of children, the obligation to submit
is abrogated by the Bible and the Constitution.

We have no Biblical basis to reject the lawfully
assigned authority of such Boards and Departments to
make or enforce ordinances. We may reject "certain
specific ordinances," where an individual ordinance
exceeds Biblical bounds. We may not scripturally object to
the "legitimate authority" of such Boards and
Departments to represent the State. Clearly we would
"prefer" local people and local control, but that cannot be
a Biblical conviction. Should your church bus get a
speeding ticket from a State patrolman, try arguing in
court that you only want local police to inspect your
speed.

Biblically and legally we have no claim to sincere
religious convictions against the "police power of the
state." The government or any of its Boards, Departments,
Commissions, Agencies or Inspectors at Federal, State or
local levels, may exercise this "police power." So long as
they are duly authorized representatives of the government
in a given field, they may inspect, control, regulate or
prosecute in accordance with the laws governing public
health, public safety and public order.

111

This is Biblical reasoning, but it is also constitutional reasoning. As early as 1885 the U.S. Supreme Court said:

> *"When we consider the nature and the theory of our institutions of government, the principles upon which they are supposed to rest, and review the history of their development, we are constrained to conclude that they do not mean to leave room for the play and action of purely personal and arbitrary power."*
> *Yick Wo v. Hopkins (118 U.S. 356, 370)*

> *"Sovereignty itself is, of course, not subject to law, for it is the author and source of law; but in our system while sovereign powers are delegated to the agencies of government, sovereignty itself remains with the people, by whom and for whom all government exists and acts. And the law is the definition and limitation of power."*
> *Yick Wo v. Hopkins (118 U.S. 356, 370)*

> *"The authority of the State to enact this statute is to be referred to what is commonly called the police power. Although this court has refrained from any attempt to define the limits of that power, yet it has distinctly recognized the authority of a state to enact quarantine laws and health laws of every description."*
> *Jacobson v. Mass. (197 U.S. 11,25)*

"It is indeed quite true that there must always be lodged somewhere, and in some person or body, the authority of final decision; and in many cases of mere administration the responsibility is purely political, no appeal lying except to the ultimate tribunal of the public judgment, exercised either in the presence of opinion or by means of the suffrage. But the fundamental rights to life, liberty and the pursuit of happiness, considered as individual possessions, are secured by those maxims of constitutional law which are the monuments . . . securing to men the blessings of civilization under the reign of just and equal laws, so that, in the famous language of the Massachusetts Bill of Rights, the government of the commonwealth——may be a government of laws and not of men."

Yick Wo v. Hopkins (118 U.S. 356, 370)

Please keep in mind that our subject at the moment is overall power, not individual points of contention. The power described here is the legitimate Biblical power granted to government by God and upheld by the courts.

"Whosoever therefore resisteth the power, resisteth the ordinance of God."

Romans 13:2

"Submit yourselves to every ordinance of man for the Lord's sake."

I Peter 2:13

113

*"For rulers are not a terror to good works,
but to the evil. Wilt thou not then be afraid
of the power? Do that which is good, and
thou shalt have praise of the same: for he is
the minister of God to thee for good."*
Romans 13:3,4

We dare not allow the church to be guilty, in any
sense, of resisting legitimate authority; this means being
subject *"not only to the good and gentle, but also to the
crooked"* (I Peter 2:18). Many times we must *"for
conscience toward God endure grief, suffering
wrongfully."* (I Peter 2:19).

Even though inspectors and regulations are unfair,
or costly, or inconvenient——even completely
unreasonable——those things in and of themselves are not
Biblical grounds to resist the power. (I Peter 2:20). The
rule is inescapable——*"Submit yourselves to every
ordinance of man for the Lord's sake."* (I Peter 2:13).

The word "every" is obviously modified by the
immutable doctrines of fundamental truth which cannot
be violated. On the other hand, "every ordinance of man"
which does not violate a clear statement of scripture is to
be obeyed "for the Lord's sake" whether we agree with it
or not. Beyond that we have a specific directive to inform
us that "the will of God" includes an attempt on our part
to seek methods of "well-doing" by which we may "put to
silence the ignorance of foolish men."

All too often Christians take an antagonistic
position toward government per se, rather than toward
specific government activities which overstep Biblical
boundaries. Remember, that to a great extent, we are the
government! "The American Caesar" is not the legislature,
or the governor, or the Congress, or the President. "The
American Caesar" is the Constitution of the United States.

114

With that in mind, we are thrown into direct confrontation with our Biblically directed accountability to God and man. The question then becomes not "How little relationship may we have to the government and get away with it?" but rather, "How far may we go to show ourselves accountable to government without violating Biblical absolutes?"

We live under "The American Caesar." The Lord Jesus said: *"Render unto Caesar the things which are Caesars."* Our "Caesar" is the U.S. Constitution. Long ago, in *Marbury v. Madison,* for all intents and purposes, the Constitution became what the Supreme Court says it is. Chapter 2 of Volume I—*The Separation of Church and Freedom*—sets forth in detail how the *Marbury v. Madison* decision made precedent law the guiding force of government.

Precedent law is the controlling element in police power. To obey God's Word we must get in line with precedent law, as established by the U.S. Supreme Court, or have a Biblical conviction against it—a conviction powerful enough to enable us to sit in prison for the rest of our life.

We are directed by the Word of God, under our system of government, to submit ourselves to EVERY ordinance of the U.S. Supreme Court for the Lord's sake or shut down our ministries and check in at the state penitentiary for the Lord's sake.

Immediately precedent law takes on the force of Biblical authority unless contradictory to the Bible. Remember, precedent law is the highest court decision available on a particular issue. U.S. Supreme Court decisions, until overturned, stand as the binding rules for

115

the government of this nation. This means God Himself stands behind every law and, without a clear Biblical mandate in our favor, we stand against God when we stand against government.

All of this background is necessary to deal with the subject of legitimate state interest in church ministries. Our premise is that there is no "wall of separation." The state does have legitimate interests in church affairs, and the church does have legitimate interest in state affairs. One determination remains to be made——how far, or to what degree, does this legitimate interest extend?

As noted in previous paragraphs, one foundational assumption can be made. In the light of clear Bible directives, we must assume that every ordinance of man is valid. This is also a basic principle of law. A statute is presumed valid until proved otherwise. Government has no responsibility to prove that it has authority over the church. The Bible, as well as law, declares that government has such authority. Our only valid recourse is to establish where such authority oversteps the God-ordained limitations.

Recognizing that government must deal with true churches and false churches is a good place to start. Unscrupulous, dishonest men are active in many religions, so we are thinking, not in terms of how much we prefer to be regulated, but where we will draw the line for society as a whole. Some of the most confusing and absurd difficulties today come from ignoring this point.

Laws cannot be localized to suit an individual building or the temperament of individual pastors. Unequal application of the law is as unconstitutional as the violation of religious liberty. We must either destroy completely the legitimate police power granted to government by Romans 13 or, on the other hand, be responsible advocates of law and order. That which we do and say must apply equally to every wild-eyed religious nut as well as sincere fundamentalists.

When we sit down to write a statute for eventual passage by the legislature we become the government. At that particular juncture the issue is not church v. state, for the obvious reason that we have become "the state." We are proposing a law, or an amendment to existing law, which will be enforced by some of our fellow citizens upon the whole of society. Tremendous responsibility comes to rest on our shoulders. Again I say, the question becomes—"How far may we go to show ourselves accountable to government of the people, by the people, and for the people, without violating Biblical absolutes?"

Legitimate authority and illegitimate authority again rise to the fore. We cannot object to the state "bearing the sword" of police power to punish those who would carelessly or willfully harm others. This is legitimate Biblical authority.

Blackstone cites a 1676 precedent as saying: "The Christian religion is part of the law itself." *[Taylor's case I, Ventris 293; 3 Keble 607, (King's Bench, 1676)]*.

The English Court said again, "Christianity in general is parcel of the common law of England, and therefore, to be protected by it." *[Rex v. Woolston, 2 Strange 832; I Barnardiston 162, (King's Bench, 1729)]*.

Romans 13 grants to "the powers that be" the authority to be "the minister of God to thee for good." In America, "the powers that be" are as follows:

117

THE DERIVATION OF GOVERNMENT AUTHORITY IN AMERICA

GOD
(The Ultimate Authority)
Granted

(Certain Inalienable Rights)
Expressed in

THE PEOPLE
(Mutually Accepted)

THE DECLARATION OF INDEPENDENCE
(Inspired and Framed)

THE CONSTITUTION OF THE UNITED STATES
(As an Instrument of Govt.)   (As a Body of Law)
Established   Established

Legislative Branch
Executive Branch
Judicial Branch

Bounds of States Rights
Control of the Three Branches
"A Government of Laws and Not of Men"

THE DERIVATION OF POLICE POWER

GOD
(Permitted)

THE UNITED STATES CONSTITUTION
(Supreme Law of the Land)
As Interpreted By

THE UNITED STATES SUPREME COURT
(Which Determines the Validity)
Of Decisions By

FEDERAL COURTS   *STATE COURTS*
(Which Oversee Laws Enacted By)

U.S. CONGRESS   *STATE LEGISLATURES*
(Which Enact Laws Enforced By)

FEDERAL OFFICIALS   *STATE OFFICIALS*
(Who Deal Directly With)

THE PEOPLE
118

As evidenced by the previous diagrams, *"The powers that be are ordained of God" (Romans 13:1).* We are bound by Scripture to obey every edict of human government unless it is unscriptural or unconstitutional. In our capacity as Christians we may challenge, in the courts, any law which violates the Law of God. In our capacity as Christian citizens we may also challenge, in the courts, any law which violates the Constitution.

For a further application of these principles, please read carefully *The Philosophy of License.*

Chapter 7

THE PHILOSOPHY OF LICENSE

"To imagine a man perfectly free and not subject to any law, we must imagine him all alone, beyond space, beyond time, and free from dependence on cause."

Leo Tolstoy
War and Peace

Across the nation State licensure of church ministries has become a major issue. Numerous states have faced proposed legislation to license pastors before permitting them to counsel their church members on various subjects.

The Roloff case was lost and refused review by the United States Supreme Court over licensing of child care homes by the State. Some states have faced licensing of Christian schools, either in fact or in principle. Most common is the problem of state licensure of Church Day Care facilities. We have fought each of these in North Carolina.

The subject of licensure must be approached carefully and in great detail lest rhetoric outrun reason. To put into perspective the principles involved, we must begin at the beginning by examining Biblical philosophy applied to the law of the land.

BEWARE THE PSEUDO CAESAR

Paul and Peter, the most prolific writers on the subject of submission to human government, and the authors of Romans 13 and I Peter 2 (examined in the previous chapter), both spent time in prison for conflict with that same government. More specifically, they were in prison for the principle we seek to uphold in this hour. At Phillipi, Paul was imprisoned by those who accused him in the following manner: They said: *"These men . . . teach customs which are not lawful for us to receive, neither to observe, being Romans."* What did being *Romans* have to do with the religion Paul proclaimed? What was the conflict between their citizenship and the convictions taught by the Apostle Paul? The answer is history.

As Professor Rushdoony has pointed out, "The conflict then and now is a war of names. Which is the name of power, Christ or Caesar?" Rome of the first century had perpetuated the "divine right of kings" philosophy of ancient Babylon. Heads of State were god walking upon the earth—-the hope of the people. They had a slogan in the Roman Empire which has a familiar ring---*"There is none other name under heaven, given among men, whereby we must be saved than the name of Caesar."* In Acts 4:12 the Apostle Peter was proclaiming a challenge to governmental authority which had overstepped the limits of legitimate authority. He heralded forth the Lordship of Christ in a society which claimed Caesar as Lord.

These men were teaching customs which were not lawful for the people to receive, neither to observe being Romans. It was blasphemy to acknowledge any authority to be supreme except the authority of Caesar. As a means of keeping civil order and with the passage of time, it became permissible to retain any personal religion, so long as an individual would give "licit" to Caesar. "Licit" is the Latin form from which our English word "license" comes. To give "licit" to Caesar meant simply that Caesar was the supreme authority. Christians went to the lions for refusal to give "licit" to Caesar. Throughout the Gospels and the Book of Acts we see this battle raging. The "divine right of kings" included both political and religious supremacy over the people. Even the Jews *"cried out"* emotionally, *"Whosoever maketh himself a king speaketh against Caesar"* (John 19:12). They said, *"We have no king but Caesar"* (John 19:15). This is the epitome of Secular Humanist religion, the belief late echoed by Hegel that the state embodies supreme authority in all matters political and religious; it is God walking upon the earth.

It is noteworthy that the chief priests of Israel said, *"We have no king but Caesar."* This was an acquiescence of tremendous magnitude to the prevalent doctrine of the religious preeminence of Caesar. These were men who, from childhood, had been taught to repeat and sing almost endlessly, *"God is the King of all the earth"* (Ps. 47:7). *"O Lord of hosts, my King and my God"* (Ps. 84:3). *"The Holy One of Israel is our King"* (Ps. 89:18). Their rejection of Christ as Messiah was not the point. They did not say, "This man is not our king." The religious-political leadership of Israel had bowed to the golden image of state worship, denying the absolute supremacy of the King of Glory in heaven, when they said, *"We have NO king but Caesar."*

Such is the attitude we oppose in the warfare of the Twentieth Century. We may teach our children as we please, but it must be in the name of Caesar--"STATE approved" schools; "STATE certified" teachers; "STATE licensed" day care centers.

Before proceeding further we should draw clear distinctions in our mind as to the situation in which we find ourselves. While the analogy of "Caesar" is a familiar comparison, it is, nonetheless, only an analogy and not indicative of our specific form of government. We are the government. Basic to our reasoning here is that we have

123

"government of the people, by the people, and for the people" as Abraham Lincoln said. "We the people" have jointly united ourselves under a system which embodies final authority in matters of government in the U.S. Constitution. The "Caesar" of Bible reckoning is the supreme authority in human government. This being true, "the American Caesar" is the Constitution of the United States. All men in office in this country are only duly authorized representatives of "the American Caesar"––the Constitution. Bureaucrats and political liberals often misconstrue the purpose of the "State" in American society, and attempt to assume powers akin to the Roman Caesar. We must not, however, mistake those activities for legitimate claims under our system of government. Our dealings ultimately are with "the American Caesar"––the Constitution, and the people it represents.

Thinking now from that root assumption, we are faced with a dilemma. We have a "Caesar" which, in most points, is a Bible-based document drawn by Bible-believing people. Coupled with that, we have a Secular Humanist system applying that document. Almost without exception, present day legal decisions affecting us are rooted in the Secular Humanist philosophy of a "wall of separation between church and state." God's Word abhors such a philosophy of government, so we begin with a less-than-ideal relationship at best.

Biblical government is a "minister of God" according to Romans 13; not an impartial arbiter between multitudes of religions. Such being the case, our question then becomes: "What degree of state interest may be tolerated by Biblical convictions as we live in a pseudo-Christian nation?"

124

Answering that question requires countless hours of serious contemplation of a myriad of ramifications.

A PERSONAL TESTIMONY

We have run the obstacle course in North Carolina out of sheer necessity. First we sought a negotiated settlement through the State Attorney General's office; we then defied certain laws on the basis of their unconstitutionality; we then had a suit filed against us in Superior Court; we staged a rally on the courthouse steps with 5,000 people; we had a full scale trial to examine our convictions; we have been in Federal Court twice over separate matters; we have needed three different stays from the N.C. Supreme Court to keep us out of prison; we have had as many as 4 suits in progress at one time. All this is important to assure the reader that at no point have we backed off from our convictions or avoided the threat of fines and imprisonment. My part in the matter has been to stand with my brethren in the front lines, to advocate a militant position as strong as any which has been litigated in any court in the nation. I have paid my dues as a fighter, so please give close attention to some advice from one who knows both sides of the story.

At the risk of being branded a compromiser, I want to suggest some logic which cannot be refuted by reasonable Bible-believing men. What you are about to read is the result of countless hours of discussion with fundamentalist leaders from across America, dozens of hours with some of the leading Constitutional lawyers in the nation—and most important, a tremendous amount of Bible study and prayer for the Lord's wisdom in writing this book. Coupled with these sessions with "a multitude of counselors," I have read and analyzed every U.S.

Supreme Court opinion ever written on religious issues, from 1789 through 1979. I have gone off alone, for weeks on end, to do nothing but think and pray and write and rewrite on these issues.

All these personal references are dangerous lest it appear that I claim some special wisdom. In reality I claim only three things; 1––to have been in the heat of the battle, rather than theorizing about how it might be, 2––to have an incredible burden from the Lord to write this book, 3––to have done my homework. We are all pioneers in a field virtually untouched by the Lord's people for generations. May God grant us the grace and the humility to think and rethink our positions as well as the courage to adjust our views when truth demands it.

THE AMERICAN WAY

Had I lived in the days of the Roman Empire I would have died rather than give "licit" to Caesar. Such an action meant Caesar was Lord and controlled the right to worship according to the dictates of conscience. We do not live under a Roman military dictatorship, and until Constitutional interpretation demands that government take the place of Caesar we must use that analogy only as an illustration, rather than a Christian conviction. Think for a moment of this definition of "sovereignty" given by the U.S. Supreme Court:

> *"Sovereignty itself is, of course, not subject to law, for it is the author and source of law; but in our system, while sovereign powers are delegated to the agencies of government, sovereignty itself remains with the people, by whom and for whom all government exists and acts. And the law is*

126

the definition and limitation of power."
Yick Wo v. Hopkins (118 U.S. 356, 370)

We are not asked by the U.S. Supreme Court, or by the Constitution itself, to acknowledge the lordship of the state. "Sovereignty itself remains with the people!" We, as individuals with individual rights protected by "the American Caesar," the U.S. Constitution, are free under our system to choose to maintain personal sovereignty or acknowledge the sovereignty of God. "Sovereignty itself remains with the people."

As the U.S. Supreme Court has said:

"The fundamental rights to life, liberty and the pursuit of happiness, considered as individual possessions, are secured by those maxims of Constitutional law which are the monuments... securing to men the blessings of civilization under the reign of just and equal laws, so that, in the famous language of the Massachusetts Bill of Rights, the government of the Commonwealth——'may be a government of laws and not of men.'"
Yick Wo v. Hopkins (118 U.S. 356,370)

We cannot be faced, under our system of government, with acknowledging the lordship of any man in office. A legislature is an expression of government by the people. Any controversy we may have is not with a man——it is a controversy with law. Law, if it is legitimate law, protects life, liberty and property. As a nation under law we are bound by the Word of God to obey every law which is not unbiblical or unconstitutional. Think about this question very deeply:

Law is the authority vested in a system of government to restrain its citizens. Any legal system is a series of restraints. You do not enjoy absolute freedom in this nation. Absolute freedom is anarchy. The law is, by its very definition, a prior restraint on the free exercise of religion. Many times the U.S. Supreme Court has said that free exercise of religion is not absolute.

A great deal of rhetoric is going forth today concerning "the principle involved." What is the "principle?" Some would tell us the "principle" is that government cannot tell the church what to do. Simple common sense dictates otherwise. Government can stop you from having 700 wives, as Solomon did. Government can stop you from burning your child on the altar to fulfill a vow to the Lord, as Jepthah did. We must be consistent, as well as Biblical, in our logic. If we stand for the "principle" of no state control of free exercise of any sort, we must go to court immediately to fight for polygamy rights and child sacrifice rights, as well as many others which could be cited.

Before any reasonable position may be reached, we must be consistent. Government does have God-given authority to limit free exercise of religion. "Religion" includes every claim to a belief of any kind. An insane man may say he believes in any sort of wild practice; immediately he has a First Amendment claim. If we reject law we reject the Bible because it is a Book of Laws, as well as the basis for our legal system.

THE ANATOMY OF A LICENSE

You say you object to a church ministry being

licensed by the state? That statement, taken alone, will not stand the test of the Bible, the courts, or even good common sense. Licensing of a church ministry is legitimate or illegitimate authority depending on several tests which are inescapable in our reasoning. Should you choose another position——Keep in mind that you must be willing to die for the difference, or you are a hypocrite.

Several years ago, when the Bishop of Maryland of the Episcopal Church was installed, his church had a party where the guests consumed 2600 cans of free beer provided by the church. Personally, I would not want to take away their freedom of assembly, their right to life, liberty, and property, or the free exercise of their "religion"——but I would want that church, forced by the state, to take a beer and wine "license" like any other tavern, before allowing them to handle and distribute alcoholic beverages in quantity.

Certainly we must agree there was a time in America when no license was required for anything in any area of life. We no longer live in those days. The issue then, becomes crystal clear. Perhaps we would prefer no license for anything, including marriage, but such preferences are a moot point and may as well be forgotten. "License" is a nationally accepted form of exercising police power. Our only decision is the point at which we will resist unto prison, even unto death, the licensing of a church ministry.

Never for one moment may we defend a position which rejects all law affecting churches. Our only logical claim is to reserve the right to challenge any law which goes too far in its restraint on the free exercise of religion. Please think about that carefully. If we accept law at all——the only possible issue is——which laws go too far!?

129

Before proceeding further, we must face certain realities. "Churches" in the New Testament had no corporate charters. Any time a church goes to court as a corporation, that aspect of defense is purely legal——not Biblical. When the courts examine beliefs and convictions they know only too well that the issue at stake is not the rights of a church building, or the rights of a piece of paper designating it as a church. Neither the Constitution nor the Bible protects anything except the BELIEFS of individuals. Always the issues hinge upon the Biblical convictions of the person or persons who go to court.

The Amish won because they were defending a total lifestyle. We dare not fall into the trap of divorcing our life into sacred and secular categories in our dealings with government. We cannot draw a distinction between the practices of individuals and the practice of a church. In every case the issues must be the rights of individuals to function individually and as a group of like-minded individuals in the practice of certain beliefs.

To develop this reasoning, consider certain questions: Do you take a license or permit from the state to preach? Would you ever take a license to preach? Would you take a license to pray? Would you take a license or permit to drive from house to house to carry out your ministry of visitation? Would you take a permit or license to preach on the steps of the state capital? If you were a missionary pilot, who could not visit your congregations without a plane, would you cease your ministry or take a license which permitted you to do what God has called you to do?

We must face these questions squarely and know why we stand. We do, indeed, get state "permission" in many forms, without which our work for the Lord, individually and collectively, would be hindered if not completely halted.

130

In the matter of "license"——every church in America has taken many "licenses." They may not have been called a "license" but they were a piece of paper, without which the church could not function as desired. One of these pieces of paper was necessary to have electricity in the church, another to have a septic tank installed or connect to city sewage, another to build a building or add additional space, another to serve food to school or day care, another to own the property by recording it with the government, another to become incorporated, etc., etc. Law requires each of these pieces of paper in order to function. We accept these "licenses" because we know the clearly defined limits, and we know they pose no threat to Free Exercise.

The issue is not "license" because law is "license." In every case the only question is——does the law go too far in proscribing Free Exercise? To accept one of these pieces of paper is to accept the terms as suitable for all of society. Always the question is——"What does the piece of paper mean?" Does it mean the heating system is safe? Does it mean the trusses will hold the weight of the roof? Does it mean the commodes will drain properly? License is law by definition of the U.S. Supreme Court, a legitimate tool of police power.

God ordained marriage and commanded it in His Word. He never authorized government to have anything whatsoever to do with marriage. Nowhere in the Bible do we find mention of a marriage "license" from the state, as a prerequisite to obeying God in the sacred rite of Holy Matrimony. Yet how many pastors would perform a wedding where the couple had no marriage license? The issue is not license. License is only proof that a law has been obeyed. The issue must be nothing more, nor less, than the PURPOSE of the license. Is it limited sufficiently in its scope, by the law it represents, or does it unduly burden the Free Exercise of religion?

Here is our dilemma. Benjamin Disraeli said, "If you would converse with me—define your terms." "License" is a term which may be construed in a broad sense or in a narrow sense. For example, I have a driver's license. Driving is a vital part of my work as a pastor. Much of my ministry involves driving; in fact—no less than 50% of my present work for the Lord would cease if I had no license from the state. This is even more true of missionary pilots. If 50% of my personal ministry as a preacher of the Gospel depends on permission from the state, and the taking of a license—I must be a compromiser. Only a compromiser would take a license which affects his ministry in any way. After all, it is the principle that matters.

Is that sound reasoning? Of course not. I take a driver's license because such a license is a legitimate tool of police power, to protect the public safety. It is a license issued under narrowly drawn statutes which clearly limit the police power to a public safety function.

THE U.S. SUPREME COURT AND LICENSE

The U.S. Supreme Court has, on numerous occasions, permitted "license" of religious activities. However, they have specified that any such action by government must be severely limited to prohibitions involving legitimate public concerns for health, safety, and order. As long ago as 1905 the Court said in *Jacobson v. Mass. (197 U.S. 11)*

> *"The authority of the State to enact this statute is to be referred to what is*

132

commonly called the police power. Although this Court has refrained from any attempts to define the limits of that power, yet it has distinctly recognized the authority of a State to enact quarantine laws and health laws of every description."
(at 25)

"According to settled principles the police power of a State must be held to embrace, at least, such reasonable regulations established directly by legislative enactment as will protect the public health and the public safety."
> *Jacobson v. Mass. (197 U.S. 11, 25)*

"A local enactment or regulation, even if based on the acknowledged police powers of a State, must always yield in case of conflict with the . . . . Constitution, or with any right which that instrument gives or secures."
> *Jacobson v. Mass. (197 U.S. 11, 25)*

"But the liberty secured by the Constitution of the United States to every person within its jurisdiction does not impart an absolute right in each person to be, at all times and in all circumstances, wholly freed from restraint."
> *Jacobson v. Mass. (197 U.S. 11, 26)*

"The right to practice religion freely does not include liberty to expose the community or the child to communicable disease or the latter to ill health or death. It

is sufficient to show that the State has a wide range of power for limiting parental freedom and authority in things affecting the child's welfare; and that this includes, to some extent, matters of conscience and religious conviction. The State's authority over children's activities is broader than over like actions of adults."

Prince v. Mass. (321 U.S. 158, 166-168)

"By its construction of the ordinance the State left to licensing officials no discretion as to granting permits, no power to discriminate."
Poulos v. New Hampshire (345 U.S. 395, 400)

"There is no basis for saying that freedom and order are not compatible. That would be a decision of desperation. Regulation and suppression are not the same, either in purpose or result, and courts of justice can tell the difference."
Poulos v. New Hampshire (345 U.S. 395, 408)

"Determination by the legislature of what constitutes proper exercise of police power is not final or conclusive but is subject to supervision by the courts."
Meyer v. Nebraska (262 U.S. 390, 400)

Stated in a nutshell you have just read the position of the U.S. Supreme Court on licensing of a religious function. Licensing is permitted, so long as it is limited to the legitimate functions of police power: public health, public safety and public order. The statutes must be narrowly drawn, and not left to the discretion of public officials. Finally, if a specific claim of police power is unreasonable——it may be fought in a court of law.

These brief quotations of precedent are not exhaustive. Page after page could be quoted to show them to be firmly entrenched principles of Constitutional law. The word "license" may be construed as narrowly as a pastor's driver's license, a missionary's pilot license, a licensed heating plant in the church basement, a licensed kitchen free from health hazards, or a licensed facility meeting fire and safety standards.

The word "license" may be construed as broadly as a licensed school, day care, church camp, Sunday School, etc., allowed to exist and function only at the arbitrary whim of an unrestrained bureaucracy. It is the latter which we must fight and may fight, with the Word of God, the U.S. Supreme Court, and the Constitution on our side.

THE "FACT" OR THE "FUNCTION"?

We must not fight confusing semantics. Our enemy is not the word "approval"——or the word "permit"——or the word "license"——or the words "letter of compliance"——or the word "certificate." The question in each individual case must be——"What does the word mean in the context of the law which it seeks to enforce?" We are not in conflict with terminology——we are at war against the power vested in the terminology by force of law.

For the reasons cited above, and upon advice of the U.S. Supreme Court, we must take the initiative. Some states have laws requiring "approval" of Christian Schools, and such "approval" power is nebulous and uncertain. These laws need to be attacked either in court, or preferably in the legislature, to make them clear and definitive.

A "license" may mean an open door to bureaucratic intrusion into a particular ministry. That "licensing" power needs to be challenged in court to obtain a written judicial limitation on what that word "license" means. Some states have been able to win a legislative victory in this regard and erase the word "license" altogether. In any event we must reduce the CONCEPT to nothing more than tightly prescribed and proscribed functions of legitimate police power, having no more effect on the training of children than a driver's license or a health certificate.

At the present moment we face a myriad of attacks from various agencies of government. We need to focus our attention on major issues such as the IRS defining a church, "licensing" programs which exceed legitimate police power, and state attempts to force Christian Schools to become public schools through too many "minimum standards." This is an appeal to reason suggesting that we may easily go too far in purist idealism by rejecting clear-cut narrowly drawn statutes designed to control enemies as well as friends of sound government.

Do not forget the definition of "conviction." A "conviction" is a Bible-based belief for which you will die. A "conviction" is something for which you will spend your life in prison. I want to suggest that we must either turn in our marriage license, or stop saying, "We will never take a license from the state to practice what God has commanded." If the state demands that you take a license or permit from the fire marshall to meet in a public building for preaching services——will you cease all preaching and go to jail if the law demands no more of you than of a local tavern? The issue cannot be the "fact" of license——it must be the "function" of license!

In every case which reaches the U.S. Supreme Court they will be asking three questions:

1--Does the statute (licensing or otherwise) have a secular legislative purpose?

2--Is the PRIMARY effect of the statute to advance or inhibit religion?

3--Does the statute produce EXCESSIVE government entanglement with religion?

Brethren, that is solid-rock First Amendment Constitutional law. It will not be overturned in our lifetime. It cannot be proven to be antibiblical reasoning in terms of our responsibility to government before God.

ILL WINDS ACROSS THE POTOMAC

We come now to consider, in more definitive terms, what elements constitute impermissible "licensure," "permit," "certification," "approval"——the terminology is irrelevant.

Since the most common area of license is Day Care we will use that as a specific example. Child care is both a mission of mercy and a ministry of religious education. *The White House Conference on Children* in its report to the President said in part:

"Day Care is a powerful institution. A Day Care program that ministers to a child from six months to six years has over 8,000

137

hours to teach him values, fears, beliefs, and behaviours."

May I suggest to you that a person's *values, fears, beliefs and behaviours* constitute the sum total of their religion! No regulation which touches the minds of these children is permissible.

Our concern is the religious liberty rights of parents to choose religious child development programs for pre-school children which are totally free from any potential for state intrusion beyond fire, health and safety standards.

> *"50% of the intellectual capacity of an adult has been developed by the age of four and 80% by age eight."*
>
> *Dr. Benjamin S. Bloom*
> *University of Chicago*
> *Director of Research*
> *Conference on Education*
> *U.S. Office of Education*

Day Care, by common definition, involves the structured supervision of children of pre-school age. The common definition is not, however, a true definition. Christian parents and educators, as well as government agencies and secular institutions of higher learning, have come to affirm that day care, in the modern world, is far more than "supervision."

In a publication entitled *Day Care——A Statement of Principles,* published by the Office of Child Development, U.S. Department of Health, Education, and

Welfare, the following quotation is given:

> *"The unacceptability of purely custodial programs and the necessity of a developmental approach have been identified by the President of the United States as Keystones of Federal policy in day care. In his address on welfare reform, the President stated: 'The child care I propose is more than custodial. This Administration is committed to a new emphasis on child development in the first five years of life.'"*

Another publication by the Federal Office of Child Development, entitled *Day Care——Staff Training*, indicates clearly that this "developmental approach" specifically involves the instruction and teaching of day care children. Under a section on page 22, entitled "How Do People Learn, Anyhow?——Approaches to Instruction," the day care staff member receives the following information:

> *"Learning——or teaching, which is the other end of the process——is crucial to every human enterprise. No one knows for sure how people learn anything. but we are all still searching for ways to make people learn better and faster. Since any training program will employ methods and techniques that grow out of a teacher's belief in how learning happens, it may be helpful to look at five of the most common theories about learning:*

1. *DEVELOPMENTAL THEORY:*
    Since human beings grow in a patterned way unique to the species ... (Evolution)

2. *THE MIND AS A COLLECTION OF ABILITIES:*
    One of the earliest ideas about learning was based on the idea that the mind was composed of a series of specialized abilities called 'faculties.' Much college curriculum was modeled on this theory and teaching practices based on it are still common to colleges and schools. (Humanism)

3. *LEARNING AS A RESPONSE TO STIMULUS:*
    Classical conditioning had a major effect on American education. John Dewey's Learning by Doing *came from these ideas about the specific nature of the learning process. (Pavlovian Progressive Education)*

4. *THE MIND AS A MAKER OF PATTERNS:*
    This principle can be recognized in many areas of everyday life, in the organization of textbooks——in the case-study method of teaching, and in the core curriculum which builds learning of many subjects around a common theme. (Gestalt Psychology)

5. *LEARNING BY REWARDING THE LEARNER: B.F. Skinner of Harvard made a series of observations which he codified into a powerful and useful theory called operant conditioning. (Behavioural Psychology)"*

(Parenthesis mine to identify the learning theories suggested.)

This lengthy quotation is given for a two-fold purpose. First, to prove conclusively that the foremost governmental center on the study of childhood development in the world says, day care is EDUCATION! It is NOT simply supervised custodial care of preschool children—it is highly sophisticated EDUCATION with staff members trained accordingly. Second, this lengthy quotation is given to demonstrate that government is involved in a multi-million dollar program to direct day care centers toward certain EDUCATIONAL goals. Each of these theories of learning included in that direction is conclusively antithetical to Biblical Christianity, and the goals of day care centers which are church ministries. A system of licensure may entangle our religious child development programs with humanistic goals and methods.

Dr. Bernice T. Cory, founder of Scripture Press, writing in "Christian Education Monographs" used the following titles:

FIRST FIVE YEARS SHAPE ALL OF LIFE

CHILDREN UNDER SIX ARE APT LEARNERS

TRAIN CITIZENS IN THE CRADLE

BEHAVIOR IS SET BY AGE FIVE

EARLY LEARNING FOUND VITAL

AGE FIVE IS OLD PSYCHOLOGICALLY

Not to belabor the point, one quotation from one section will suffice:

> *"Educators and scientists are affirming that a child's learning and remembering abilities are greater during his preschool years than they will ever be again. According to these specialists, the first 5 or 6 years of a child's life are his most sensitive, receptive and crucial period of development——in fact, the optimum learning period of his entire life! These years are the most critical in which to develop his will to learn, his creativity, and his ability to perform. They affect all his subsequent learning."*

A BATTLE FOR THE MIND

With the foregoing testimonies from the highest forms of expertise available in both government and religious contexts, I will now draw on their definition of day care to substantiate our own. Day care is EDUCATION. In our churches it is CHRISTIAN EDUCATION. Day care is CHILD DEVELOPMENT. In our churches it is specific RELIGIOUS DEVELOPMENT, as a part of the mission and ministry of our churches. Day care is both, a mission of mercy to needy children and parents, and an evangelistic tool which formulates beliefs and values to be carried over into elementary grades. Day care is a mission of church service provided to our school teachers, church members, and others, with the church staff acting in loco parentis for religious training of the children involved.

In summary, our day care is only day care by statutory definition. Our day care is a private, religious endeavor which would not exist apart from the church.

No compulsory attendance statutes cloud the issues. Parents are not obligated to avail themselves of this decidedly religious ministry and, indeed, many choose not to do so when they see the extent of Biblical indoctrination involved. The primary goal is to provide for the children of our own church members and church employees an early childhood development program which is distinctly religious. We seek others for evangelistic purposes.

Day care is not a business enterprise. It would not exist apart from the church. Our purpose in going to court over day care statutes should be primarily to obtain clarification of the purpose of legitimate police power provisions, and to have any vague or open-ended regulations struck down. A second goal would be to establish by legal precedent the religious character of the activity. One final goal would be to challenge any provisions which intrude, beyond public health, public safety and public order, into the minds of children.

While the chance of eliminating the "fact" of license in a court of law is virtually non-existent, the legislature is a different matter. Both Virginia and Indiana have won replacement of "license" with another means of satisfying police power. When such an "alternative means" is unacceptable to a state legislature the only solution is a court challenge to force a written, judicial limitation on the scope of license.

No "license," "certification," "permit," "approval," etc. can be accepted if the meaning of that document exceeds the Biblically authorized police power.

We must be willing to turn in licenses, go to court, go to prison, whatever is necessary to stop any permits, certification, licenses, and approval which are unbiblical and unconstitutional. But unless you are prepared to turn in your marriage license do not say——"I will never take a license from the state to do what God has commanded."

Remember——we are formulating law, not only applicable to true Christians, but also to religious charlatans. We should be just as interested in the safety and health of children as any state agency. In actuality, we should be more interested in children and their welfare, because of our Biblical knowledge of God's special interest in children. We should uphold and advocate any reasonable efforts of society to curb irresponsible activities by foolish men who act in the name of religion, and hide behind the First Amendment to jeopardize the lives and safety of children. Our goal is to uphold religious liberty and, at the same time, act as responsible citizens who cooperate with administration of legitimate government functions.

A CONTINUING BATTLE

With these principles intact our final consideration is the abuse of police power. Attorney William Ball has said that the future battlegrounds will center on education and welfare of children. We must prepare our thinking in these areas. We cannot Biblically object to the police power of human government, nor may we hope to win even one case in court which denies such power.

Statist thinkers and Secular Humanists of every stripe know, only too well, the mountain of precedent law available on this score. As a result, we see more and more regulation tending in this direction. Safety of children, in some states, is said to depend on the qualifications of staff members. In Texas the Department of Human Resources said: "Health" includes MENTAL health, and it is injurious to "threaten a child with the displeasure of Deity." This is, indeed, the wave of the future. Only two thoughts are important on this subject:

Number one——do not panic over possibilities. Because abuses are possible, or even visible, never go to the courts or to the legislature in an attempt to eliminate the general police power——it simply cannot be done. Fighting inspections of buildings, or authority to make regulations, or powers of enforcement, is like spitting into the wind. There is no such thing as a guarantee against such abuses. The power to regulate public health, public safety and public order is here to stay and, therefore, abuses of such power are here to stay.

Number two——Any person or group, at any time, may challenge a particular ruling or law which they feel goes beyond legitimate police power; in fact, this is the ONLY method of combating attempts to control our ministries in these areas. You say that's expensive? Yes it is. You say that's time consuming? Yes it is. You say that's unreasonable? Yes it is. But it is not nearly so expensive, and time consuming, and unreasonable, as attacking the general police power and losing major decisions which hurt every church and Christian school in America.

In spite of all we say or do——government will retain the right to do a safety inspection on the facilities of "The Temple of Divine Dopeheads." There is such a thing

145

as equal application of the law. If the state may inspect "The Temple of Divine Dopeheads," they may inspect my church and yours. I will not spend 30 seconds fighting against the right of government to pass a regulation against keeping rabid dogs in church day care rooms, as they seek to protect the health of children. If they may pass a "health" regulation against rabid dogs, they may pass a "health" regulation against Bible verses which cause insanity; but when they extend police power that far, you may rest assured they will see me in court at the time appointed. We have no recourse against illegitimate extensions of fire, health, and safety except hand to hand combat over a specific regulation which violates our religious convictions.

This is, and will be, a continuing battle. There is no such thing as a piece of legislation, or a court decision, which will stop forever the abuse of police power. Certainly we must fight all open-ended claims to "approve," "zone," assign "permits," "certify," "accredit," "license,"——anything designed to improperly intrude into our ministries by controlling statutes. In the past two years I have put more time and money and sweat into that cause than 99% of the fundamentalists in America. But PLEASE read carefully the last section of this chapter.

A CALL TO CONSISTENCY

We are in SERIOUS danger of allowing rhetoric to outrun reason. We can only hurt our cause by public statements and court cases which assert that government cannot regulate the church in any way. We MUST draw a clear distinction in our minds between legitimate power and illegitimate power. We MUST understand that law is an agreement among reasonable people as to proper restraints to be placed upon all of society. Some of our people have a tremendous blind spot in this regard——and remember brethren——your attorney is not going to jail for you if you lose in court. Of course, going to jail is not the issue; if it is right we should be willing to die for it, but what a tragedy to close your ministry and go to jail for faulty reasoning. If the "principle" for which we stand is——

> *"No license——ever——to do what God has commanded!"*

> *"No permission from the state to practice our religion!"*

any state attorney worth the powder to blow him up, can make a fool out of us in court. He could easily say:

> *"You already accept licenses to do what God has commanded. Have you turned in your marriage license yet? Is it not a part of your religion to believe in marriage as a God-ordained, God-commanded practice? Your Honor, I submit that this man is a hypocrite! He says——"No license from the state--ever--to do what God has commanded" and yet he accepts a license which allows him to live with his wife. As a matter of fact, the only reason his children are not illegitimate is that licensed relationship.*

> *Your Honor, this man claims to be standing for a "principle." He says he does not need permission from the state to practice his religion under any circumstances. I want to suggest, your*

147

Honor, that we live in a society which has 'a government of laws and not of men.' Suppose he says his 'god' has commanded him to exterminate 'the enemy,' as in Old Testament times, and he considers 'the enemy' to be the church in the next block. Suppose his church was in court today opposing the liquor license laws of this state on the grounds that the Bible says 'Give strong drink unto him that is ready to perish.' *This man claims to believe in justice and order and yet he asks this court to rule that religious liberty means— —'no man needs permission from government to do what God has commanded.' I suggest to Your Honor that this man is a fool. He asks us to believe that anything may be done without state permission if someone's 'god' commands it. He asks, in principle, that we no longer license church credit unions, church missionary pilots, church real estate ventures, church restaurants, church gambling operations, church bus ministries, church wineries, or any of the many other activities engaged in by the major denominations of this nation. His principle is— —'no license— —ever— —to be required of a church.'*

"The U.S. Supreme Court has, in some cases, upheld a 'license' or 'permit' requirement to preach the Word of God. The right to preach is not absolute. You cannot walk into a man's bedroom at 3 a.m. and preach him the Gospel. You cannot hold an evangelistic meeting in the

148

middle of Interstate 75 anytime you please. By the same token you cannot 'worship' in your church according to your 'religious beliefs' if those beliefs include snake handling, child sacrifice, use of illegal drugs, or a thousand other things not permitted by law. Law is license. Law is permission. How, in the name of sanity, may he contend for the right of all Americans to do as they please, without permission, in the practice of 'religion'? His principle is, 'no license——ever——to be required of a church.' That contention will neither stand the test of literally hundreds of precedents at all court levels, nor will it stand the test of common sense. I rest my case."

Brethren, that day is coming unless we know why we are in court. We are not fighting a WORD——the word "license"——WE ARE FIGHTING ILLEGITIMATE POWER! A license is only as powerful as the law with which we must conply to meet that standard. Our whole system of law is a license; it is permission to live and practice beliefs within a framework of restraints——the violation of which bring imprisonment.

It is true that we must totally reject any license, permit, approval, certificate, accreditation, etc. which deals with anything other than public health, public safety, and public order. Even then we may go to court and fight individual regulations or regulatory systems which go too far. My only concern is that we not verbally paint ourselves into a corner. The tracks we leave coming out will be visible for a long time.

Obviously individual conscience must prevail. You must decide before God when to go to court or prison for your beliefs. All I suggest is careful study of the implications of your position.

> *"The government is not going to require anything of my day school they don't require of my Sunday School."*

Is that your position? Would you close down your ministry and go to jail because government requires fire drills where children meet daily and does not require them where children meet only on Sunday?

Did the brethren in Virginia compromise because they agreed to Day Care standards for health and safety not required of children meeting only on Sunday? Of course not. In Indiana they also need "permission" to operate. They must obtain certain certificates which prove they are in compliance with the reasonable demands of "government by the people." They *are* "the people." They have agreed that any of "the people" with unsafe facilities should be shut down, no matter what their religious beliefs. The new laws, in both Virginia and Indiana, are "victories" even though they do not eliminate state "permission" per se.

We do not have a right before God to put 300 people in a 10 foot by 10 foot room, just because it is a church service. Neither do we have a command from God to object to human government stopping such a meeting. If the government "by the people" has a law against meeting under these conditions, the burden of proof is upon us to show that our "rights" override the law in question. The authority of American government to make such a law is beyond debate. Is our task to go to prison because we believe in the "principle"—not the size of the building? Of course not.

If human government has the power to stop a church from gathering 300 people in a 10 foot by 10 foot building, they also have the power to stop 5 people from meeting in that same room. But if they try it——we go to court. Government has the power. Always, in every case, the question is——"Does the power go too far in its effect on prohibiting our ability to obey God?"

Law is license. It is permission to practice a lifestyle within certain restraints. Our purpose is not to do away with all law pertaining to churches, but rather, to be certain that all the laws in our state which allow us to operate are confined to legitimate rules of health, safety, and order. We can only hurt our cause by fighting the POWER of government to issue a building permit, license, missionary aviation, approve or disapprove health conditions, or license the heating system and the purely physical aspects of church or school facilities.

Again——it is true——we may need to fight an unreasonable building permit, or the wrong construction of zoning statutes, or a license on health and safety which goes too far. But the AUTHORITY to require those things of churches is a settled fact in American jurisprudence.

To summarize, the U. S. Supreme Court has taken osition that even Secular Humanism is a religion. They have acknowledged the rights of all Americans to believe in anything or nothing and agreed to protect those rights. At the same time they have said——the states may pass laws, regulate, license, permit, even stop an activity carried out by an individual or group in the name of religion.

However, such state control and intervention must deal only with public health, public safety, and public order. Even then, the laws which regulate the activities of religious groups and individuals must pass a three-fold test:

1. Is the law designed to accomplish a purpose which is sufficiently secular in nature? (Such as protecting the safety of the general public in a reasonable fashion)

2. Is the primary, not potential or theoretical, effect of the law to advance or inhibit religion? (Does the law go too far in aiding a religious group? Or does it go too far in unreasonable demands which would unduly burden the practice of religion when weighed against the common good?)

3. Does the law produce excessive government entanglement with religion? (Some entanglement is permitted——excessive entanglement is not)

Remember——in America——we do not obtain permission from "Caesar" to obey God. We do, however, agree among ourselves that all "religions," true or false, will be subject to "a government of laws and not of men."

Chapter 8

THE PHILOSOPHY OF LAW BREAKING

"Laws are better unmade than unkept"
Henry Smith
The Puritan

We are often accused of "lawlessness" when we fight these battles. The answer to the charge is that any government agency or legislature is the "lawless" entity when they make a law applicable to a church, if that law oversteps the bounds of legitimate police power.

U. S. Supreme Court Justice Douglas, with whom Justice Black concurred, put it very well in *Poulos v. New Hampshire, (345 U.S. 395, 1953),* a religious liberty case:

> *"When a legislature undertakes to proscribe the exercise of a citizen's constitutional rights . . . it acts lawlessly; and the citizen can take matters into his own hands and proceed on the basis that such a law is no law at all." (at 423)*

> *"The reason is the preferred position granted freedom of speech, freedom of the press, freedom of assembly, and freedom of religion by the First Amendment." (at 423)*

153

"The command of the First Amendment is that there shall be NO law which abridges those civil rights. The matter is beyond the power of the legislature to regulate, control or condition. The case is therefore quite different from a legislative program in the field of business, labor, housing and the like where regulation is permissible." (at 423)

"The Constitution commands that government keep its hands off the exercise of First Amendment rights. No matter what the legislature may say, a man has the right to make his speech, print his handbill, compose his newspaper, and deliver his sermon without asking anyone's permission. The contrary suggestion is abhorrent to our traditions." (at 423)

There are no (First Amendment rights) in the sense of the Constitution when permission must be obtained from an official . . . that is a previous restraint condemned by history and at war with the First Amendment." (at 426)

"Those who wrote the First Amendment conceived of (First Amendment rights) as wholly independent of the prior restraint of anyone. The judiciary was not granted a privilege of restraint withheld from other officials. For history proved that judges too were sometimes tyrants." (at 426)

Romans 13 was never intended to command Christians to disobey the Bible in the name of submission to government. Moses disobeyed Pharoah, Shadrach, Meshach, and Abednego disobeyed Nebuchadnezzar. Daniel disobeyed Darius. New Testament Christians disobeyed plain commands from government not to preach or teach in the name of Jesus, etc., etc., etc.——all because they had a command from God which overruled. Those who find in Romans 13 a reason to stay out of the battle, in the name of submission to government, will find no support from the heroes of the faith in Bible times, nor will they find support in common sense.

We would do well to observe the progress of the black minority in this generation. By becoming vocal advocates of their poor treatment under the shadow of the U. S. Constitution, they have changed the face of America. While they have been gaining their liberty through activism and lobbying, we have been losing our religious liberty through apathy and indifference. Many fundamental preachers need to stop hiding behind Romans 13 and, at least, rise to the level of Martin Luther King, Jr., who once said:

> *"I believe in the beauty and majesty of the law so much that when I think a law is wrong, I am willing to go to jail and stay there."*
>
> *New York Times*
> *October 16, 1966*

THE HIGHER LAW

Vital to our thinking, at this point, is to develop in our minds how we, as fundamentalists, will stand. Attorney William Ball has said:

"One of the great struggles in which we are engaged today is the conflict in jurisprudence between the concept of a 'natural law,' or 'higher law,' and 'state law.' There is a very important school of thought (and it is dominant in Communist countries and was, too, in Nazi Germany) which says that the state is the final source of all rights, and that what the state says IS law. The opposite school of thought considers that all man-made law is subject to a 'higher law,' or immutable principles of justice and right. We, as Christians, say that those immutable principles have their origin in God. But there are non-Christians who at least acknowledge that the state law is not the final word, and that there is, overall, an injunction to 'do good and avoid evil.' "

To be certain there is no confusion fostered by the preceding pages, I must elaborate briefly on several points we, as fundamentalists, take for granted.

Any man-made law, whether it be a local regulation with the force of law or the Constitution of the United States, is just that——man-made law. When we postulate the fact that any law "respecting an establishment of religion, or prohibiting the free exercise thereof" is an unlawful law, we are correct. Equally true is the Biblical admonition that, *'We ought to obey God rather than men.''* (Acts 5:29).

"The higher law" is to be contrasted with "state law" in the sense that our rights are a gift from God, rather than a concession granted by the state. While it is true that the U. S. Constitution is the ultimate expression of law from the body politic, and binding upon every citizen of the United States, God has a written expression of his law in the Bible which takes precedent over any contrary law of man.

What I have attempted to express in the preceding pages is the practical reality that a law fashioned by the principles of democracy is THE final word in America. Suppose, for example, that the Constitution was amended to declare that families may have only one child as a means to prevent over-population. The amending of the Constitution would establish such a practice as the ultimate law of the land, binding on the fifty states. Any aberrant practice sanctioned by an individual state would eventually be held unconstitutional and illegal.

Suppose, further, that you, as a Christian, say to yourself——"This is an unlawful law. It violates the laws of God which command us to be fruitful and multiply; therefore, I must obey the higher law and have my children." The premise of the preceding sections of this book is that we would be entirely correct to take such a position. However, to understand the American Constitutional system is to realize that our belief in the premise of a "higher law" in no way negates the consequences.

We are free in our conscience to say at any point——"My beliefs in the application of God's law conflict with the law of the state——this new constitutional amendment is not the final authority in my life." Over that point we go to court. But do not diminish for a moment the thought that, having reached the U. S. Supreme Court, having had that Court declare the law to be Constitutional, you have reached the final authority in this nation.

God is not the final authority in America. Certainly he could be, but He has chosen not to be (at least for the present), if His Will is rejected by the people. God, for example, does not sanction abortion on demand. The U. S. Supreme Court says the Constitution does sanction abortion on demand. Therefore, in present day America, we have abortion on demand. To say that a higher law refutes that position is a moot point. The Supreme Court has rejected the "higher law" in favor of its own view of the Constitution.

Theoretically, such a ruling by the Court could come in any area, or the Constitution itself could be altered through ratification by the states. Potentially, the First Amendment could be changed to allow only federally sanctioned churches in the states. We could challenge that, as violative of the "higher law," but after losing in the highest court in the land, where do we go? We go to prison if we choose to violate the law of the land.

It is true that certain basic rights come from God and not from the state. It is true that ultimately, the law is not what the majority chooses to make it——law is what God says. However, it is equally true that our God-given rights may be championed only from a prison cell if society, through the Congress, the Constitution, and the United States Supreme Court, agree to negate some of those rights.

To summarize, we should keep ever before us the following principles:

—God is the ultimate authority in the universe.

—Government has LAWFUL authority only

as God stipulates in His Word

—Government has UNLAWFUL authority
to any degree which God permits

Considering these factors, we must differentiate in our minds, between laws which are LAWFUL, and laws which are UNLAWFUL, from God's point of view. There is a "higher law." Man-made law, in any form, is not the ultimate authority. We may resist, and must resist as a matter of principle, any attempt by the government of man, to make or maintain laws violative of the "higher law."

However, we must acknowledge as a practical reality, that while God does not SANCTION, He does PERMIT the laws and governments of many lands to make and uphold unlawful laws; sometimes to the imprisonment and even to the death of those who resist.

The Constitution of the United States is the ultimate law of the land, but it is not the ultimate law of the universe. We may be imprisoned for violation of the law of the land, by the courts of this world, but our position will be vindicated in the Court of Heaven if that position is Biblical. As Christians and as citizens, we may reject any additions to the U. S. Constitution which violate the "higher law." We may further reject U. S. Supreme Court interpretations of the Constitution which transgress the higher law, if we are prepared to pay the price in time with an eye toward eternity. The path of liberty has never been easy or cheap. It is stained with the blood of fools and martyrs. Some have defended their own stubborn, self-willed ideas; others have defended the principles of liberty embodied in the Declaration of Independence, the U. S. Constitution, and the Word of God. We must pray diligently and think carefully to assure that the positions for which we stand are God-blessed and Biblical. We must be willing to pay any price to uphold truth, yet wise enough to avoid the pitfalls laid by Satan, even in the realm of defense of liberty.

Chapter 9

THE PHILOSOPHY OF EDUCATION

*"Christ . . . in Whom are hid all the
treasures of wisdom and knowledge. And
this I say, lest any man should beguile you
with enticing words."*
                                   Colossians 2:2-4

As a result of our controversy with the State over
the regulation of Christian schools, many people have been
forced to express opinions, who would never have done so
under normal conditions. It is always true that in times of
crisis, attitudes and opinions come to light, which might
not otherwise appear. The most revealing comments come
from those in churches, schools, and religious entities of
various sorts. Shocking to the point of great concern is the
fact that, in many cases, there is a great similarity between
the opinions of religious leaders and the opinions of
Secular Humanist state officials.

A leader of the Baptist State Convention (Southern
Baptist), in North Carolina, wrote the following words for
the most politically influential daily newspaper in the
state:

> *"I have serious reservations about a church
> being in the school business today. When so
> much is said of separation of church and
> state, I wonder to what degree a church
> infringes on states' rights and obligations*

when it assumes the role of teacher for history, math, English, chemistry, biology and literature. The church seems to get off the track of its New Testament spiritual redemption ministry and mission as related to the Kingdom of God. The total programs of these churches, including the morning worship hour, gyrates toward the school, especially during these days of controversy with the government. The trend is more toward the purely secular."

This man is all too typical. He is, to an extent, echoing a point of view which is held by a great many who name the name of Christ. While they may not express the thoughts verbally, in the minds of many Christians there is a reservation concerning the validity of a Christian education ministry for the church, as well as a strange mental separation between the secular and the sacred aspects of human endeavour.

In the remainder of this chapter, we want to establish several ideas which may seem radical and disturbing at first glance, but which are crucial to understanding a Biblical philosophy of education.

1. The Bible allows for no division between secular and sacred in the life of the child of God.

2. The State has no authority or obligation to educate children.

3. The work of the church has never been anything other than education.

162

THE SECULAR AND THE SACRED

Most professing Christians readily accept the idea of a clergy and a laity. We have those who are in "full-time service for the Lord" and those who are out in the "secular" business world. The "clergy" is to be distinguished from the "laity" by various methods and attitudes. Such a distinction is totally foreign to the Word of God. Speaking from the Biblical viewpoint, a person's occupation has no bearing on their spiritual condition. Some of the most worldly, ungodly men on earth are "clergymen" of great standing in society. A man may be a plumber, an executive, a carpenter, a brain surgeon or a streetsweeper, but before God he has as much obligation to be holy and spiritual as any "preacher" or "full-time Christian worker" on earth.

Differences do indeed exist. There is a difference between the roles of parent and child, husband and wife, elder and deacon and pastor. There are differences in the gifts which are sovereignly bestowed by the Spirit of God. But none of these differences divides life into "secular" and "sacred." Every Christian, from the day that he or she is born again, is in "full-time Christian service." Looking at the "full-time Christian service" of many Christians may not encourage us, but we should never make experience the basis for truth. Truth is what God says about a matter. God's Word authorizes certain Christians to be leaders of other Christians, but the dedication, godliness, and spiritual power to which we are to attain does not vary from person to person or occupation to occupation. When the Bible sets special qualifications for elders and deacons, it would be absurd to say the will of God is for others to have lower standards. He is simply saying——accept nothing less than "normal" Christianity in appointing your leaders.

163

Every Christian, from the day he is born again, is in "full-time Christian service." If it is somehow more holy to be a missionary, then every Christian who fails to go to a foreign field is a fool. If it is possible to get more "credit" from God for being a preacher than for being a housewife, then God is, indeed, a respecter of persons. The truth of the matter is that it is a sin against God to be a traveling evangelist if His will is for you to be a janitor in a local church. It is wicked, instead of spiritual, to be a pastor when God wants you to be a farmer.

There is no such thing as a "higher calling" by God's definition. The highest calling for any life is the will of God, whatever and wherever that will might be. "Full-time Christian service" may be carried out in the home, the office, the factory, the school, or the church. But every Christian, from the moment he is born again, is in "full-time service." Every moment of every day is to be spent walking with the Lord Jesus Christ, doing His will, and there is no higher calling; there is no more spiritual work. There is no more important endeavor on the face of the earth, than to be a child of God, living in the will of God, wherever that will may lead.

New Testament Christianity is not bringing people to church to meet the preacher, it is going out into the streets and shops and factories and homes to witness and win souls and bring them back for fellowship. Unless you hold such a view of Christiantiy as just described, you cannot hold a *Philosophy of Christian Education* which is consistent. We must never suppose there to be a distinction between one area of life and another for the Bible-believing Christian. Sitting in a church service, hearing the Word of God preached, is no more "holy" than dressing the family for Sunday School. In fact, there is more opportunity to be a testimony and a blessing under

164

those hectic pre-church conditions. Of course, getting ready for church is no substitute for attending. Both are necessary. Both are a part of the will of God.

The following chapter, entitled *The Classic Secular Humanist* defines the word "secular" in the only fashion acceptable to those who believe the Bible. "Secular" means "without the True God and the true religion." It is a sin for a Christian to attempt to do anything divorced from his God or his religion. Some areas of life may be more important than others, relatively speaking. Praying may be more important than mowing the grass at times. The fact remains, however, that if a Christian has grass he should cut it. His testimony will be damaged if he refuses. This is not to say that he should cut grass when he should be praying, but neither should he be in the closet praying when it is the will of God for him to mow the grass. Mowing grass is not a "secular" work for the Christian——it is a part of his Christian testimony.

The Bible says that whether we eat or drink or whatsoever we do we should do all to the glory of God. Washing clothes is not a "secular" work for the believer. Taking care of the house, planting a garden, washing windows, none of these things is "secular" under any circumstances. In the business, in the home, in recreation, in the school——anything we cannot do for the glory of God we have no business doing.

Since these thoughts are true, in view of the Bible's teaching, why do we naturally divide life into "sacred" and "secular"? The scripture preceding this chapter, from Colossians 2:4, explains:

> *"And this I say lest any man should beguile you with enticing words."*

165

No one was born with a concept of "sacred" and "secular." Somewhere along the way in life they heard someone speak, or read a book, or were taught in school, this belief about the "sacred" and the "secular." Someone *beguiled (us) with enticing words."* In verse 8 of that same second chapter of Colossians, we get the rest of the picture:

> *"BEWARE lest any man spoil you through philosophy and vain deceit, after the traditions of men (that is humanism), after the rudiments of the world (that is secularism), and not after Christ."*

Imagine that! The Bible specifically warns Christians to beware of being spoiled and deceived by the philosophy of Secular Humanism. *"The traditions of men"*−−that is Humanism. *"The rudiments of the world"*−−that is Secularism. Yet, is it not true that in churches across America this philosophy is preached? God's people are beguiled into thinking there is a difference between the "sacred" and the "secular" and especially in matters of education. Men and women have been deceived, by the traditions of men, into thinking that education is the states' business and religion is the churches' business.

WHAT IS EDUCATION?

What is education? Is education something you receive by attending a state school from first grade through college? Certainly that definition is not correct, since the champions of state-controlled education acknowledge that 80% of the adult mental capacity of a human being is developed and set by age 8. What of all the education a child receives before attending school, or the education following graduation, which continues through life?

What is education? Professional educators do not agree. They do not agree for the simple reason that they do not know. The Secular Humanists who influenced the thinking of most of us have always said, quite mysteriously, "Education is going to school." The Baptist State Convention leader, quoted earlier in this chapter, reflected that thinking. He said:

"What is the church doing interfering with the rights and obligations of the state to teach history, math, English, chemistry, biology, and literature?"

State education is Secular Humanist education. Education "without the True God and the true religion" is taught in the public schools of America. The U.S. Supreme Court has recognized public education as secular education; in fact, they have mandated it to be so by, in effect, outlawing any prescribed system of beliefs to be included in the education of children. Public education is, and has been for decades, synonymous with the term "secular education."

What is education? "Secular education," by anyone's definition, is education without the God of the Bible. The Southern Baptist leader quoted above, as well as the myriads who follow his line of reasoning, are saying: "Man without God can be educated." "Education is possible in a secular environment, because education per se has nothing to do with the church or religion." If you read the chapter in this book entitled *The Classic Secular Humanist* you will see that what we are discussing here is nothing less than a system of belief rooted in "the other religion," Secular Humanism.

What is education? What you are about to read is THE definition of education. Notice this is not A definition, this is THE only valid definition of education. Biblical logic demands that there be no other definition of education.

"Education: The acquisition of true wisdom and true knowledge."

Modern educators have no consensus on a definition of education, because they are searching for truth. Most are not even sure truth exists. They search for truth——they search for a definition of education, but you cannot find something until you look in the place where it is. As long as they are looking in all the wrong places they will find no valid definition for education. Truth may only be found in the Bible. There are no non-interpreted facts. We cannot define education until we have a basis from which to evaluate empirical knowledge——a basis which we know to be the source of truth.

What is education? "Education is the acquisition of true wisdom and true knowledge." Someone may ask——"What about the acquisition of false wisdom and false knowledge? Is it not true that a person is educated by his mistakes?" The Bible's answer is, "No!" The Word of God teaches that someone may live his whole life and never begin to know wisdom. *"The fear of the Lord is the BEGINNING of wisdom"* (Proverbs 9:10). *"The fear of the Lord is the BEGINNING of knowledge"* (Proverbs 1:7).

The way this works in practice is quite simple. False knowledge has no meaning of any value until and unless it may be compared to true knowledge. For men to comprehend reality there must be some truth which is standard in the universe for comparison. Make a mental note of this because you may need it sooner than you think.

Suppose a child wants to compute 3x5. He sits down and goes to work and, on the first try, gets an answer of 13. He works the problem again and the second answer is 16. He works it again and the next answer he gets is 10. Question: Has that child yet been educated on the issue of 3x5? The answer is––of course he has not. For all he knows, 3x5 may equal 13. Sixteen or ten may be the correct answer. After all––he sincerely tried to find the answer and who is to say that he was wrong? But, once he knows the truth, even his mistakes take on meaning. The moment he is certain, beyond any doubt, that 3x5=15, he can look anybody in the face and say, with all the confidence of an educated man, "3x5 is NOT 13!––3x5 is NOT 16!––3x5 is NOT 10!––3x5 is 15!" He may say that because on that particular problem he has become "educated,"––"The acquisition of true wisdom and true knowledge."

One other example is sufficient. This time we will consider the greatest intellectual, philosophical and practical question the human mind will ever entertain. Suppose a man wants to become educated concerning how to have eternal life. He goes to one source and they say: "My belief is that you must be baptized to be saved." He goes to another source and they say: "Be sincere––just do the best you can." He consults one final source and they say: "Live right, obey the Ten Commandments, and help your fellow man." Question: At this point in time, is the man educated on the subject of how to obtain eternal life? No. For all he knows, any one, none, all, or a combination of some of those statements could be correct. Should others come along with divergent views, he is no nearer the answer. But, when he learns "true wisdom and true

169

knowledge,"——when he learns that salvation is the free gift of God, given to those who renounce their sin and trust in the finished work of the Lord Jesus Christ upon the Cross as the only hope of salvation——he is educated on that subject. Someone comes to him and says: "I believe you must live by the Ten Commandments to be saved." He says: "No! That is error. I can say dogmatically that it is error because I have come to THE knowledge of THE truth——I am educated on that subject."

Secular Humanist educators cannot define education for an excellent reason——they know very little for sure. They postulate the fact that the dust on the moon, by evolutionary scientific standards, should be 15 to 30 feet deep. What a shock to arrive and find it a few inches deep. It is correct to say that even Secular Humanists know some "true wisdom and true knowledge," such as the current price of eggs in China, but true intellectualism goes beyond such superficiality to the heart of man's purpose and existence.

Our Secular Humanist society, educated by the "experts," is a disaster area of 220 million opinions. Public educators, who are so dedicated to such nebulous terms as "education" and "knowledge," are adrift in a sea of confusion scientifically, morally, economically, politically, and philosophically.

SHOULD THE STATE EDUCATE?

Is capital punishment right?——Yes
Is alcoholism a disease?——No
Should we accept homosexuals as an alternate life style?——No
Is abortion right?——No
Is the Bible God's Word?——Yes
Is there a true religion?——Yes
Should we trade with communist nations?——No

170

Every major secular university in America spends millions of dollars and thousands of hours in search of truth on those subjects. We have the answer to every one. In less than a decade our economy is in shambles for one reason---ecological implications of natural resources as they relate to the economy. The Secular Humanists believe we will choke to death, or starve to death, or run out of oil, or destroy the world with nuclear weapons. We know, from the Word of God Who made the environment, that everything will be just fine when the Lord Jesus comes again.

The only pollution to fear is when the oceans, lakes and rivers turn to blood and the fire and brimstone begin to fall. The problem then will not be mining coal out of the mountains, but rather, men crying for the rocks and mountains to fall on them and hide them from the wrath of God. When the sun becomes black as sackcloth of hair, solar panels will do no good--yet billions have been spent, and our economy destroyed, by those who plan to conquer disease and sickness and aging and live forever in a world made glorious by the evolutionary ascendency of Secular Humanism, without the intervention of God.

Dewey promised a nation without poverty or prisons, through state controlled and state financed education. Instead, today, tens of thousands are graduated from state schools who are unable to read the wording of their diplomas. Perhaps, in the view of some, the state should be in the business of education, but you would never deduce that from the condition of the nation today. *The Separation of Church and Freedom* has come about through the actions of men educated without God and *The Separation of America and Freedom* is not far behind.

Personally, I would prefer that a man not be able to write, if he uses his ability to write state statutes to take away my liberty. An ignorant man can till the ground and grow his food, but you will never find him in Washington selling wheat to Russia. Education without God is a disaster, not only to the man who has it, but also to those who must cope with his ungodly ideas in the community and the nation.

Jefferson to the contrary, education in the religion of Secular Humanism does not preserve liberty and strengthen the nation. To advocate compulsory attendance laws and public education in our generation, is to advocate a citizenry forcibly indoctrinated in a religion which is not the one true religion of the Word of God. Those who believe the Bible must maintain that the ONLY acceptable form of education is Christian education. We have discovered in court, with our beliefs on trial in North Carolina, that to say that we "prefer" Christian schools, but public schools will do under some circumstances, is to negate any claim defensible on the grounds of religious liberty. No Christian would send his children to a Jehovah's Witness church or a Hare Krishna church 5 days a week for instruction.

Secular Humanism is a religion—(see *Torcaso v. Watkins (367 U.S. 488)* in chapter 10. It is THE religion taught daily in the public schools of America. Pastors who appease their congregations by refusing to preach Christian education as the only form of education acceptable to God, have no claim to First Amendment protection for their schools. We must believe and preach that our children WILL NOT be educated by the State in public schools.

THE CHURCH STRIKES AGAIN

For many decades, in this country, the only education was Christian education. School classes, teaching basic subjects, were held in churches or adjacent buildings, with the pastor often being the teacher. With the passage of time, the Lord's people, for the usual economically expedient reasons, gave in to the idea of state supported schools. This was done with the vain hope that the Bible would continue as the major textbook and the Christian religion would never lose its stronghold in public thought. As with most departures from the Word and the will of God, all proceeded slowly. Only in recent decades have God's people begun to wake up and repent and obey God in the education of their children.

Deuteronomy 6 is an example of many passages in the Bible charging parents with the responsibility for the training of their children. No passage in the Bible authorizes or allows children to be trained by the government. As parents obey the Word of God by trusting the Lord Jesus Christ as their Saviour, and gather in local churches for fellowship, the only reasonable course of action is to band together under the banner of the Word of God. To train children in the faith is to train them that the faith touches every field of intellectual endeavor known to the mind of man.

What is education? "The acquisition of true wisdom and true knowledge." With this firmly fixed in mind, we may set out to examine the logic behind the place of the church in education. What of the current movement toward the local church establishing a school? What of a pastor standing in the pulpit in a "worship service" to discuss education? Our reasoning goes like this: If you desire to learn "true wisdom and true knowledge" where do you go to seek it? Certainly not to a state university. The chairman of practically every philosophy department of every state school in the nation will tell you he is searching for truth. No philosopher, worth his salt, will tell you he has found the truth. These are the men who educate the people who educate people in other state schools, whether they be elementary, secondary, colleges or universities.

To make a long story short, there is one place in all the world to go for "true wisdom and true knowledge"——that is the Bible. Obviously you may go to other books and find a mixture of truth and error, but only one book is the Book of Truth. Such a view of truth sounds strange in our Secular Humanist world, but in times past this philosophy was not uncommon.

As Sir Walter Scott lay dying, he said to the man attending him: "Bring me the Book!" His servant said: "What Book, sir?" Scott said: "Man, there is only one Book!" The Bible is not A book, it is THE Book. No other is infallibly the source of "true wisdom and true knowledge" which is imperative for education. State educators, with rare exceptions are searching for the truth. Christian educators have found it. Christian educators have found the truth, and yet there is still confusion in the minds of many as to where to go to find "true wisdom and true knowledge."

At this juncture let me say something which may shock you, but you will never refute it. "The work of the church in the world has never been anything other than education." Our first goal, for example, is to educate men and women, boys and girls, concerning the need and the way of salvation. Our second goal is to educate them into how to live a life in the world which is pleasing to God. This is a process of education. The work of the church in the world has never been anything other than education.

Surely, we seek to help people. We have various obligations to our neighbors as we find them in need, but the Lord Jesus Christ set an example when He was here. At the Pool of Bethesda (John 5), there was a great multitude of impotent folk, blind, halt, withered, waiting for the moving of the water. The Lord Jesus went to one man out of the great multitude. Neither He nor we have a mission to feed the hungry, except in a very limited sense. We are not here to heal the sick, help the dying, alleviate suffering, except in a very limited sense, and that limited sense is this: Any help we give is a teaching tool. By a process of education, we are to teach those whom we help that help comes only from the Lord Jesus Christ.

Show me a man who takes credit and receives glory for the help he gives to others, and I will show you an ego maniac instead of a Spirit-filled Christian. We, as obedient Christians, meet the physical needs of others for one stated purpose——to teach them, to educate them to the fact that the Lord Jesus Christ is the source of all help. *Every good and perfect gift is from above." James 1:17.*

Certainly we worship the Lord along the way, but that is not the work of the church in the world. If our purpose was primarily worship we would die immediately. Worship of God may be accomplished much more effectively in heaven, with the restraints and limitations of this world removed. Our worship and praise are things we do along the way, as we move toward heaven——but the only work of the New Testament church in the world is education . . . . first, to educate others concerning the need and way of eternal life; second, to educate those who have received eternal life in how to live in the world and function in a fashion well-pleasing to God.

Each person who reads these words, and is saved, was saved through Christian education. Someone opened a Bible and taught you "true wisdom and true knowledge." When you acquired a knowledge of the efficacy of the Precious Blood of Christ, you were instantaneously "educated" as to the salvation of your soul. Each person who reads these words and is strong in the Lord, a decent citizen, a credit to the community and the nation, became such through Christian education. Someone taught you, you taught yourself; in any case, the Lord taught you by "the acquisition of true wisdom and true knowledge."

As pastor of a church for the past eleven years, I have never preached a sermon which was not on the subject of Christian education. The word "education" may never have been mentioned, but the purpose of each message was education. Teaching the lost how to be saved––teaching the saved how to live––educating both by "the acquisition of true wisdom and true knowledge."

The words "wisdom" and "knowledge" and their derivatives are found almost 2000 times in the Bible. It is a Book of "true wisdom and true knowledge" from cover to cover. The logic behind this is found in the Scripture quoted at the beginning of this chapter:

> *"Christ . . . in whom are hid ALL the treasures of wisdom and knowledge."*
> *Colossians 2:2&3*

Education is impossible without Him in Whom are hid ALL the treasures of wisdom and knowledge. We must come to the Lord Jesus Christ and His Word. Any educational system which ignores this truth will not impart education.

Education received in the home is only valid with the Lord Jesus at the center of the home. Any education imparted in the church will only be valid when the Lord Jesus is the center of that church. Education taught in a day school will only be valid to the degree the Lord Jesus is the center of the school. Any education received by you or your child later in life, when formal education is ended, will only be valid to the extent that the Lord Jesus is the center of the life. This is the philosophy of Christian education, because in Him and Him alone are hid ALL the treasures of wisdom and knowledge.

"The fear of the Lord is the beginning of knowledge but fools despise wisdom and instruction. Proverbs 11:7.

God says fools despise the Bible as the only basis for truth. Fools despise the Christian schools of America because only there, on a consistent basis, is true wisdom and instruction to be found.

Question: If the church has the key to "true wisdom and true knowledge" and, therefore, to education——why do we not preach on English literature in the Sunday morning service?

If this is not some hair-brained philosophy I have contrived to defend the Christian school movement, why do I not hold math classes from the Bible on Sunday night?

If there is no secular education for the Christian, why not integrate chemistry and accounting and trigonometry and biology into sermons from the pulpit?

The answer may hurt your feelings if you are an educator and academic, beguiled with enticing words. The pulpit ministry does not include chemistry because, in the economy of God, chemistry is relatively unimportant. If algebra occupied four chapters in the Word of God, we should preach on it several times a year. If English literature were of great importance, the Bible would be filled with it.

Education, which comes from the pulpit, deals with the vital aspects of education. We deal with the true story of origins in Genesis. We teach the outline of history——past, present and future——as seen from the vantage point of heaven. We teach health when we speak of the evils of liquor and tobacco. We teach government as related to the government of God. In summary, we teach people how to live now and forever in a spiritual, moral, social, and political framework which is pleasing to the God Who made us.

This is not to say we do not believe in detailed education. This is why we have a Christian school for children who have never learned the less important details of science, history, math, English, etc. If a church is doing its job, it has a primary and a secondary education program. The church must train its people to be well-rounded individuals who understand that calculus is for time, and godliness is for eternity. The pulpit ministry does not lower itself to teach the "theory" of the atom. Instead, we proclaim Him Who "upholds all things by the Word of His power." Rather than waste valuable time on the "hypotheses" of science, or the "probabilities" of math, or the "possibilities" of physics, the pulpit ministry of education holds to the absolute certainties of infallible truth.

For what shall it profit a man if he becomes an accountant, a doctor, a lawyer, a chemist, an engineer, or by those means gains the whole world and loses his own soul?

What shall it profit to educate a child to the point that he has the tools to become rich and famous, and have him die and go to hell forever? Modern society has lost its values and its perspective. The god of America is money—the goddess of America is education. Even God's people have somehow forgotten that a man with a Ph.D. from Harvard or Oxford is a walking disaster area if his sins have never been washed away by the blood of Calvary's Cross.

Chapter 10

THE CLASSIC SECULAR HUMANIST

"The day will come when the account of the birth of Christ as accepted in the Trinitarian churches will be classed with the fable of Minerva springing from the brain of Jupiter."

Thomas Jefferson

Absolutely imperative to an awareness of the nature of the conflict in which we are engaged is a working knowledge of Secular Humanism. Throughout this book, with tireless repetition, you will find attempts to define and analyze this religion, with its almost total acceptance by society at large.

Thomas Jefferson is the classic Secular Humanist and his philosophy will serve us well to illustrate the dangers and complexities of the problem.

The terminology, in itself, is a deterrent to understanding. When the word "secular" is commonly defined, it means "without God or religion." For the Christian this is not a valid definition. For those who believe the Bible, a proper definition must be——"without the One True and Living God, or, the true religion."

Consider for a moment the case of *Torcaso v. Watkins (367 U.S. 488)*. Torcaso was a citizen of the state of Maryland who wished to become a notary public. The

181

Maryland Constitution required that any person seeking this position must affirm his belief in God. Torcaso was an atheist and refused, which caused his appointment to be denied. Torcaso appealed to the U.S. Supreme Court, which struck down the Maryland decision with these words:

> *"The power and authority of the state of Maryland thus is put on the side of one sort of believers——those who are willing to say they believe in 'the existence of God.'"*

> *"Among religions in this country which do not teach what would generally be considered a belief in the existence of God are Buddhism, Taoism, Ethical Culture, Secular Humanism and others."*

The Supreme Court held that, in spite of the fact that a system of belief excludes a god, it is still a religion. It may be "secular" and "religion" at the same time. Secular Humanism IS a religion. It is simply not the "true" religion.

My contention is that pure logic takes us one step further. The Bible presents only one God as a sacred God. He is the God of the Bible. Any other god is a secular god, a god fashioned by the mind of man.

Secular Humanism is a religion, a system of belief. It is the belief that without the One True and Living God revealed in the Bible——man is the final arbiter of truth. In his own mind, man may decide to believe in any deity he chooses, or no deity at all, and his decision is ultimate and valid for him personally. Briefly stated, "Secular Humanism" is the religion which declares "the ultimacy of the mind of man."

"Dispute as long as you will on religious tenets, our reason at last must ultimately decide, as it is the only oracle which God has given us to determine between what really comes from him and the phantasms of a disordered or deluded imagination."

Thomas Jefferson
Letter to Miles King— —1814

In a well-researched article entitled "The Faith of America's Presidents," published by Bob Jones University, Rebecca Lunceford gives the following enlightening quotation:

"To his nephew Jefferson wrote, 'Fix reason firmly in the seat and call to her tribunal every fact, every opinion. Question with boldness even the existence of God, because if there be one, He must more approve of the homage of reason than that of blindfolded fear. Read the Bible then as you would read Livy or Tacitus . . . Your own reason is the only oracle given you by heaven, and you are answerable not for the rightness, but uprightness of the decision."

Jefferson believed in "the ultimacy of the mind of man." "The true religion" is Bible Christianity. "The other religion" is Secular Humanism in its hundreds, if not thousands, of forms. Jefferson believed in a god "if indeed there be one" who has given "reason" as the "only oracle" to determine truth. His god was not the only sacred god known to man——the One True and Living God of the Bible. His god was a secular god of his own choosing——his personal definition of deity.

Such a Secular Humanist belief is completely foreign to the true religion. The Only True God reiterates scores of times in His Word that the Bible, and not human reason, is the only oracle given to determine truth. The existence of God is a fact. The existence of the Word of God is a fact. These are not issues open for discussion.

The Bible says: *"The world by wisdom knew not God!"* Human reason was given by God for one end only——to "acknowledge" truth. The Secular Humanist, on the other hand, sees human reason as a faculty which allows man to sit in judgment upon truth.

We must give careful consideration to this point, or the subtlety of the battle for the mind will escape us. "Truth" is God the Son, the Lord Jesus Christ, Who said: *"I am the truth."* No man will ever know truth without first coming to know Him. Truth is not a set of facts, it is a Person——the Lord Jesus Christ. Secular Humanism defines truth as an unknown entity in a vast ocean of suppositions. The great philosophical question of the ages is, "What is truth?" When Secular Humanists ask that question, they presuppose a knowledge of supposed facts. They suppose they exist. They suppose life is real and not illusion. They suppose 2+2=4. They suppose a tree is, in fact, a tree. What they cannot determine is WHY they exist; what makes life real; for what purpose does 2+2=4? Hence the question: "What is truth?"

Essentially the true things around us in the world are only true relating to one another. Unless they have some all-encompassing external meaning, they are random eventualities in a world evolved by chance. The true meaning of human existence escapes the Secular Humanist, even if he believes in some sort of god, because that god, be it the stone idol of the pagan, or the creator-god of a Jefferson——is the product of pure empirical knowledge.

184

In spite of the agnostics and atheists of our day, *"the fool hath said in his heart, there is no God."* Common sense looks at a watch and concludes the existence of a watchmaker. This is not a truth revealed from heaven, it is a logical approach to observable facts. To look at a man and conclude the existence of a manmaker is an intellectual belief, based on the power of the mind of man to form an hypothesis. When Jefferson said, "We are endowed by our Creator with certain unalienable rights"––he went no further than the Babylonians, or the Greeks, or any "religious" societies of ages past which acknowledged the "gods" and the need to seek their favor. In the previously cited article from BJU, another quote substantiates this:

> *"Concerning the doctrine of the Virgin Birth Jefferson wrote, 'The day will come when the account of the birth of Christ as accepted in the trinitarian churches will be classed with the fable of Minerva springing from the brain of Jupiter.'*
>
> *"In an earlier letter to another friend, Jefferson referred to such 'artificial systems invented by ultra-Christian sects' as Christ's deity, creation of the world, and virgin birth as well as the doctrines of 'the Trinity, original sin, atonement, regeneration, election.'"*

Some of the most "religious" periods of history have included belief in personal gods which were by no means the One True and Living God revealed in the Bible. To believe in a "maker," to whom all further relationship is a matter of personal choice, rather than Bible-mandated intellectual prostration to His glory and authority, is nothing more than a subtle form of Secular Humanism.

Much controversy related to Jefferson has centered around the question of whether or not he was a "deist." Here again, any confusion is a result of semantics. Those who lean toward explaining away his questionable religious views say "no." The common definition of "deist" is: "One who believes that God exists and created the world but thereafter assumed no control over the lives of people." However, those who have read and studied philosophy, know that in the study of philosophy the word "deist" has another definition, as found in most comprehensive dictionaries. In philosophy, "deism" is: "The belief that reason is sufficient to prove the existence of God, with the consequent rejection of revelation and authority."

Jefferson was indeed a "philosophical" deist. His belief in the existence of a god was, to him, a fact established only by his reason, and, consequently, he rejected the revelation of an infallible Bible and the authority of God's revealed truth.

We must come to grips with this simple thesis. Only two religions exist on earth——the revealed religion of the Bible, from the mind of God, and the revealed religion of human reason, from the mind of Satan. Bible Christianity——advocating the ultimacy of the mind of God; Secular Humanism——advocating the ultimacy of the mind of man.

If we develop this philosophically, we must do it from Bible perspective. Man has given many labels to many things in an attempt to fit the unbelief of man into specific categories. This is the source of all confusion surrounding deism, scientism, Buddhism, Confucianism, and even

186

Methodism, Presbyterianism, etc., when they depart from a belief in the revealed truth of the Bible.

Actually, a good Bible name for "the other religion" would be "the Philosophy of Babylonianism." We find it from Genesis to Revelation, in principle, if not in name. Since it would take another book to explain that thoroughly, we simply adopt the current name given to the age-old philosophy, which is "Secular Humanism."

Secular Humanism, when defined as: "A belief that without the sacred God of the Bible, the mind of man is the ultimate measure of all things," is "the other religion." Jefferson believed in a secular god, who was not the sacred God of the Bible. He believed that "our reason . . . must ultimately decide . . . as the only oracle." Since Jefferson believed in a secular god, who has left us to the ultimacy of human reason, I define him as *The Classic Secular Humanist;* in other words, one who is able, under the cloak of "the other religion," to espouse Secular Humanist principles in a religious setting.

The most specific Bible passage on "the other religion" is Romans, chapter one. There we find man who sees the existence of God in creation but will not glorify Him as God. The result is several-fold:

1. Man says, "Reason tells me there is a God."
2. "But I refuse to glorify Him as the true God to whom I am responsible for my sin."
3. His thoughts become vain.
4. His heart becomes darkened.
5. He claims to be wise.
6. In reality he becomes a fool.
7. He changes God's glory into something definable by man.

8. He changes the truth of God into a lie
9. He worships and serves the creature—
   man——more than the Creator——Jesus
   Christ.

In other words, he becomes a full blown Secular
Humanist! The end result of secularizing God into
something other than the sacred blood-stained Saviour of
sinners Who arose from the dead——is to worship and serve
man——the creature. That is Secular Humanism.

As you can see, Secular Humanism is like cancer.
While it appears with various symptoms at various stages of
the disease, it is always Secular Humanism from the day it
first infects the human mind. A religious Secular
Humanist, professing some sort of belief in a deity which
he refuses to glorify as the One True and Living God, is the
most dangerous sort. He appears to be a reasonable and
righteous man while, in the name of religion, advocating
irreligion. The Secular Humanist believes that truth is
unknown and unknowable.

> *"I inquire after no man's religion and
> trouble none with mine; nor is it given us in
> this life to know whether yours or mine,
> our friends' or our foes' is the right."*
>> *Thomas Jefferson*
>> *Letter to Miles King——1814*

The sacred God of the Bible would take issue with
the secular god who made this Secular Humanist
philosophy known to Thomas Jefferson. The sacred God
of the Bible says, *"Now is the day of salvation"* (II Cor.
6:2). And how are we to be saved "NOW"? This same
sacred God of the Bible says He would *"have all men to be
saved and come to THE knowledge of THE truth"* (I Tim.

188

2:4). Being saved is coming to THE knowledge of THE truth NOW——in this life where truth is both known and knowable. But it is only known to those who reject the philosophy of Secular Humanism and trust the Lord Jesus Christ Who said: *"I am the truth"* (John 14:6) to save them "NOW" from their sins.

Another tenet of the Secular Humanist religion is "the wall of separation between church and state." Jefferson authored this phrase, as previously demonstrated in Chapter 2 of this book. As with any good Secular Humanist, he wanted the church and its doctrine kept completely out of both politics and education.

> *"On one question I differ. The right of discussing public affairs in the pulpit. The mass of human concerns, moral and physical is so vast, the field of knowledge requisite for man to conduct them to the best advantage is so extensive, that no human being can acquire the whole himself, and much less in that degree necessary for the instruction of others. It has of necessity, then, been distributed into different departments. Thus we have teachers of languages, teachers of mathematics, of natural philosophy, of chemistry, of medicine, of law, of history, of government. Religion too is a separate department, and happens to be the only one deemed requisite for all men however high or low."*
>
> *Thomas Jefferson*
> *Letter to Mr. Wendover——1815*

While the general logic of preachers not preaching on chemistry is true, it is also overstated in an attempt to justify the principles of Secular Humanism. Notice carefully, two of the Secular Humanist views which have contributed heavily to *The Separation of Church and Freedom* in our lifetime. Jefferson was against "the RIGHT of discussing public affairs in the pulpit." He also considered religion to be "a separate department" from all other branches of knowledge. He advocated history, law, medicine, government, philosophy, etc., etc., as needing no theological guidelines from the teaching of the Word of God. Such is the position of Secular Humanism toward those areas today.

Another Secular Humanist view, which is believed but seldom spoken, much less written, is found in the Jeffersonian "Education Bills of 1782":

> *"The bill for Virginia proposes to lay off every county into small districts ... and in each of them to establish a school for teaching reading, writing and arithmetic. These schools will be under a visitor who is annually to choose the boy of best genius in the school and to send him forward to one of the grammar schools of which 20 are proposed to be erected in different parts of the country, for teaching Greek, Latin, geography, and the higher branches. Of the boys thus sent in any one year, trial is to be made at the grammar schools and the best genius of the whole selected and continued for 6 years and the residue dismissed. By this means, 20 of the best geniuses will be raked from the rubbish annually, and be instructed at the public expense so far as the grammar schools go."*

Yes, that is what he said. In doing the research I had to re-read it the third time before I could believe my eyes, to be sure nothing was misunderstood. "20 of the best geniuses will be raked from the rubbish annually."

Jefferson believed, as do the Secular Humanists today, that the average man is just so much "rubbish." The elitist Secular Humanists must rake through the "rubbish" of humanity to ferret out the superior intellects. Nietzsche was in search of the "superman" to build a Humanist society on the glories of man. Only a Secular Humanist would refer to precious souls, created in the image of God——souls for whom the Lord Jesus died——as "rubbish."

This analysis of *The Classic Secular Humanist* might continue indefinitely with the wealth of evidence available. One other quotation is sufficient:

> *"The general objects of this law are to provide an education adapted to the years, to the capacity, and the condition of every one. Instead, therefore, of putting the Bible and the Testament into the hands of the children at an age when their judgments are not sufficiently matured for religious inquiries, their memories may be stored with the most useful facts from Grecian, Roman, European and American history. The first elements of morality, too, may be instilled into their minds: such as, when further developed as their judgments advance in strength, may teach them how to work out their own greatest happiness, by showing them that it does not depend on the condition of life in which chance*

191

has placed them, but is always the result of a good conscience, good health, occupation, and freedom in all just pursuits."

Notes on Virginia
Thomas Jefferson——1782
The Jeffersonian Cyclopedia

High sounding rhetoric indeed. But a philosophy born out of the pits of Secular Humanism. Notice the outstanding elements:

1. Education without the Bible.

2. Children capable of learning Grecian, Roman, European, and American history but with "judgments" not ready for religious inquiries. Why? Because, in his view, human reason sits in judgment upon revealed truth.

3. Morality instilled in their minds without the Bible.

4. Man works out his own greatest happiness.

5. "CHANCE" and not God placed them in their condition of life.

6. Happiness "is ALWAYS the result of a good conscience, good health, occupation and freedom." Change the environment and change the man.

How did Jefferson learn these modern principles of Secular Humanism? He learned them by Satan's revelation to his reason, which he exalted above the revelation of the written Word of God. The modern principles of Secular Humanism are as old as the garden of Eden. Only the name is new. In Eden under the "tree of KNOWLEDGE"——a most appropriate location——Satan appealed to human reason and said——without the One True and Living God——"Ye shall be as gods——KNOWING . . . . !" "Adam, what you need is to exalt your mind above the mind of God——ignore His Word and come let me educate you to the way of true happiness." That is the virgin form of Secular Humanism, and it came into full blossom with the passage of centuries, as seen in the philosophy of Thomas Jefferson——*The Classic Secular Humanist.*

"Secular Humanism" has a system of basic doctrine being taught pervasively throughout the educational system, media outlets, and religious institutions of the world. Those who are believers in the "other religion" evangelize and witness for the faith with uncommon zeal. Watch for the fundamentals of the faith" of Secular Humanism, and you will understand the impact being made on our society. The basic doctrine is as follows:

Basic goodness of man

Human reason as the final arbiter

Science as the source of all truth

Infinite potentiality of nature

Amoral value systems

World interdependence

Human government as the ultimate authority.

Chapter 11

THE BATTLE BEFORE US

Rousas John Rushdoony

For some generations now, the church has been in steady retreat. The Puritans had made as their battle principle "The Crown Rights of Christ the King," and had sought to conquer every area of life and thought for Jesus Christ. After 1660, the churches retreated from their world-wide and total calling to dominion to the "spiritual realm." (In the United States, this same retreat took place in the 1800s, especially after 1864. Step by step, the church conceded one area after another to humanism: politics, economics, the arts and sciences, vocations, health care (hospitals were once all Christian), education, and more. Humanism was rapidly becoming the true catholic faith of Western man, and the churches a fringe cult.

But the churches slept on, and complacent congregations rejoiced in retreat, as long as the building fund prospered, and the church socials were successful. They prided themselves on being better than the Puritans, because they were exclusively concerned with things "spiritual," and they regarded their growing irrelevance as a blessing and a mark of spirituality.

But humanism was determined to leave no area to the church. Its goal being the obliteration of Biblical faith, humanism was not satisfied with possessing the world and men's material lives. It wanted their souls as well. Freud supplied the answer. Religion, he said, meaning Biblical faith, cannot be destroyed until guilt ceases to be a religious problem and is treated as a scientific and medical one. Guilty men crave God's grace and forgiveness; they will seek a *theological* answer to the problem of guilt, unless we convince them that guilt is simply a relic from primitive man's soul and can be determined to be scientifically comprehensible. Freud launched the attack on the last corner of the universe left to Christian man, his soul. "Catholic" humanism insisted on its right to control every area of life and thought, and it denied to Christianity any area whatsoever.

After Freud, all that remained of the church was ready for burial. As John Whitehead pointed out, in *The Separation Illusion,* after World War II and in the early 1950s, the U.S. Supreme Court apparently decided that Christianity was dead and became more and more openly humanistic. Only the funeral of Christendom remained.

But something else happened at about the same time. In 1950, the only church schools were Roman Catholic, Christian Reformed, Lutheran, Mennonite and Amish, and Seventh Day Adventists, with a limited number of others. Many of these were to close in the 1960s. Everywhere, however, without organization or direction other than from the Holy Spirit, men began to establish Christian Schools. There was, of course, opposition. Christian Schools were seen as an "unspiritual" concern by many complacent Pharisees in the church and were bitterly opposed. But they grew.

No one knows the extent of their growth. No statistics exist. Estimates run between 10% and 30% of the grade school population as the number in Christian Schools; the second figure is probably closest to the truth. Losses in the public schools have been dramatic; some have been shut down entirely. Many state schools dishonestly pad their rolls with non-existent pupils in order to gain more funds. The growth has been substantial, enough to alarm and anger the humanists and their educators.

The implications of the growth of Christian Schools are revolutionary. Given their present rate of growth, by the end of this century the public or state schools will have virtually disappeared. The result will be a devastating change, as far as the humanists are concerned. The Christian Schools, already training the coming leadership with their superior instruction, will remake America. The citizens of the future will be a Bible-believing people, fundamentalists! The very thought of such a future horrifies the humanists. As a result, we have their counter-attack, their desperate affair to save America for humanism before it is too late!

The humanists thus see the issues: America (and the world) are at stake. It is a battle unto death, a war of obliteration, in which the winner takes all. It is for them especially unsettling to find that these Christian School people will not compromise in so many cases; that many are like the Rev. Kent Kelly, ready to go to jail rather than to surrender. Men like the Rev. Levi Whisner have gone to jail, and then fought to victory. Dr. Lester Roloff has been thrice sentenced, twice in jail, and he refuses to lose, because Jesus Christ is his Lord, and Christ is King of Creation. *"This is the victory that overcometh the world, even our faith"* (I John 5:4).

In the battle before us, we thus face a powerful humanistic establishment in state, church, and school which has no intention of surrendering its power. Only by long, steady, and costly legal and political battles will they be blasted out of power, step by step.

Already, however, Christian men are hearing the call to re-enter every field for Christ the King. The world and all things therein belong to our Lord, not to the enemy, and the enemy must be blasted out of his every stronghold. The politicians are beginning to feel the heat and the pressure of aroused Christians.

But the humanists are not the only enemies we face. Dead churches, *"having a form of godliness, but denying the power thereof"* (II Tim. 3:5), talk much of winning by love rather than contention, but their lack of love for any fighting fundamentalist is conspicuous! Such men and churches rush to the state-house and to Washington, D.C., to assure one and all that they are content with any and all chains, being too spiritual to feel concerned about slavery. At every opportunity, they turn on God's soldiers to slander them and to revile them. This should not surprise us. The stand made by the Lord's faithful soldiers troubles their conscience and gives them no peace.

Thus, we have a double-fronted war: against the humanists, and against the church Pharisees. But in this war we have a great ally, the Lord God of Hosts. Our Commander tells us that *"the gates of hell shall not prevail"* against His army and Kingdom (Matt. 16:18). He speaks of an attack against the very walls of hell, and of hell's inability to hold out against us! Take your children, and your grandchildren for a walk, or a drive. Take them by city hall, the state-house, the courts, the schools, and the universities. And tell them every time you go by, that these are the Lord's and, in due time, He will claim and possess them all. Tell them to prepare themselves in Christian School for conquest. Read to them the Lord's Commission to Joshua, which is restated in summary form by our Lord to His disciples in the Great Commission (Matt. 28:18-20):

> *Every place that the sole of your foot shall tread upon, that have I given unto you, as I said unto Moses . . . .*
>
> *There shall not any man be able to stand before thee all the days of thy life: as I was with Moses, so I will be with thee: I will not fail thee, nor forsake thee.*
>
> *Be strong and of a good courage: for unto this people shalt thou divide for an inheritance the land, which I sware unto their fathers to give them.*
>
> *Only be thou strong and very courageous, that thou mayest observe to do according to all the law, which Moses my servant commanded thee: turn not from it to the right hand or to the left, that thou mayest prosper whithersoever thou goest.*
>
> *This book of the law shall not depart out of thy mouth; but thou shalt meditate therein day and night, that thou mayest observe to do according to all that is written therein: for then thou shalt make thy way prosperous, and then thou shalt have good success.*
>
> *Have not I commanded thee? Be strong and of a good courage; be not afraid, neither be thou dismayed: for the Lord thy God is with thee whithersoever thou goest.*
>
> *(Joshua 1:3,5-9)*

Tell them that, having placed the soles of our feet in education, it is ours in the Lord, and we will not retreat. Tell them that they must plant their feet in still further ground, conquering one area after another for Christ the King.

Troubles? Of course. Enemies? Certainly. *"What shall we say to these things? If God be for us, who can be against us?"*

VOLUME III

THE PRACTICE OF WAR

PREFACE TO VOLUME III

In this section, *The Practice of War,* we come to the mechanics of getting the job done. Each chapter speaks of the practical "nuts and bolts" techniques which have been successful in bringing North Carolina to life in the defense of liberty.

Before a legislative study commission in 1974, Mr. Calvin Criner, Director of the Office of Non-Public Schools in North Carolina, and senior director of non-public schools in the nation, said: "North Carolina is the most heavily regulated state in the nation in potential control over private schools." Contrast that statement with Attorney William Ball's evaluation of our new law for private church schools, passed in 1979. He called it: "The Magna Carta of religious education for the nation."

Every iota of glory belongs to the Lord Jesus Christ Who said: *"Without me ye can do nothing."* It is, however, clearly observable that the Lord used means and men to get the job done. The men are immaterial. "God's best method is always a man," but WHICH man really makes no difference. When God needs a burning bush any old bush will do, with availability being the only criterion.

This section points out the techniques available to men in every part of the nation; techniques tested and proven in the school of experience to get the job done. Another entire book would be needed to catalogue our failures, our discarded ideas, our blind alleys. Before you, in the following pages, are eight chapters, each of which cost us no less than $20,000 and hundreds of man-hours. Your cost for the use of this information is the price of this book, and the time to read these next chapters carefully.

Chapter 12

ORGANIZING FOR BATTLE

*"Whenever the legislators endeavor to take
away and destroy the property of the
people, or to reduce them to slavery under
arbitrary power, they put themselves into a
state of war with the people."*
                                    John Locke

THE PURPOSE OF STATE ORGANIZATION

Without question, the most effective means of
defense is an organized defense. The organization of
independent, fundamental churches and schools is
sometimes a battle in itself. Many states are fragmented by
issues totally unrelated to reason in the face of conflict.

Each of us is concerned about quality education.
To organize for purchasing power, sports, and fellowship
are legitimate pursuits. The height of absurdity is to allow
such peripheral issues to dominate a state organization. No
state organization can control educational quality in
independent schools. At best it can only set standards and
require member schools to show prima facie evidence of
compliance. To develop a "Christian school bureaucracy"
with inflexible leadership is disastrous to the defense of
Christian liberty. Older state organizations, established
before government intrusion became so rampant, must
reaccess their goals and purposes if they are to serve the

needs of the hour. We must have Christian schools before there is any need to raise educational quality. You cannot be concerned about academics in schools which do not exist, as will be the case, unless we defend our liberty.

Far and away above any other purpose, we must organize for defense of liberty. If there is an organization in your state with this purpose, join it. If not, an organization with this stated goal should be formed immediately. Certainly unnecessary division among brethren is against Bible principles; every effort should be made to obtain a meeting of the minds. It is, however, impossible to effectively fight a war with a football team. Football teams are organized to play ball and armies are organized to wage war. This is not to say that soldiers don't play football on suitable occasions——it is to say that every organized effort known to man has a primary purpose which overshadows any other goals they may pursue. Each state in this nation needs a state organization of Christian schools, the primary purpose of which is to defend our freedom.

THE PLACE OF STATE ORGANIZATION

At the beginning stages, a state organization must follow the address of its secretary-treasurer out of economic necessity. His mailing address becomes a central contact point for communications in written form. As the organization grows, a full-time Executive Director, who lives in the state's capital city, and maintains an office there, is the ideal. In the meantime, as many activities as possible should be centered in the capital. Scheduled meetings of the membership, board meetings, special called meetings——all of these focus attention on the purpose of the organization when held in the state capital. Pastors and administrators should not be allowed to remain strangers to the seat of government.

Periodic visits to the state legislature should be a normal part of the agenda of every pastor in the state. Legislators need to be aware of who we are and what we stand for, in advance of a confrontation on specific issues. Those in positions of leadership in the state organization must work patiently and tirelessly to educate fellow pastors to the political necessities of these times.

THE PEOPLE OF STATE ORGANIZATION

Every person in the state who is a pastor or Christian school administrator needs to be involved. Of course, this is much easier suggested than accomplished, but that is the goal. Christian schools are under attack as a prelude to soon-coming assaults on local churches. In some areas these assaults have already begun through zoning problems, health departments, and building and fire codes.

You will find that some men see the issues and are eager to join. Others hesitate, through lack of information, fear of controversy, etc., as will be discussed in the next section. Ignoring the problems, suffice it to say that when all is said and done——"Never will so many have owed so much to so few."

State organizations cannot be built on potential, they must be built on reality. Those who could do the most, often do the least, which is no new piece of knowledge to men who are familiar with local church life. Some pastors are like some of the members of your church——if they are not on the board, or in charge in a visible way, they seldom attend the meetings. If they must work with Brother So-and-So who has a church near theirs——forget it.

All such childishness aside, you will find in your state a central core of dedicated men with enough humility

205

and discernment to work together, give together and pray together to get the job done. Others will see the need with the passage of time and get involved unless you brand them as compromisers while they are learning. We need each other desperately. Any Bible-believing fundamentalist, with enough guts and desire to start a school, is a likely prospect to be recruited to defend his freedom to continue that work.

Most state organizations are run by democratic process as we commonly know it. One school——one vote with a Board of Directors elected by the membership. This is fine WITH ONE CAUTION: never set up a board in such a way that the entire leadership can be replaced in one election. Experience is still the best teacher and new men can make old mistakes without advice from those who have been in the battle.

The Board of Directors has officers consisting of a president, who leads all meetings, a vice-president to preside in his absence, and a secretary and treasurer either as a combined office or separate offices, depending on convenience. Some state organizations have an Executive Director (usually ex officio on the Board) if finances permit. As stated in the chapter, *Meet the Press,* there is a great need for one or two men designated as responsible to deal with the media. Their job is facilitated, to a great degree, if they are also on the Board of Directors.

THE PROBLEMS OF STATE ORGANIZATION

Perhaps the best way to approach the subject of "problems" is to consider them individually, because they are many and varied.

MONEY

Money is usually a serious problem for state organizations. From the beginning, dues should be set high enough to cover the monthly cost of operation. This means keeping monthly costs commensurate with the size of the membership. To hire employees, or rent buildings, etc., beyond the reach of income, will cripple the organization for years to come.

Board members should understand at the outset that one of two things is expected of them:

1. Do the myriad of tasks personally––travel, research, lobbying, recruiting, contacting media, etc.
2. Raise enough money to hire someone to carry out these responsibilities.

For a new state organization, the only hope is a Board of determined, tenacious friends of liberty––men who will sacrifice at the expense of their church ministries to get the job done. This means spending a great deal on telephone calls, printing, travel, and many other expenses which are the cost of the privilege of serving on the Board, and which the organizational funds cannot afford to repay.

Older state organizations, with larger memberships, may be able to distribute these costs among the schools, as well as employ secretarial help and a paid lobbyist in the form of an Executive Director.

Once again, dues and volunteer help should cover monthly operational costs if at all possible. With that issue settled, the time to begin raising money for legal defense is last year. In other words, any time you start will not be soon enough. One of the greatest blights on the testimony of fundamental Christianity today is states where people retain attorneys and do not pay their bills. Brethren, it is an ungodly thing to bring in a man from a distant state to do a job and, as in some cases, not even pay his plane fare to come and defend your liberty. Beyond that, it is equally ungodly to set an agreement to pay him any amount for his services and fail to meet that obligation. These attorneys do not take Master Charge or Visa. They offer no "dollar down and dollar a week" easy payment plans. God says, *"Thou shalt not steal,"* and to contract verbally or otherwise and not pay is stealing. When we join a state organization, or when we even align ourselves philosophically with this warfare, we automatically shoulder the cost of the battle, whatever that cost may be. If your church must suffer, let it suffer. If the missionary payments must be cut for a few months, let them be cut. If it becomes necessary to take a special offering every month, we should take it.

Church members, missionaries, pastors, and everyone else should not be allowed to sleep well at night, knowing God's people owe thousands of dollars for the freedom to carry on our ministries and cannot pay. You see, the problem is——we WILL not pay! How do I know that? Because God says He *"will supply all our need according to His riches in glory by Christ Jesus."* Defense of liberty is not a luxury, it is a need. God has promised to supply. His only means of supply is His people. Our business is not to rest until we find out which of His people are holding on to the money God intended to be used to pay our debts.

Any time you start raising money for legal defense will not be soon enough. Once the fight is on, your reserves will be wiped out no matter what they are. Any church with decent leadership, and a proper pulpit ministry on the cause of freedom, should have no objection to a special offering for legal defense at least every six months. Even better would be a special offering, plus a set monthly allocation to fund the fight.

National organizations, such as the American Association of Christian Schools or causes in other states, need periodic contributions. Monthly or annual dues should be a part of tuition or registration fees. Make the parents with children in the school pay those fees as a part of the cost of Christian education. That leaves the church free to get directly involved in the thick of the legal battles.

In 18 months of legal battles in North Carolina, my church, with a Sunday morning attendance of 225, gave $32,000 in cash to finance the warfare. No rich people giving large sums; all hard-working men and women with families and payments just like those in your church. They were simply taught systematically from the pulpit that we have no choice but to sacrifice until we feel the pain, or the iron hand of state and federal government will control our children and our liberty.

SPLITS AND SPLINTERS

Some states are divided in ways which present serious problems to the existence of a state organization——A.C.E. vs. traditional; denomination vs. independent; personality vs. personality; alma mater vs. alma mater. These are only a few of the problems to be reckoned with. Just remember, Brethren, were it not for the Mormons and Roman Catholics and Jehovah's Witnesses keeping the Supreme Court hot while Fundamentalism was asleep, we would probably have no religious liberty in this country.

You need the help of every warm body which is inhabited by a conservative mind, to stop abortion, defeat liquor, block ERA, etc. We can be separatists without being political isolationists. If our country were in physical warfare, you would never kick an atheist out of your foxhole. Given any compassion at all, you would try to win him to Christ as you fought side-by-side. The same principle exists in working with conservatives of every stripe, who may not be regenerate, to accomplish political goals.

Of course, working with them and having them in your state organization are two different matters, just as having a man in your state organization and having him on your church board are two different matters. Surely you see the point. A foxhole is one situation. A rally to defeat an abortion bill is another. A state organization of Christian schools is still a different situation. A question of joining someone for the Lord's supper is yet another matter.

We are born again, blood-washed, separatist, independent, baptized by immersion, anti-New Evangelical, fundamental, pre-millennial, Bible-believing, anti-ecumenical, friends of liberty. Everybody say "Amen"! But, I am not a Baptist. If you would exclude me from a state organization on that basis, you do not understand the war. I did not graduate from Bob Jones University, Tennessee Temple, Baptist Bible College, or the Tiddly-Wink School of Theology. If you would exclude me from a state organization on that basis, you do not understand the war. If you would rather have your child in a public school than an A.C.E. school, you do not understand the war. Almost every state is plagued with prima donna Pharisees like those described in "The Epistle Dedicatory" to the King James Version:

210

*" ... self-conceited Brethren, who run
their own ways, and give liking to nothing,
but that which is framed by themselves,
and hammered on their anvil ... "*

This battle will not be won unless we humble
ourselves and get on our faces before God to admit that
such a condition does exist, and it is nothing less than sin
of the first magnitude. Brethren, a satisfied sheep wants no
other pasture—or pastor! If you cannot work with the
fellow across town to defend your liberty—God help
you—you will soon have no liberty!

A well-taught Christian should have sense enough
to hear aberrant doctrine and discern it. This is a coalition
of leaders, not a nursery school for new-born Christians. If
you are unable to work with a man with whom you
disagree to some extent, you are not mature enough to be
in this battle. If you cannot stand shoulder-to-shoulder
with ANY man who believes in an infallible Bible, the
deity of Christ, a blood-bought salvation, and who lives a
holy life, you belong in a monastery instead of an army.
Go somewhere in a corner and be a doctrinal thumbsucker
until the Secular Humanists come to cart your
super-separated carcass off to jail. This is a battle for men
who "have an understanding of the times"—not fiddlers
who split holy hairs while Washington burns.

THE UNINFORMED AND THE UNGODLY

A final problem confronting us as we seek to
organize for battle is one of the most crucial. To varying
degrees, 90% of the fundamentalists in America are still
uninformed on the factors relevant to the conflict; some
are not aware of the extent of government encroachment
into church affairs; others were themselves educated in

Secular Humanist school systems and are like Lazarus of old——*"Bound hand and foot with graveclothes."* Still others were taught, as Dr. Al Janney has characterized them, that "F.D.R. and the New Deal heralded the impending millennium and the Democratic party would bring in the Kingdom of God——therefore Christians could forget politics." Still others were taught, as Prof. Rushdoony has characterized them, that "since we live in the last days we should abandon hope and retreat into the churches to wait for the end."

Whatever the reason, be it "pre-mill"——"post-mill"——"a-mill" or "wind-mill," God's people have not been hearing Scriptural preaching on the responsibility of the child of God to be the "salt of the earth" and the "light of the world." This means no facet of human existence——be it the voting booth, or the halls of the legislature, or the business office, or the factory, or the home, or the church is to be excluded from the effort and influence of born again believers.

Many pastors cannot immediately lead their people into the fight, because their pulpit ministry has not included "all the counsel of God." Christian education is no longer a luxury, it is a necessity. The only parents who do not have their children in a Christian school are the uninformed and the ungodly. Either they are not informed about the condition and the goals of public education, or they know and do not care. Sadly, this tremendous company of "the uninformed or the ungodly" includes many pastors and Christian leaders who are desperately in need of information.

The death of a state organization, in terms of growth, is to become known for branding those on the outside as compromisers. Seven years ago my children were in a public school. I was a fighting fundamentalist, against sin, for the Bible—— yet completely unaware of "the other religion" being taught in public school. I had never heard the term "Secular Humanist." Had I encountered a group of men who called me their enemy because I was not in the fight, or a compromiser because my children were in public school, serious damage would have been done.

We need compassion and concern for men who need information. Even when they criticize and malign those who take a stand, we need to pray for them, and discuss the issues, and solicit their help. We have men in our state, even now, for whom my heart breaks because they want to be involved and are afraid such a move would split their church, or cost them their job. Personally, I would prefer to split my church or be without a job rather than to be caught in a position where I could not do the will of God as I know it. The sin comes when I begin to condemn them and resent them because they assess the situation another way. It may be that they are on the verge of turning their church around. Perhaps I have been remiss in supplying the information which would show them the seriousness of the conflict. In any event, if our true desire is to help people and have them join us, the tirade of a Pharisee is not God's appointed method.

As a pastor, or school administrator, the process of becoming informed begins with you. Certainly we should never give up preaching the Gospel to change the world politically. Equally certain is the fact that unless we change some things politically we will soon lose the freedom to preach the Gospel. If you believe the Word of God, you have some things to "render unto Caesar." A certain portion of your time must be spent learning God's will concerning the Christian and government.

Surely a reasonable assumption would be that we would need to preach a sermon every six months on Christian citizenship. Neither would it be unreasonable to spend two days a month, in the capacity of a Christian leader, seeking to determine the actions of society concerning pornography, abortion, homosexuality, religious liberty, liquor laws, Christian education and related matters.

Two sermons per year——two days per month——since these are areas of Christian responsibility it is sin to ignore them. But what about preachers who have been in the ministry for ten years and never preached a sermon on Christian citizenship; never spent even one day of serious inquiry into the politics of the state and nation? Brother——you already owe God 20 sermons and 240 days of intense study. Why, by the time you catch up on your disobedience to God, your congregation may say you have become a political radical! On the other hand, you could confess your sin publicly and say: "Brothers and sisters——we have seriously neglected an area of responsibility covered in the Bible, but with God's help that will be changed immediately. For the next eight weeks, on Wednesday night, we are going to do a series of Bible studies on Christian citizenship; and if most of you skip Wednesday night, I will change it to Sunday morning."

You see——we as leaders must get fired up about this thing. We must not go off to conferences and meetings, or listen to tapes, and go back to a congregation which has heard nothing, only to wonder why they are not concerned. Most of your congregation will know what you teach them, and nothing more. Becoming informed begins with you. Your church will give to this cause to the extent that you inspire them to give. They will write congressmen, and senators, and state legislators, to the degree that you convince them of the importance of such action. Every war is won or lost on the basis of leadership. The greatest tool to pry the troops out of complacency is information; and you cannot disseminate information until you have it for yourself.

The time to begin is now. Nothing could be more foolish than to wait to train an army until the legal bullets begin to fly in your state. Until the Humanists took control, a basic principle of Americanism was military preparedness. We knew that a mighty army, trained and ready for battle, was the greatest insurance against enemy aggression and all-out war. Americanism has not changed. America has changed——but we can still use the old methods in our battle for Christian liberty.

THE POWER OF STATE ORGANIZATION

Congressman Larry McDonald has said, "Organization and not numbers is the key to influencing government." No truer words were ever spoken. Our liberty has not been lost to great masses of Americans rising up to request more regulation by the Internal Revenue Service. National public policy did not remove prayer and Bible-reading from the schools. The private school laws of your state were not written because thousands of telegrams flooded the legislature asking government to take over. Small——at times extremely small——organized minorities have done more to shape the laws of this nation, in our lifetime, than any other single factor.

Coupled with this is a new philosophy of government which has taken hold. Bureaucrats set the

215

policies of this nation and they measure the validity of new controls by a strange yardstick. Instead of looking at the support "for" government intervention, they look at the opposition. The basic assumption is that the government must control all areas of life. If there is no opposition to entering a certain area, they assume that to be tacit endorsement by the people.

We must have an organized voice or we will not be heard. Every state needs a Christian school organization as a rallying point for Christian liberty. This gives us, not only a place of fellowship and information, but an organized voice for fundamentalism in the state. Why a Christian school organization? Because this is the front line of attack to bring about *The Separation of Church and Freedom.*

No general worth his salt would launch an open ground assault on the front lines. The flank is the point of vulnerability because the troops have their eyes in another direction.

If precedent law will establish the church school as a secular entity run as a business, the process of definition and division used in the Soviet Union will be complete. In Russia they said, "We believe in religious liberty; you may have religious liberty, but the state will define that which we will allow as religious, and divide it from all other pursuits." The very first church ministry in Russia defined as secular, and divided from the protection of religious freedom, was the education of the children!

We have the power through state organization and national organization to prevent, or at least delay, such an eventuality. There are approximately 10,000 Christian schools in America. No more than 5,000 are fundamentalist schools which could be expected to stand. Christian schools are beginning at the rate of an average of 3 per day and no end is in sight. True, we are a minority, but we have no less than one million students in these schools. Those students have one or two parents in the home; parents concerned enough to pay public school taxes and pay again for a Christian education. Those parents would also be concerned enough to register and vote if we urged them to do it. They would write their senators and congressmen, if we urged them to do it. Can you imagine the effect if 100,000 letters went to a politician's desk to encourage him to vote for, or against, a bill? We have the power, if we have the organization, so why not begin today?

5,000 gather in Raleigh, N. C. for Christian school court hearing.
April 24, 1978–Photo by Cooper Francis

Chapter 13

MEET THE PRESS

"It is by the goodness of God that in our country we have those 3 unspeakably precious things: freedom of speech, freedom of conscience, and the prudence never to practice either of them."

Mark Twain
Pudd'nhead Wilson's
New Calendar

Will Rogers was not the only American who could lay claim to knowing nothing except what he read in the papers. One of the facts of life is the effect of the media on modern society. Regardless of personal opinion about the prevalence of liberalism, or the question of managed news, note carefully the following statement: "You will be covered by the media for good or for ill!" Not too profound, you say? Patently obvious? Think again!

One of the most serious mistakes made in the beginning stages of church-state conflicts is to ignore the media. Presuming bad coverage, assuming a clandestine, secret-agent-type posture, the path of least resistance seems to be a hale and hearty—"No comment!" More deadly words were never spoken.

"WE HAVE MET THE ENEMY AND THEY ARE US!"

A great general never said that, but many should have said it. We are, all too often, our own worst enemies when it comes to public relations. Lower the boom on

219

bureaucrats, critical letters to the editor, apostate preachers, and external criticism of every sort. Such alien creatures provide a catalyst to tell the story and such conflict is news. But never, never, never, make an enemy of a newspaper editor. Never purposely antagonize reporters or TV and radio interviewers under any conditions.

Vital to any serious attempt at winning in the press is a basic assumption; most newspapers, magazines, radio and TV stations, wire services, etc., are predominately liberal. We preach that man is totally depraved, then get offended and outraged if he acts like it. Our basic presupposition is bad coverage; our goal is to turn that around.

Every editorial, in every newspaper great or small, should be answered in a letter to the editor. Those who speak in favor of our position should be commended and reinforced in their views. Those who speak against us need to be answered with information, and not criticism. Personal attacks erect psychological barriers which good ideas cannot penetrate. The man may be an "enemy of freedom," or a "tool of the devil," or whatever you perceive him to be. To tell him so, and compound the offense by expecting him to print it in his newspaper, is foolish.

Thinking men and women read "letters to the editor" in any given newspaper more frequently than any other portion. Responding to editorials is like being in a mental boxing match. Any editor worth his salt will never be offended by clean blows, even if they hurt. By the same token, boxers and editors both recognize a low blow, and to lose their respect is to lose their newspaper as a forum.

PUBLIC RELATIONS

Frightening as it may seem, most of what the general public will ever know about our position comes through the media. Such being the case, the media MUST be penetrated at all costs. Mr. William Ball has said: "There is a court higher than the U.S. Supreme Court——it is the court of public opinion." Any case going to the State Supreme Court, U.S. Supreme Court or even the State Legislature must reach the minds of the decision-makers well in advance. Objectivity is a myth. We have created a national consciousness of the Christian School movement by our activities in the various states. To suppose that Supreme Court Justices and legislators do not read newspapers, listen to radio, and watch TV is illogical, to say the least. They sense the climate of public opinion and lean toward the temperature of the times.

Public relations will determine the tenor of media coverage. Public relations will determine the volume of mail flowing against our cause. Public relations affect the courts, the legislature, the Congress as well as actions by regulatory boards and bodies. Equally important is the fact that public relations affect the morale of the people in our churches——people who must be solidly convinced of the value of the cause. Many a pastor has seen his church split, or fail to support his stand, or decrease in spiritual vitality, through poor public relations.

THE POINT OF BEGINNING

Media people are suspicious out of necessity. They are besieged, with great regularity, by unknown strangers seeking publicity for ridiculous issues. Never be surprised if you get the cold shoulder until they know who you are and consider you a reliable contact. Good press relationships do not occur by accident. They are a result of a tremendous amount of effort and a constant series of contacts.

Every pastor should build a working relationship with local newspapers, TV, and radio. This means reasonable, informative letters to the editor, a willingness to put off other business to grant interviews, and a reputation for complete openness and cordiality toward media staff. If no friendly relationship can be established with local editors they can, at least, be made to respect you as a man ready and able to defend your cause against frivolous comments. Once the battle begins in your state, every pastor with a school is subject to unannounced visits from the press and, as the issues broaden, this will include all pastors with and without Christian schools. Many a preacher has done great harm to the cause by failing to educate himself on the issues and arguments. There is no time to call a state leader or read a book when the press comes knocking on the door. Refusing to grant an interview is no solution since, in most instances, the story will go out with or without your comments. "You will be covered by the media for good or for ill!"

THE NEXT STEP

As individual pastors lay the groundwork for good press relations in local communities, the next step is statewide. Without question, the bulk of major press contact will come through the state organization. Media interest generally leans toward group activities with individual pastors, churches, and schools coming under scrutiny as an offshoot of the efforts of the group. Such being the case, immediate dangers begin to arise. Several rules will nullify the dangers:

1. Never become dependent on official spokesmen.
2. Never believe a bad quote is accurate until you check with the man quoted.
3. Never fail to have a man responsible to deal with the press.

A few comments on each of these rules tell the story.

BRONZED BABY SHOES

"Never become dependent on official spokesmen." If you want to kill your press relationship by an act of premeditated murder, the method is simple: Allow your state organization to become bogged down in the same bureaucratic quagmire found in the hierarchy of state government. The state organization must be absolutely flexible. Nowhere is this more important than in dealing with the press. Keep in mind that "Baby shoes may be bronzed for posterity but newspaper pages are not!" "Exposure" is the key word in public relations, not accuracy. 99% of the material printed or aired on TV and radio will be forgotten within 2 weeks; only an awareness of the issues will remain.

Officers and board members will speak officially in dealings with state officials, courts, attorneys, filing formal press releases, etc., as they should. General press contacts can not, and should not, be limited in this fashion. If contacts are restricted in this way, members of the media quickly tire of calling the "spokesman" for a comment, only to find that he is in parts unknown and cannot be reached until after their deadline. They react by assuming, all too correctly, that it is a waste of time to call 98% of the men and receive "no comment". It is then a further

223

waste of time to call the very busy "spokesmen" only to find them gone. Such activities create a pavlovian aversion to the idea of frequent attempts to obtain our point of view.

Some will object, from unfounded fears, that unqualified men are not capable of handling the press. That, my friend, is Secular Humanism in sheep's clothing! Supposedly it is the other crowd who believes in an elitist aristocracy controlling the masses who are incapable of acting reasonably on their own. Every man who heads up a Christian school should be able to speak kindly and forcefully of his personal convictions to any other human being under heaven. Should there be exceptions, far more harm is done by no press than by occasional bad press.

Contrary to popular belief, the media does not seek out those who will misrepresent your cause. State attorneys will stoop to that, but not the media, as a general rule. In fact, news people prefer someone who uses correct English, speaks pointedly to the issues, and is able to articulate a strong case contrary to the views of the other side. News thrives on controversy. To hedge and double-talk and play down the issues is to cause them to make a mental note to find someone else to state the case in the future. In summary, the Lord will raise up spokesmen (usually 3 or 4 in a statewide movement) and the press will gravitate toward them for most public comment and interviews. Danger comes when we resist the judgment of the media as to those with whom they can best communicate.

LOVE THINKETH NO EVIL

The second rule mentioned previously is: "Never believe a bad quote is accurate until you check with the man quoted". Satan is the accuser of the brethren, and one way to instant defeat in any war is for the troops to fight among themselves. Just as surely as any man is quoted in the press, he will be misquoted. Satan promotes jealousy and fear in the heat of battle. Many dangers lurk in the shadows of good public relations with which the uninitiated are unfamiliar.

Pastors are leaders or they would not be pastors. When leaders get together, a volatile situation exists to say the least. Independent churches are like corporations with a board of directors and a president. Pastors of these churches are thoroughly acclimated to carrying out the normal function of a corporate president which, in particular, involves having the final word over every statement of policy. Paramount to your understanding of the danger at this point, is to realize the diversity and sincerity of your brethren. Statements to the press are not statements of policy. If they appear to be, the man has been misquoted, or had a statement taken out of context, in 99% of the cases. He may not state the facts or answer the questions as you would have done, given the opportunity. Just remember you were NOT given the opportunity. The Lord permitted that man to be at a certain place at a certain time when an interview was conducted, and we know that Romans 8:28 is still in the Book. We do everything humanly possible to act rationally and answer correctly, but only the Lord knows what happens when the information reaches an editor's desk or the editing room of a TV station.

Beyond the problem of misquotes is the problem of poor judgment. We all use poor judgment at times; hindsight is always better than foresight. Please keep in mind that the goal is exposure of the issues. Never intimidate a brother or discourage his sincere efforts on

225

behalf of the cause. Some bad press is absolutely unavoidable if a media blitz is to be successful. Should one of your number make regular mistakes which you consider to be harmful, get on the telephone and discuss it with him personally. Never become guilty of the very gossip you preach against by impugning his motives and assaulting his character while sowing discord among brethren.

Closely related is the danger of jealousy. Professional jealousy is rampant among preachers under normal circumstances. This is war, and such childishness must be laid aside for the good of the cause. Example: "Have you noticed how Brother So-and-So loves to be in the limelight? He goes out of his way to get his name in print as much as possible". The man who says such a thing is filled with fleshly jealousy. You need to discern his threat to the cause, and mark him until his humility returns.

Perhaps you say, "How can you know that to be true?" "Are you not judging him unfairly since someone may indeed be a publicity-seeker?" The answer is clear to those who have been there. One of the first lessons learned through extensive contact with the press, is their uncanny judgment of personalities. Media people can spot publicity hounds a mile away, and avoid them like the plague. In fact, the most certain method of NOT appearing frequently in the newspapers, TV, and radio, is to be even slightly pushy about interviews. The statewide press is a closely knit community. When the word gets around through the grapevine that a man is uncooperative, or critical of their integrity, or most especially, eager to be interviewed, he is blackballed to a very great degree. The greatest compliment is frequent interviews. The greatest insult is to be ignored. Never allow Satan to convince you that a brother makes arrangements to get his name in the papers and his picture on TV. Such a course is absolutely impossible apart from the will of the news people themselves.

MANAGED NEWS

The third danger mentioned previously is as follows: "Never fail to have a man responsible to deal with the press." Much of the material covered thus far speaks to spontaneous press relations. This danger involves assuming such spontaneity to be sufficient. We hear a great deal about managed news today, but we would do well to remember that there is no other kind.

Our country has poor government because we sit back and leave it to the other guy. America is controlled by liberals because conservatives are too involved in other interests to change the drift of the times. Much the same conditions explain the danger here. Reporters cannot report what they do not know. With the exception of newspaper editors, most media people are genuinely interested in telling both sides of the story, if they know both sides. The concept of news management is the awareness that objectivity is a myth. Reporters sincerely attempt to be objective, in most cases, but sincere attempts at the impossible accomplish very little. Personal biases creep into reporting as surely as a teacher's values affect the student. To deal with the subject of managed news effectively, we must look at the two areas mentioned thus far.

First——the mechanics. At least one and perhaps two men in a statewide battle should have a leading from the Lord, and a specific responsibility, to cultivate press interest. Again, this is not to ask for interviews, or force coverage in any way. The man is to be a mechanic, above

227

anything else. Should circumstances dictate that he also be the subject of interviews, well and good, but his primary function is as a conduit for press awareness. This man, or men, should compile a list of every major newspaper, news service, TV station and radio station in the state. He needs phone numbers, mailing addresses, and the name of at least one key person in each news department. Also important is contact with the national media, but that is an entirely different ball game with which we will deal in another section.

As preachers, and not politicians, we sometimes get the impression that the world is waiting to hear what we have to say. You are no doubt familiar with the fellow who told everybody the Lord had given him the gift of preaching but he couldn't find anybody with the gift of listening. Never think for one moment that calling a press conference means the press will come. One or two key men must become known to media people as reliable sources of information regarding times and dates of press conferences, rallies, court proceedings, etc. Every major news outlet in the state should be kept aware of progress through periodic phone calls, mailouts, and personal contacts. News management, first and foremost, involves the consistent, timely dissemination of information through an individual known to the press as a reliable source. They cannot report what they do not know.

Second—the ministry. Perhaps "ministry" seems like a strange word, but all that we do should be an attempt to proclaim a message of truth and righteousness. Not only "the mechanics," but "the ministry" as well, plays a vital part in news management. As mentioned previously, the only news is managed news. Objectivity is a myth, perpetuated by those who fail to understand that all thought, with its attendant outward expression, stems from personal presuppositions.

News reporting displays the feelings of the reporter in subtle ways. One example would be an imbalance of material. Fourteen paragraph articles, which contain nine paragraphs of one position and five paragraphs of the other, are managed news. Another example would be unanswered criticism. In a radio interview two sound clips are used as a news report. One man says, "Our school bill before the Legislature is based on sound legal principles." This statement is followed by an antagonist who says, "This piece of legislation opens the door for cults to establish schools." One statement is general, the other is specific, raising a major doubt with no response. Any attempt at fairness would cite a specific objection, followed by a specific response to the objection, and let the two comments stand on their own merits.

Management of news is done most effectively in radio and TV, where an interview lasting ten minutes is often reduced to 15 seconds. News management is done most destructively, however, in newspapers, because of the extended coverage involved. Only a few words scattered throughout the article set the tone and create an impression. A few examples tell the story: "In a tense, two-hour meeting Wednesday . . . . . " "He is waging a strong race for one of the two seats available . . . . . " "No matter what anyone does, the place seems jinxed . . . . . " "The angry crowd assembled outside the courthouse . . . . " Obviously, how "tense" the meeting, or how "strong" the race, or how "jinxed" the place, or how "angry" the crowd, is purely a subjective opinion.

Reporters would legitimately say, in their own defense, that they reported the facts as they saw them, which is precisely the point. "How they see" the facts determines the tone of the article.

Vital to the philosophy of having one or two men specifically assigned to the press, is what we might call "friendly education." We have a valid position, not only in terms of Biblical mandate, but also in terms of a common-sense approach to perpetuating a free society. Press people are intelligent and tenacious. Should they ever become convinced of the relationship between preservation of our First Amendment rights and theirs, the tone of the articles will change.

The man assigned to the press should work earnestly and diligently to get printed material into their hands, with a personal request that they read it. He should seek to develop a cordial relationship, majoring on frank discussion of the issues, as well as free exchange of ideas. Important to note is the fact that media people seldom have more than a passive detached relationship with state officials. Bureaucrats do not trust press people, and they know it. If we come to them seeking no special favors, but promoting an honest and open association, they cannot escape preferring us and our sincerity above that which they find to be true of the artificial nature of the bureaucracy.

Witnessing to the press may also be a part of our ministry. Come on like a human bulldozer who just finished a crash course in soul-winning, and everything you have worked for will be destroyed. Wait for the Spirit of God to lead to His time and circumstance, and the Lord will honor His Word. Keep in mind that if you blow it, you do not walk off down the street and knock on another door, mumbling about the reproach of Christ. You may be dealing with these people for years to come, so to antagonize them, or harass them about the condition of their soul, is inexcusable. They interview the Moonies, Jehovah's Witnesses, Mormons, and religions of every stripe. To witness to them before you have convinced them you are different, is an exercise in futility, without a most unusual leading from the Lord.

To summarize: managed news is nothing more nor less than a fallible human being reporting events as he or she perceives them. This perception is colored by personal preference, availability of facts, and relationships to the participants. A good public relations man can affect all three and thereby "manage" the news.

NATIONAL COVERAGE

National coverage of your problems is an entirely different situation. In the first place, you must begin by going against the inviolable rule laid down for state coverage, and ask the national media to cover your story. Such action is made necessary by the inaccessability of those who decide which stories will be covered.

When you speak of the *Wall Street Journal*, the *New York Times*, the *Atlanta Constitution*, the *Chicago Tribune*, CBS-TV news, National Public Radio (aired on over 200 stations nationwide), NBC and CBS radio––all of which covered the North Carolina story, only the Lord could bring it to pass. You do not make plans to be on the front page of the *New York Times*, or the front page of the *Wall Street Journal*. A phone call to Washington will never get an hour-long special broadcast aired twice on 209 radio stations from coast to coast. We count those among the many miracles the Lord wrought on our behalf in North Carolina.

Obviously, we must pray as if everything depended on the Lord, and work as if everything depended on us. Certain things are humanly possible, which often serve as catalysts to promote others. Local affiliates are important. Your state has CBS, NBC, and ABC TV news affiliates. These are the local news departments which carry their programming. Your state has an affiliate of the Public Broadcasting System aired on radio across the nation. From the news departments of these local stations you may obtain phone numbers, and possibly names of people to call in New York, or Washington, or Atlanta, or Chicago, or wherever national coverage decisions are made. Once you have names of those with whom you have communicated by phone, they need local press clippings and a brief typewritten summary of what you face. Here again, one or two men in charge of media contacts need to know this advance work to be their responsibility.

Another avenue is contact with nationally syndicated columnists and conservative writers such as J.J. Kilpatrick, Russell Kirk, or for that matter, any who may be known in your part of the country. Here again, the only means of obtaining coverage is a straightforward request for their help. While a phone call may establish contact, they will invariably ask that you send them clippings and material to review before committing themselves.

Just a word about hospitality is in order. When a man flies in to cover the story, offer to pick him up at the airport and take him out to dinner. If he comes to examine your church and school, invite him into your home for a meal or a cup of coffee. National media people are admittedly a different breed from the local press but they are not creatures from another planet; you will find them to be just as susceptible to the "news management" of friendliness and sincerity mentioned in the previous section.

232

One other point on national coverage is the need to be on the lookout for opportunities. National media people coming to your area to cover other stories will provide an occasion to meet them personally and hand them materials to read on the plane ride home.

At a crucial point in the North Carolina conflict, President Carter, President Sadat of Egypt and Prime Minister Begin of Israel were meeting at Camp David, Maryland for peace talks. Over 300 members of the press from every major news outlet in the world were on hand for several days with little to do but twiddle their thumbs. I sent my wife and my aunt to the meeting 400 miles away, armed with press clippings, legal briefs, and a firm resolve to make our story known. Several days later we received a phone call from a pastor in Maryland. One of his church members was working inside the Camp David complex and found some of our material in the President's cottage. Of course the President has nothing to do with national press coverage, but such an occurrence graphically demonstrates the power of the printed page to reach into otherwise inaccessible places.

As a final note, some national exposure may be obtained through Associated Press and United Press International, both of which have offices in your capital city. These wire services, which cross the nation, are staffed by those with whom you may deal as you would with any press representative in your state.

REFLECTIONS

A free press is as much a part of the First Amendment as religious liberty. We have nearly lost our press to the liberals, as we have our government, by a refusal to acknowledge our responsibility as Christian

233

citizens. "The pen is mightier than the sword" is more than a slogan, it is the truth. Our war is a war of ideas above all else. Our freedom will live or die, not in the U.S. Supreme Court but in the court of public opinion. Get on your knees. Get out the Bible. Meet the attorneys. Meet the issues. But don't forget to meet the press!

Chapter 14

SEARCH AND RESEARCH

"Facts are stubborn things; and whatever may be man's wishes or inclinations he cannot alter the state of facts and evidence."

John Adams
Defense in Boston
Massacre Trial—1770

This chapter will have application only in certain circumstances, but the advantages and disadvantages should be weighed carefully. Research, as any lawyer will tell you, is important to a well-rounded case. Any law firm, worth its salt, makes frequent use of research assistants. Since these people usually cost $40.00 per hour, or more, there is good reason to offer your services. One word of caution is in order. Never insist—only volunteer. Some legal research demands legal training and the money saved is not worth mistakes.

The ideal situation is where a local church in the state organization is able to take on this responsibility. Here again, the leading of the Lord is imperative. You must have a church which is able and willing in terms of finances, as well as having personnel suited to this type of work. My church took the job in North Carolina and, as a result, you may profit from our mistakes.

Essentially research involves two areas. Information related to the state in which you reside and national research which indicates an overview of the situation in education. Most lower courts pride themselves in showing disdain for what is happening in other states. However, any such information has a tremendous effect in higher state courts or in federal courts, so the important thing is the court record. To include research in testimony it must, obviously, first be available. Your state organization could begin, even before any sign of trouble, to compile a file of relevant data.

As a point of beginning, contact should be established with other state organizations to pool resources on national research. Items such as the two national surveys in the Appendix of this book are examples. Any higher court would be impressed with the fact that only four states in the nation require state certification of Christian school teachers. Even more impressive is that the same figure also applies to secular private schools. With the upsurge of mandated competency testing for high school graduation, we need the information showing only two states which include Christian schools, and even those, failing to enforce the requirement.

National research pertaining to laws in the fifty states must be done in a law library. Usually the Supreme Court building in the state capital has the best sources, and librarians are most helpful. Any local attorney with a large practice would know the location of needed information. Outside the legal area, you may need documentation on the condition of public education nationwide. In North Carolina we used the following sources:

Options in Education
   2025 M Street, N.W.
   Washington, D.C. 20036

FLS (Foundation of Law and Society)
   15th St., N.W.
   Washington, D.C. 20005

National Humanistic Education Center
   Springfield Road
   Upper Jay, N.Y. 12987

America's Future, Inc.
  542 Main St.
  New Rochelle, N.Y. 10801

Mrs. Ruth Feld
  P.A.C.A. (Parent and Child Advocate)
  Rt. 4, Emerald Drive
  Watertown, Wisconsin 53094

The Barbara M. Morris Report
  P.O. Box 412
  Ellicott City, Md. 21043

News and Views
  Wheaton, Illinois 60187

The Right Woman
  410 First Street S. E.
  Washington, D. C. 20003

Accelerated Christian Education
  Box 2205
  Garland, Texas 75040

American Association of Christian Schools
  1017 N. School St.
  Normal, Ill. 61761

Christian Schools of Ohio
  6929 W. 130th St.
  Cleveland, Ohio 44130

Organized Christian Schools of N.C.
  Box 27723
  Raleigh, N.C. 27611

Center for Independent Education
P.O. Box 2256
Wichita, Kansas 67201

Chalcedon Report
P.O. Box 158
Vallecito, Ca. 95251

Christian Focus on Government
P.O. Box 681
Lubbock, Texas 79408

Christian Law Association
P.O. Box 30290
Cleveland, Ohio 44130

Christian Legal Defense
P.O. Box 2396
Garland, Texas 75041

Council for Educational Freedom in America
2105 Wintergreen Ave., S.E.
Washington, D.C. 20028

Temple Times
2560 Sylvan Road
East Point, Ga. 30344

The Heritage Foundation
513 C Street, N.E.
Washington, D.C. 20002

National Christian Action Coalition
Box 1745
Washington, D.C. 20013

National Assessment of Educational Progress
700 Lincoln Tower
1860 Lincoln St.
Denver, Colorado 80295

Library of Congress
Washington, D.C. 20540

Church League of America
422 North Prospect Street
Wheaton, Ill. 60187

Freemen Digest
P.O. Box 116
Provo, Utah 84601

Aspen Institute for Humanistic Studies
717 Fifth Avenue
New York, New York 10022

Educational Resources Information Center
Washington, D.C. 20000

Office of Child Development
H.E.W.
Washington, D.C. 20000

Office of Education
H.E.W.
Washington, D.C. 20000

Office of Career Education
U.S. Office of Education
Washington, D.C. 20000

Division of Resource Development
  National Institute on Drug Abuse
  11400 Rockville Pike
  Rockville, Md. 20852

U.S. Supreme Court
  Documents Dept.
  Washington, D.C.

The National Institute of Education
  U.S. Dept. of HEW
  Washington, D.C.

Institute of Government
  University of N.C. at Chapel Hill
  Chapel Hill, N.C.

National Center for Education Statistics
  Washington, D.C.

U.S. Civil Service Commission
  Educational Technology Office
  Washington, D.C.

Superintendent of Documents
  U.S. Government Printing Office
  Washington, D.C. 20402

Research Triangle Institute
  Research Triangle Park
  North Carolina 27709

National Center on Child Abuse and Neglect
  Dept. of HEW
  Washington, D.C.

U.S. Dept. of the Interior
Washington, D.C. 20240

Environmental Education Staff
Washington, D.C.

Perhaps more relevant to most cases is local research. Each state is unique in terms of history of education, passage of pertinent legislation, condition of public schools, etc. If you are willing, much of the legwork can be done by your own people and save the cost of legal research assistants, local attorneys doing their own research, or even worse, the research being left undone for lack of time. Because of the varying facilities from state to state we will touch only general areas.

The person in charge of research should familiarize himself thoroughly with public information laws and relay that information to his staff. Approach public officials and their office staff kindly but firmly. There should be no private files in state government unless specific laws exist to the contrary. The following sources appear by a similar name in your state:

Department of Education
State Library
State Archives
Legislative Library
Division of Research
Department of Administration
State Education Library

Most state libraries or state archives contain microfilm files of all major newspapers. These may be viewed through a machine available to the public at no cost. Newspaper articles which establish actions by the legislature, the State Board of Education, or other agencies may be most helpful. In some cases, the microfilmed records go back beyond the turn of the century. While there is no cost to view the newspapers, a charge is made to reproduce any articles needed for your own records. If such articles are to be admissible in a court of law, they must be marked and notarized at the facility under North Carolina law; a similar situation may exist in your state.

If your task is to obtain a legislative history, the source would be either the state archives or a library in your state legislative building. One of these two facilities should have copies of all bills introduced and, in many cases, a record of discussion by related committees. A friendly legislator with some years of experience can guide you to the resources available.

Any document must follow one of two procedures to be acceptable in court. The opposing attorneys must stipulate to the authenticity, or someone must take the stand to validate the document. State attorneys will usually accept any government publication, whether from Washington or the State, without controversy. Unless such an agreement can be reached, it will be necessary to place someone on the witness stand who is closely associated with the document and can confirm its validity.

When compiling documentation, always obtain no less than eight copies of anything you intend to use in court. This may seem expensive and unnecessary but, I assure you, it is most practical. An additional trip to Washington, D.C. to pick up extra copies is more than convincing. We

242

needed one set of documents for our local counsel, one set for out-of-state counsel, one set for an attorney's working copy, one set for state attorneys, one set for the judge, one set for filing with the court, and one set for our files. Even then, we came up short, because a janitor who worked in the superior court building mysteriously entered the judge's chambers, removed his wood-grained hardboard box of neatly ordered documents and burned them in the incinerator as the trial began. Our State Board of Education now requires 50 copies of any document brought before them, which would tend to suggest that one of the members must own stock in a paper mill.

Partial documents are not acceptable in many courts. In other words, a chapter from a book or a section from a study would not be sufficient. The document should be produced in its entirety, and reproduction should be avoided where the original is available. Unmarked copies, while not absolutely required, are preferred by fussy judges. Underlining and notations should only be done in copies for study.

As to the types of documentation available, a representative list is suitable for our purposes here:

Newspaper articles

Early education statutes

Papers from governors and state officials relating historical views of church schools

Reports from legislative study commissions

Minutes from State Board of Education meetings (Ask about tape recordings as well)

Official state publications on education policy

Textbooks and classroom materials reflecting secular humanism in public education

Computer printouts on teacher certification and personnel evaluation

State assessments of educational progress at various grade levels

Books evaluating the place of private education in state history

Copies of state regulations and statutes

Books published by "experts" on either public or private education

Any and all of these types of documents, as well as others you may uncover along the way, could be helpful should the need arise. To begin now to compile a library of such items for your state organization would be most advisable.

The time consumed in research is staggering. Often when searching for precedent law against your cause, the ideal situation is to find nothing after weeks of research. This should be explained to those who labor in this area, lest they be discouraged. Research is the epitome of looking for the proverbial "needle in a haystack," and thousands of pages must be covered to find a powerful piece of material. This is a thankless task for which there is no glory or earthly reward. All "volunteers" will soon fall by the wayside but those who are "drafted" by the Spirit of God will do the job for you admirably.

Chapter 15

LEARN ABOUT LAWYERS

"The man who defends his own case has a jackass for an attorney and a fool for a client."
Abraham Lincoln

Critical to the warfare which faces us, is a need to prepare an adequate defense of our position. Surely our ultimate criterion should be the Bible, followed by the United States Constitution and the State Constitution, if the latter speaks to the subject of religious liberty; but our defense must be carried out by competent legal counsel. We would do well to think first of all about the place of the attorney in the total picture.

The Bible recognizes the need for a mediator between man and his government in matters of law. *"We have an advocate with the Father, Jesus Christ the righteous."* I John 2:1. *"For there is one God and one mediator between God and men, the man Christ Jesus."* I Timothy 2:5. These Scriptures point us, not only to the principle of needing an "advocate," but also to the Ultimate Legal Counsel, the Lord Jesus Christ Himself.

An attorney is not a mediator between God and man. The Lord Jesus is the only mediator. Many make the mistake of seeking out an attorney to consult him on their convictions. Religious convictions are a matter, first and foremost, between the Christian and God. The fact that laws are involved, or that government precipitates the problem, is irrelevant. The purpose behind retaining an attorney is never to formulate your beliefs around his philosophy. Only after our beliefs are settled in our minds and hearts, is there a need for someone to defend them.

The attorney may be a friend, an advisor——even the enunciator of your beliefs in legal terminology. He is, however, an employee who has been carefully taught to remain in that capacity at all times. This is particularly important when crucial decisions confront you and the way does not seem clear. To do his job properly, he must advise you of the alternative courses of action in an impartial fashion. Simply because an attorney states a position does not mean that he is advocating such a position. His aim is to defend policy, not formulate it. In any case he will not serve your jail sentence, or pay your fine, or guarantee that your church will stand behind the position you take. For all these reasons, whatever his value as an advisor, you must retain final decision-making power.

Across the country much discussion has taken place as to the wisdom of using attorneys who are not fundamentalists by our commonly accepted definition of that term. All argument is put to rest if we understand two factors:

1. There are not, nor will there be in the forseeable future, enough lawyers who carry our trademark to meet the needs.

A fundamentalist attorney who is too busy to take your case, or who is too far away for immediate problems, might as well not exist as far as you are concerned. Our chickens have come home to roost in terms of our Secular Humanist views of "full time Christian service." (See chapter on *Philosophy of Education*.) We have not taught young people that a Christian attorney witnessing in America, is as acceptable as a Christian missionary witnessing in Outer Mongolia. As a result, fundamentalist attorneys are virtually non-existent as to their impact on the total legal profession today.

2. An attorney is not hired to be your "theologian in residence." He is a mechanic who must take the tools of statutory law, precedent law, and the Constitution, and repair the damage to our religious liberty.

If your car has serious mechanical problems, you want a technician, not a shade-tree mechanic. He may not be a card-carrying member of the fundamentalist inner circle, but that does not mean he is unqualified. When you go to the hospital, you would prefer a fundamentalist brain surgeon, but the first question should be——"Can he fix brains!?" This, however, should not be the only question. Unless he is a man guided by Christian principles and a strong conservative view, he may consider you expendable and withdraw the life support systems at a most inappropriate moment.

The parallel in attorneys is obvious. His overall philosophy of life will bear heavily on the case at hand. He must believe implicitly in the cause for which he is fighting, or he may retreat in the heat of battle. If he is to go the second mile and be strong when others would be weak, he must be a man of unusual fortitude and dependability. As we well know from sad experience, some men talk the language of the faith and then proceed to act in a manner decidedly antithetical to Christian philosophy. For these reasons skill must be interwoven with an unyielding conviction that the cause is just. Two dangers are ever present when seeking the man for the job; zeal without knowledge and knowledge without zeal.

Another matter, which may come as a shock, is the money. Rest assured that when you hire an attorney his fees will seem astronomical. As in other realms of life, we usually get what we pay for. The difference between a well-used pick-up truck and a Rolls Royce is obvious. One is a means of transportation; the other is a means of intimidation. This will be discussed further in the section on "Expert Counsel" later in this chapter. Vital to an understanding of the money, is to realize that attorneys are not retained as individuals, in most instances. His fee represents the price you pay to get the services of his law firm. This includes a law library, high-powered legal secretaries, research assistants, and much more——as well as the man himself. Please read carefully the section on *Money* in the chapter on *Organizing for Battle*.

LOCAL COUNSEL

Each local church should have an attorney in the city or county, available for immediate consultation as needed. Each state organization of Christian schools should have an attorney on full time retainer, to oversee the legal affairs of normal operations. Since the former is seldom involved in statewide litigation, we will speak only to the latter in detail.

The state attorney must be selected and taught with great care. A man who has been out of law school for a number of years is as ill-equipped to handle constitutional theory as you are to speak the Latin or Spanish you learned in high school. First Amendment religious liberty cases have been rare until recent years. They are not at all comparable to bent fenders and divorce settlements, which are standard fare for the average lawyer. The fact that an attorney is a friend of yours, or the fellow with the lowest fee, should have no bearing on the selection process.

Perhaps you already have an attorney. Perhaps you need to shop around and be sure you have the right man. Nothing is more disastrous than to find yourself in court without adequate defense. To choose a doctor on the strength of his "bedside manner," rather than his skill, may be hazardous to your health. To choose local counsel on the basis of his personality, or reputation, may be hazardous to your freedom. Keep in mind that unless your state has already been plagued with church-state problems, the reputation of a local attorney has nothing to do with your needs. He may be a nice fellow, with a great reputation in murder trials and corporate law, and be a dud when you get him in court to defend your liberty.

Local attorneys are important, since they often lay the groundwork in a given case. No harm can be done to check around and have the best man available. A good place to start would be the early chapters of this book. Read and study carefully the analysis of Supreme Court thinking.

Constitutional law is a specialized field. First Amendment Constitutional law, dealing with religious liberty, is an even more highly specialized field. The lawyer's stock-in-trade consists of two things: 1——his accumulated knowledge; 2——his mind. As you are well aware, some men are geniuses when it comes to accumulating knowledge, but they do not have enough common sense to get in out of the rain. For our purposes, you are not looking for accumulated knowledge. Any that he may have is probably on all the wrong cases, or on totally irrelevant areas of litigation.

First and foremost, you are seeking a man with a MIND which readily adapts to Constitutional principles. Please read that last sentence again. As you will discover, what we might call a "Constitutional Mind" is extremely rare. Attorneys, generally, are the product of Secular Humanist educational institutions and, as such, are not original thinkers. "The Constitutional Mind" is a blend of the philosophical and the practical, which enables a man to evaluate the new ground of church-state conflicts. He must perceive the impact of centuries-old principles on present day issues and bring original, forceful arguments to the maze of precedent law. The difference between general practice of law and First Amendment Constitutional law, is as great as the difference between checkers and chess.

Local counsel is no problem if you get the right "type" of man. Those who have "The Constitutional Mind" will devour, with great interest, any material supplied them, and will soon educate themselves, if the right information is made available. The state attorney should be constantly advised of cases across the nation to keep him abreast of the type of litigation he may encounter as your attorney. He must be well-supplied with copies of court cases, legal briefs, trial transcripts, court opinions, and related materials, as sources of constant education. Someone in your state organization should be responsible to obtain these from other state leaders and put them in his hands. (Ask him periodically if he has read them.) You must assume the need to acquaint him with everything from fundamentalist theology to recent precedent law.

EXPERT COUNSEL

From the beginning, local counsel should be advised of the probability of outside help being brought in at any time. A local attorney who has little experience in First Amendment Constitutional law MUST NOT argue your case before the U.S. Supreme Court. Remember, the higher your case goes, the more you affect the whole nation. A sloppy defense may set a precedent which will harm the whole Christian school movement.

Expert counsel is necessary because First Amendment law is highly specialized. You would not want open-heart surgery performed by a general practitioner, and the difference IS THAT GREAT, even though some lawyers will tell you otherwise. Only a handful of men in America are specialists in Constitutional law as it specifically relates to religious liberty. Earlier, we mentioned the difference between an old pick-up truck and a Rolls Royce. One is for transportation; the other is for intimidation. "Expert counsel" is only "expert" by having earned that reputation. The legal profession is elitist by its very nature. Those who rise to the top in the media are clowns and showmen. Those who rise to the top in the estimation of their peers do so by ability only. For that reason, a man who enjoys the unique position of "expert", in a world sustained by giant egos, may cost like a Rolls Royce, but he also operates like one. Judges, from obscurity to the U.S. Supreme Court, know such a man and, being only human, they are intimidated by his very presence on the case. He stands before them, not as a novice who must be evaluated as to his legal ability or, as in the case of today's radicals, his sanity, but as one who is presumed a winner until proven wrong. This is a tremendous advantage when the opposition is usually an obscure State Assistant Attorney General. Some backlash is always possible in the lower courts. A judge without a national reputation may resent a lawyer who has one, and rule against him to sustain his self-esteem. Keep in mind, however, that lower court decisions mean little or nothing. Appeal is almost automatic by either side, and petty bigotry against "Philadelphia lawyers" and their reputations is almost nil in the higher courts.

WHAT COMES NEXT?

Having an attorney is one thing; getting your money's worth is another. You must take the initiative, through your state organization, to keep the lines of communication open and hot. No more than four men should be selected to meet with the attorney at regular intervals, both to get his views and give him yours. Any more than four men will present a multitude of problems, ranging from getting everyone together at a given hour, to extraneous questions eating up valuable time.

While the attorney formulates a legal framework from which to operate, this small group from your organization must set policy and enunciate convictions. The attorney will need materials. (See the chapter on *Search and Research.*) If his staff must obtain them it will cost you $40 and hour. Most, you can do with volunteer help. Should you go to trial, he will need witnesses. (See the chapter on *Courting the Courts.*) The attorney will look to you to supply him with suitable candidates who have already been screened by you. Four things must not be neglected under any circumstances:

1. Keep the lines of communication open.
2. Know your convictions and express them.
3. Volunteer your help unhesitatingly.
4. Pay the bills!

Chapter 16

COURTING THE COURTS

"It is NOT true that the function of law is to regulate our consciences, our ideas, our wills, our education, our opinions, our work, our trade, our talents, or our pleasures. The function of law is to protect the free exercise of these rights, and to prevent any person from interfering with the free exercise of these same rights by any other person."

Frederic Bastiat
THE LAW

Far and away the most important consideration in the battle is the courtroom. Because of the immeasurable impact of precedent law mentioned previously, potentially every case could affect the nation. Everything takes on new perspective when we contemplate the reality that we enter the courtroom on behalf of the entire Christian School movement. Frivolous cases, ill-prepared cases, poorly argued cases, all speak forth a message to the nation concerning our testimony.

"Preparation" is the key word. The preparation of convictions, attorneys, research, witnesses, and publicity are our main considerations and we shall discuss them in a moment. First, we would do well to do some preparatory thinking about the court system generally. Court names and functions vary so widely from state to state that this

253

volume is inadequate to deal with them individually. Certain factors are worthy of note, however.

Lower courts seldom speak to constitutional questions. On the whole, judges are also former attorneys who have been taught to make every attempt to settle a case on grounds other than the U.S. Constitution whenever possible. State statutes must be presumed valid and Constitutional until proven otherwise, as a principle of law. This means the burden of proof is always on the challenger to overcome those presumptions. Lower court judges are often more politically motivated and, in some cases, are even appointees of your opposition.

It should be interjected here that procedure demands that under normal circumstances, State "administrative" remedies must be exhausted before a matter can be heard by a federal court. Once all avenues prescribed by the State Legislature for resolution of an issue have been cleared, the judicial process may begin. In order to reach a federal court a "federal question" must be raised. This is normally done in education cases by charging a violation of the First, Fifth, Ninth, and Fourteenth Amendments and, in particular, the "Due Process" and "Equal Protection" clauses of the Fourteenth Amendment.

Anytime a court reporter is present a record is being made. The words "preliminary"——"pretrial"——etc. all evoke an attitude of apathy in the minds of those who have seldom been there. In retrospect, we erred greatly in North Carolina on at least two occasions. Given a choice to have a court reporter present or absent, we chose the latter, when involved in what seemed to be relatively unimportant hearings. In one case the state made numerous hasty statements which could have been used against them in the press, if nothing else. In the other the judge made outrageously biased comments which could have seriously damaged the credibility of his subsequent blanket decision against us. In both instances we could have insisted on the presence of a court reporter, and did not, so there was no official record available.

Another factor is the temperament, (by reputation), of the judge. This information is available from attorneys who have appeared in his court, the media, or even fellow judges if any are friendly to your cause. Discreet inquiries, and they must be discreet, may be of assistance in planning your approach. Some judges are hypersensitive toward any action they consider to be an attempt to influence the court. Others thrive on publicity and see it as an indicator of their fairness and openness in a free exchange of ideas surrounding the case. One judge may be impressed by a full courtroom in a preliminary hearing. Another may see this as an effort to intimidate him.

Someone should investigate in advance and know the size and seating capacity of the courtroom, the policy of the judge on reserved seating for press and litigants, as well as the availability of facilities such as meeting rooms should you need to confer with the attorneys when court is in recess. Your people should be advised in advance that most judges insist on a first-come, first-served basis for seating. This may mean that those who are interested enough to arrive 2 to 3 hours early are the only ones who will have a seat for the proceedings.

PREPARATION OF CONVICTIONS

Long before you go to trial the preparation of convictions should begin. Many church members scoff inwardly at the possibility of the state taking a church to court. We discovered, much to our consternation, that some pastors stood in danger of splitting their churches at the most crucial moments when the eyes of the media were watching every move. With the Lord's blessing, 63 churches entered our original case and 63 stood to the end. This is the exception rather than the rule in spite of our fundamentalist emphasis on "standing."

The media always contains some "vultures" who hover tirelessly over the situation, waiting to swoop down on any sign of weakness or vacillation on the part of those who have made a public stand. To avoid such a disaster we must begin as early as possible to school pastors and people on the U.S. Supreme Court policy that "convictions" are defensible, "preferences" are not.

The pastor is the place to begin. He should read every book and article, listen to every tape, study all appropriate statutes and regulations, until clear-cut Bible-based conviction emerges in his mind. This is dangerous business. A "conviction" is something you will not change under any conditions. Prison or death may be the easy way out. The real question is——"What happens when you present your convictions to the staff and ¾ of them threaten to quit if that is to be the policy of the school?" (We have seen this in North Carolina.) How will your backbone bend if you come to the church with your "convictions," and they vote to get a new pastor if you fail to reconsider? If your congregation is not willing to see you put in jail, that has many ramifications. To take a stand for your convictions may not mean going to court to contend for the faith——it may mean simply that you get fired, and become nothing more than an unemployed preacher or school administrator, with no involvement whatsoever in Christian education.

256

A "conviction" is a Bible-based belief which will not change under any circumstances if it costs you your job, staff, freedom, wife or life. Until you reach such a position on any given issue, you have only "preferences" which the U.S. Supreme Court says are not protected by the First Amendment. Not only is it imperative that pastors and school administrators prepare these convictions in advance—teachers, parents, board members and church members must be prepared as well. To a great degree this depends on two factors—leadership and teaching. Without the information which has given you convictions being communicated to your people, you cannot expect them to hold similar convictions. This is a long and arduous process which, if undertaken after the legal battles begin, may lead to serious internal problems.

Keep in mind that this is a collective effort. You may control the witnesses your attorneys call to the stand, but the state may call anyone they please. Every pastor, with you or against you, is subject to subpoena. Every teacher, school board member, deacon, elder, parent, church member, or student is a potential candidate for the witness stand. In one of our cases, the state went into detailed discovery tactics to search out and interrogate school personnel from the worst circumstances. They sought out small schools, weak schools, churches with known moral problems or financial problems. Fasten your seat belts, gentlemen, and prepare for a bumpy ride.

"Convictions" must be defined and taught from one end of your ministry to the other. Following is a questionaire we used to survey the convictions of our men and church members. If some of the questions offend you, rest assured that the attorney for the prosecution will get even more offensive in an attempt to prove that you hold only "preferences" and not "convictions"——or that you are biased and unreasonable in your position.

QUESTIONNAIRE

A. BACKGROUND
  1. Can you affirm without question that you have eternal life? ....
  2. How long have you been saved? ....
  3. Do you accept without question the Bible as the infallible Word of God? ....
  4. Are you fully convinced that your wife/husband/children would display a good testimony if placed on the witness stand? ..
  5. Could your children honestly say, under oath, that you live a consistent Christian life? ....
  6. Is there any circumstance under which you would allow your children to attend a public school? ....
  7. Could you immediately put into words why you believe the Bible teaches a definite need for Christian education? ....

B. SAMPLE QUESTIONS WHICH MAY BE ASKED BY A PROSECUTOR TO PROVE OUR CONVICTIONS ARE NOT VALID.
  1. Do you read the Bible and pray daily? ....
  2. Do you faithfully attend every service of your church with your family? ....
  3. Do you give a significant portion of your income to the Lord's work? ....
  4. Do you smoke? ....
  5. Do you attend movies? ....
  6. Do you allow your children to attend movies? ....
  7. Do you have a television? ....

8. If you have a television do your children ever see a program containing sex, violence, profanity, use of alcohol or drugs? ....
9. Do you allow any magazines or literature in your home which contain profanity, sex violence or immoral acts? ....
10. Would you object to your children attending school with blacks? ....
11. Would you object to blacks joining your church? ....
   (Questions 10 and 11 will no doubt be asked in an attempt to prove the Christian schools are operated to avoid integration.)
12. Have you ever been in court for violations of law other than traffic citations? ....
13. Do you owe any back taxes? ....
14. Do you have more than $200 in past due business or personal debts? ....
15. Is there anything in your pre-conversion life which could be damaging as circumstantial evidence, such as dishonorable military discharge, psychiatric care, divorce, bad debts, criminal charges, alcoholism, etc.? ..
16. Suppose the school your children now attend closed tomorrow. Would you quit your job, if necessary, and move to a town where they could attend a Christian school?
17. Suppose your income were cut in half tomorrow. Would you put your children back in public school? ....
18. If you were offered a job making $48,000 a year is there any possibility you would move to a town which had no Christian school? ..
19. Would you allow your children to attend a secular college after high school? ....
   (Questions 16-19 could be used in an

259

attempt to prove that Christian education is a preference and not a conviction.)

SECTION II

Questions for the School Administrator or Principal

A. **VIOLENCE AND PERSONAL SAFETY**
1. How many rapes have you had in your school in the past year? ....
2. How many robberies? ....
3. How many assaults? ....
4. How much vandalism? (dollars estimate) ..
5. How many drug related incidents? ......
6. How many cases of alcoholic beverages used on campus? ....
7. How many student pregnancies? ....
8. Interview your teachers and ask how many are in the following categories:
   a. Assaulted by students ....
   b. Afraid of students ....
   c. Unable to control class ....

B. **EDUCATIONAL COMPETENCY**
1. Do you feel that your staff is adequate? ..
2. Are your textbooks suitable? ....
3. Can you give an overall grade level average for your students based on recent tests? ..

C. **POINTS OF DEFENSIBLE CONSISTENCY**
1. Is your school a separate corporation from the church? ....
2. Are all checking accounts in the name of the church? ....
3. Do church and school have identical WRITTEN statements of faith? ....
4. Does every teacher and school board member adhere as a conviction to every

belief of the church? . . . .

5. Do all board members of the church and school have their children in Christian school? . . . .

6. Are all teachers members of the church operating the school? . . . .

7. Are all policies, such as dress code, abstinence from tobacco and alcohol, etc. required of every staff member, Sunday School teacher, deacon, elder, school board member, or any office holder of both church and school? . . . .

8. How many teachers do you have? . . . .

9. How many of these teachers would you be satisfied to see on the witness stand as an example of your desired quality of Christian testimony? . . . .

10. Do you have a woman in charge of your school as Administrator or High School Principal? . . . .

11. Do you give free tuition to any students who are unable to pay? . . . .

12. Is entrance testing the final determining factor in who will receive a Christian education in your school? . . . .

13. Does the Pastor of your church preach that Christian education is the ONLY acceptable form of education without exception? . . . .

14. Do you receive any aid or assistance from Federal, State, or local government? . . . . .

15. Does your church have a WRITTEN statement of its Biblical position on the philosophy of Christian education? . . . . . .

16. Have you ever applied for or received a zoning variance from local government? . .

17. Do you do any fund raising for your school of a type you would not do for the church?
18. Do you accept approval or accreditation from any State or Federal agency? ......
19. Does your School Board contain all members of the governing body of your church? ....
20. Are all doctrines of the Church consistently taught in the school chapel and Bible classes? ....
21. Can any statement be found on sermon tapes, in Minutes of Board Meetings, or in the conversation of Pastor, Board Members or staff indicating any separation of Church and school? ....
22. Do any of your teachers accept or seek state certification for their teaching ministry? ....

We used these questions to give us advance knowledge of the condition of the troops BEFORE selecting the men and ministries to represent us on the witness stand. All this effort was preparation to find the most consistent convictions to uphold our cause. Again——keep in mind that we had no power whatsoever over who would be chosen by the state. No doubt, one reason God has permitted these attacks on church ministries, is to remind us that *the time is come that judgment must begin at the house of God.* Neither God nor the courts will tolerate hypocrites seeking a constitutional defense of beliefs they do not consistently practice.

Now is a good time to use these examples in sermons, staff meetings, board meetings, etc. Preparation of convictions must be settled well in advance of a day in court.

PREPARATION OF ATTORNEYS

The chapter, *Learning About Lawyers*, will help you here but these further thoughts could be added. Hiring an attorney is in some ways like hiring a building contractor. It is not his business to tell you what you want built. He expects you to have a general idea of your purpose so that he can take your specifications and suggest how to implement them based on his expertise. The contractor has no idea whether you want two bedrooms or five, a cottage or an apartment building, plush carpet or dirt floors. You must prepare the attorney by advising him of your convictions and how you see them to be in conflict with laws or regulations being imposed on your school. He should be very candid and frank in his assessment of the reasonableness of your position as related to precedent law.

Out-of-state attorneys should be apprised of the situation surrounding the case. Two means can best accomplish this. 1——A series of meetings with the fundamentalist leaders involved and 2——close working relationships with local attorneys. Court procedures and policies are so complex and variable from state to state that it is virtually impossible for a "foreign" attorney to understand local rules without local help. When lawyers come to town for a meeting with your organization, or when they come for a court appearance, travel and accomodations must be prepared in advance. Some attorneys prefer to have their own staff do this, while others do not. Someone in your state organization who is familiar with airports, car rentals, men available to provide transportation, quality of motels, distance to the courthouse, etc. should contact the attorney or attorneys involved and offer assistance. Under no circumstances treat him like a visiting evangelist and presume to tie him up in meetings with the press, parties in the case, or public eating arrangements. His most important pursuit is mental preparation and only absolute necessity, or mutually agreeable arrangements, should prevent him from being alone as much as possible.

Advance preparation over a period of months is covered in the chapter entitled *Learning About Lawyers.* Final preparation will come at the request of the attorney. He will expect you to speak pointedly and authoritatively in the final weeks before trial. All internal problems should be resolved and representatives should be authorized to speak and make decisions. He has every right to assume that you have done your homework, and every question need not be taken back to the state organization for resolution. This will save a tremendous amount of time and money.

The attorney will need names and addresses of individuals you have selected in advance as potential key witnesses. He will need time set aside at his convenience to interview these people and make them aware of the type of questions they may expect on the witness stand. Preparation of attorneys is a vital factor and their familiarity with the principals in the case will be the last step in that preparation, and perhaps the most important.

PREPARATION OF RESEARCH

While this is dependent on the issues in the case, and may or may not be crucial, you should keep it in mind. The chapter entitled *Search and Research* provides all the details on how and why. Research should be completed well in advance of the case so that all documentation will be available to the attorneys and witnesses for study. The attorney will decide which points should be stressed, and his decisions should be coordinated with the overall education of witnesses. Since this book contains an entire chapter on research our only purpose here is to reflect the need to get the information into the hands and minds of those who will introduce it on the witness stand. The attorney will assign documents and subjects to various witnesses, who will be vehicles for introduction of this vital information into the court record.

PREPARATION OF WITNESSES

Witnesses are the heart of any trial. Attorneys must present clear arguments, research should be thorough, but in the final analysis the case will stand or fall with the testimony of the people involved. Obviously the court will be most interested in the individual spokesmen who feel their rights have been violated, as well as the sincerity of the beliefs, since these are cases in defense of religious liberty.

Witnesses should be chosen with great care. When a large number of schools are involved, a wholesale shakedown is in order. The survey in the early pages of this chapter is a sample of how this may be done. In any event, if you ever studied James 2:9 in your life, this is the time to put it into practice. *"If ye have respect of persons ye commit sin."* DO NOT PLAY GAMES WITH THE WITNESS STAND. Forget who is the biggest contributor to the state organization. Make no false assumptions about the condition of the fastest growing church in 50 counties. Allow no concessions for Brother So-and-So, who is known for his far-reaching ministry. My freedom is at stake, and before God, you are obligated to be impartial about this——the most important of all decisions.

Turn on the heat. If a man says he has the ideal parent witness, make him prove it. Never take anybody's word for something this serious, without investigation. If a man says his church is a good church that means nothing. To him it may be wonderful——to the Supreme Court of the United States it may be a joke. On the witness stand under oath is no place to explain carnality and backsliding. The court record from day one, even the lowest courts, is THE record which follows you to the Supreme Court.

Turn up the heat. Sift, and question, and probe, and discuss. Be ready to take off your coat and fight before you allow anyone on the witness stand who does not believe and preach that Christian education is the ONLY acceptable form of education. Someone who thinks Christian education is nice, but would change to public school if a depression comes, has no religious conviction about Christian education. It then becomes a personal preference with no more meaning to the U.S. Supreme Court than a belief in padded pews.

A world of difference exists between a case involving an individual and a case with churches and schools under scrutiny. What YOU believe may be great, but since the *Yoder* decision the gut issue has become——"Does your church collectively hold to absolute beliefs, and demonstrate those beliefs with observable consistency as a way of life?" Not you as the pastor will be on trial, but the overall effect of your ministry on the lives of the entire congregation as a whole. We will put a case in the U.S. Supreme Court one day, in which Fundamentalism will be compared to the Amish, to test our claim to the defensible nature of our movement. We must be able to show a lifestyle which singles us out as a "community of faith," as distinct, productive, and unusual as the Amish, or we will be thrown into the lion's den and devoured by the fact of our concessions to worldly Christianity. Witnesses are the determining factor in all of this.

In North Carolina we said to the court——We are not to be compared to the other so-called fundamentalists of North Carolina. We are not to be compared, through the testimony of the state's expert witnesses, to historic fundamentalism. We are a particular type of fundamentalists who are collectively a "community of faith" as distinct as the Amish. We are a minority within a minority. We are a peculiar type of people whose religion demands that we have clear cut standards of dress, morality, lifestyle, and most particularly——education, which cannot be compromised under penalty of imprisonment. We do not accept Christian schools as an alternate form of education, but rather as the ONLY form of education permissible to us, and to our people. The Court found that these were, indeed, our sincerely held beliefs.

Perhaps you say this is unrealistic. The Court, in our case, found it to be realistic. Perhaps you say, "That

267

would split my church to say it is against God and the Bible to send any of our children to public school." In North Carolina, 63 churches went to court and 63 churches were still standing on that belief when we finished. The Court found, based on the testimony of our witnesses, that an entire class of 63 churches sincerely upheld the absolute necessity of Christian education for our children. To retreat from that position is certain judicial death, and we need witnesses in cases across this country who will not waver from these principles.

Selection of witnesses must be done carefully and impartially. As previously stated, we must "turn on the heat." As previously stated, we must "turn up the heat." As previously stated, we must say to one another: "If your church, and your teachers, and your board members, and your parent witnesses, can't stand that kind of heat——get them out of the kitchen——and out of the courtroom as well." This is a life-or-death struggle. PLEASE——PLEASE——do not go to court to defend Christian education unless you intend to defend it. That means you must be willing to shut the doors of your church and check in at the state penitentiary, or move to another state, before you will give up the right to educate your children in an environment totally founded on the Word of God.

We cannot overstress the fact that, barring extremely unusual circumstances, there will be only one trial. Any points of argument, documentation, testimony of witnesses, or facts you wish included in the record——must be included at the time of trial. The attitude of the lower court judge is ultimately immaterial, so long as the record is complete. The State Supreme Court and the U. S. Supreme Court will hear attorneys'

268

arguments only. The court record, made months or even years prior to the case coming before them, will be their only access to your testimony.

Preparation of witnesses begins with their selection, as stated previously. Once they have been selected, someone familiar with the overall intent of the case should discuss, in great detail, what may be expected on the witness stand. The pressure is tremendous by the time the actual trial begins. Every word is important and, in a packed courtroom with state and national media out in full force, you must have people who can stand an immeasurable amount of stress in a strange situation.

Expert witnesses are almost a necessity. As you well know, modern society lives and dies by its "experts." These men must be prepared for hostile cross-examination and should, therefore, either be well-known to you or thoroughly examined as to their beliefs. It is possible, and has occurred in some states, that a man will give outstanding support to our position on direct examination and kill us on cross-examination by the exposure of his liberal views. Expert witnesses must have impeccable credentials as men of NATIONAL standing in the academic arena. They will be assigned, by the attorney, to specific areas of expertise, such as testing, church history, national research, etc.

We made a mistake in North Carolina, which you may avoid. If your expert witness is from out of state, get all materials such as curriculum guides, public school textbooks, etc. into his hands for study, well in advance of the trial. Have him come to your state two or three days prior to the trial to visit public schools. His testimony

269

concerning Secular Humanism in public education will be greatly nullified if attorneys for the opposition bring out that he has no PERSONAL knowledge of conditions in your state.

To give a practical example of the type of people involved in a typical case, the following is a brief profile of witnesses in our trial in North Carolina.

WITNESSES FOR THE STATE
(First Day of Trial)

Glenn Ruellman, Principal——St. John's Lutheran Day School in Winston-Salem, N. C.: M.A. degree from UNC at Greensboro; Member of Council for American Private Education; President of Southeastern District Lutheran Teachers covering 6 states. Testified to having no objection to the state's then existing regulation of church schools. (Responded to 57 questions——14 pages in the record).

Sister Mary Barbara Sullivan, Supervisor of 10 Catholic schools in North Carolina and Florida: Nursing degree from Sacred Heart College; Masters degree in educational administration from UNC at Chapel Hill; Former director of field services for National Catholic Education Association in Washington, D. C. Testified to having no objection to the state regulations. (Responded to 36 questions——12 pages in the record).

Dr. A. Craig Phillips, Superintendent of Public Instruction for the State of North Carolina. Testified to his views of the scope and meaning of the state regulations.

(End of First Day of Trial)
(Begin Second Day of Trial)

Dr. A. Craig Phillips, Superintendent of Public Instruction——completion of testimony. (Responded to 156 questions——47 pages in the record).

J. Arthur Taylor, Director of State Division of Teacher Certification. Testified to the value of, and need for, teacher certification, as well as state policies in this area. (Responded to 198 questions——41 pages in the record.)

Calvin L. Criner, Director of the Division of Non-Public Schools, State Department of Public Instruction. Testified to the extent and practices of state regulation of Christian schools. (Responded to 198 questions - 41 pages in the record.)

Dr. Carl Dolce, expert witness: B.A. from Tulane University; M.A. from Loyola University of the South; Doctorate from Harvard University; Dean of the School of Education, N.C. State University. Testified to the value of teacher certification. (Responded to 49 questions——12 pages in the record.)

Dr. Samuel Holton, expert witness: B.A. degree from Duke University; B.S. degree from New York University; Masters degree in school administration from Duke University; Masters degree in secondary education from Yale University; Ph. D. from Yale

271

University; Professor of Education, U.N.C. at Chapel Hill; author of one textbook and co-operating editor of another; participant in many national education organizations. Testified to the purpose and value of teacher certification. (Responded to 45 questions——20 pages in the record.)

Dr. H. Shelton Smith, expert witness: B.A. degree from Elon college; Ph.D. from Yale University; former Professor at Columbia University and Yale University; author of seven books; former president of the American Theological Society; former president of the American Society of Church History; Professor at Duke University for 32 years. Testified on the history of fundamentalist Christianity. (Responded to 44 questions——24 pages in the record.)

William Vogdes, one of our men called by the State: Principal of Hanover Christian Academy, Wilmington, N.C.; B.A. degree from Baptist Bible College of Pennsylvania. Questioned on his objections to state regulation. (Responded to 96 questions——13 pages in the record.)

Douglas Davis, one of our men called by the State: Principal of Berean Christian School, Fayetteville, N.C.; attended Tennessee Temple Schools and Temple Baptist Theological Seminary. Questioned on his objections to state regulation. (Responded to 85 questions——12 pages in the record.)

Pastor Gene Woodall, one of our men called by the State: Pastor of Bethany Baptist Church, Concord, N.C. (educational background not mentioned in testimony). Questioned on his objections to state regulation. (Responded to 82 questions——13 pages in the record.)

272

Pastor Charles Arrowood, one of our men called by the State: Pastor of Bible Baptist Church, Matthews, N.C. (Educational background not mentioned in testimony). Questioned on his objections to state regulation. (Responded to 83 questions——12 pages in the record.)

WITNESSES FOR THE CHRISTIAN SCHOOLS

Dr. David Bayless, hostile expert witness: Senior statistical scientist with the Research Triangle Institute; head of team which conducted the "Violent Schools——Safe Schools" study for the U.S. Congress; testified to the validity of this document. (Responded to 7 questions——3 pages in the record.)

Dr. Donald Erickson, expert witness: B.A. degree from Bob Jones University; M.A. and Ph.D. from the University of Chicago; Professor of Education at the University of San Francisco; Director of the Center for Research on Private Education; Professor at the University of Chicago for 11 years; author or co-author of 5 books; Research Director of CAPE; member of the Board of Directors of the National Catholic Education Association; etc. Testified to the fallacy of teacher certification, as well as problems with state law in N.C. (Responded to 234 questions——78 pages in the record.)

Pastor Kent Kelly, Pastor of Calvary Memorial Church and Administrator of Calvary Christian School, Southern Pines, N.C.: High School graduate; spokesman for the schools in the area of religion and its relationship to education. (Responded to 276 questions——74 pages in the record.)

273

Dr. Rousas J. Rushdoony, expert witness: B.A. degree and M.A. degree from the University of California; B.D. degree from the Pacific School of Religion; two honorary doctorates; missionary to the Paiute and Shoshone Indians; researcher for the Center for American Studies; President of Chalcedon, an educational foundation; author of 25 books. Testified on church history. (Responded to 62 questions——24 pages in the record.)

(End of Third Day of Trial)
(Begin Fourth Day of Trial)

Donald Wells, Principal of a Quaker School: B.S. degree from Dartmouth College; M.S. degree from Wesleyan University. Testified to the agreement of Friend's Schools with the position taken by the fundamentalist schools in the case. (Responded to 37 questions——13 pages in the record.)

Rev. Henry Brown, Principal of Wilmington Christian Academy, Wilmington, N.C.: B.A. degree from Bob Jones University; Master of Divinity degree from Bob Jones University; spokesman for the schools in the areas of testing and educational proficiency. (Responded to 178 questions——43 pages in the record.)

Pastor Dan Carr, Pastor of South Park Baptist Church in Winston-Salem, N.C. and administrator of South Park Christian School: B.A. degree from Tennessee Temple; President of Organized Christian Schools of N.C.; spokesman for the schools in the area of conscience versus regulation. (Responded to 85 questions——13 pages in the record.)

Dr. Ed Ulrich, Executive Director of the North Carolina Association of Christian Schools: (Educational background not specified in testimony); spokesman for the schools on the history of Christian schools in N.C. (Responded to 17 questions——11 pages in the record.)

Elizabeth King, educated at Northfield School, Northfield, Massachusetts and Greensboro College with a B.F.A. degree from East Carolina University: parent with 3 children; Christian school teacher at Calvary Christian School in Southern Pines, N.C. Testified both as a teacher and as a parent with children in a Christian school. (Responded to 20 questions——5 pages in the record.)

Peter King, educated at Georgetown University with a B.A. degree from American University in Washington, D.C.: M.A. degree from East Carolina University; member of the N.C. National Guard; served in the U.S. Marine Corps; parent with 3 children; Christian school teacher at Calvary Christian School in Southern Pines, N.C. Testified both as a teacher and as a parent with children in a Christian school. (Responded to 41 questions——8 pages in the record.)

Rachel Ulmer, student: Friendship Christian School, Raleigh, N.C.; 14 years of age; formerly attended public school. Testified to the differences between public and Christian education. (Responded to 42 questions——7 pages in the record.)

Dixie Ulmer, Registered Nurse: husband is staff engineer with IBM; parent of 2 children. Testified as parent of Rachel Ulmer mentioned above. (Responded to 42 questions——8 pages in the record.)

Jordan Simmons, III, Manager for Hanes Corporation: B.S. degree from South Carolina State University; Black parent of 3 children; one child old enough to attend school and he is a student at South Park Christian School in Winston Salem, N.C. Testified as a parent to satisfaction with Christian education and absence of racial bigotry. (Responded to 35 questions——6 pages in the record.)

Nancy Biggs, parent of 3 children: employed in a cotton mill, High Point, N.C. (educational background not covered in testimony). Testified as a parent to necessity for, and satisfaction with, Christian education. (Responded to 25 questions——4 pages in the record.)

James Biggs, parent of 3 children: employed as a cloth cutter at W.J. Rives Company, High Point, N.C. (educational background not covered in testimony). Testified as a parent to corroborate testimony of his wife mentioned above. (Responded to 19 questions——3 pages in the record.)

(End of Fourth Day of Trial)

From the preceding example you may deduce, by inference, the types of witnesses and the subjects assigned for testimony. You also see the comparative lengths of time devoted to each subject area. Obviously every case is different in detail but, where a class action involving many schools is at issue, this would be a typical example.

Again, the preparation of witnesses is a crucial part of any case. To take it lightly is to imperil the court record which may stand for, or against, the Christian school movement nationwide.

276

While a chapter on dealing with the courts may seem a strange place to speak of publicity, such is not the case at all. Publicity may have little or no effect on the decision itself, but in the "court of public opinion" publicity is essential. General publicity should be in full swing long before the issue reaches the courts. (See chapter—*Meet the Press*.) Specific publicity pointing to the trial itself must be timed properly. All the usual media outlets should be contacted and directed to the specifics of the case, before they hear them in the courtroom.

Most major newspapers, and some T.V. and radio stations, assign their people to different areas, This may mean that after months of working with individuals assigned to cover education, you now find yourself with an entirely different set of reporters assigned to cover the courts. These newcomers need printed materials and much conversation to acquaint them with the complex intricacies of First Amendment litigation.

A rally which attracts public interest is an excellent publicity vehicle. This is where timing becomes especially crucial. To determine the Lord's will in the matter is the only possible hope, since the variables are innumerable. Nothing could be worse for publicity than to hold a rally where nobody comes. The same media which gives you great coverage for success will give you the attendant bad publicity for failure. They do not like to be called out expecting a story and not get one.

In North Carolina we coordinated our rally with the pretrial hearing. The sheriff's department estimated the crowd in front of the courthouse at 5,000. This is comparable to the Ohio rally of 10,000 since the population there is almost exactly twice that of North Carolina. From these figures you may get a general idea of what to expect in your state should the need for a rally arise. Because of the variation from judge to judge, state to state, and state organization to state organization, there are no guidelines to follow. We chose the preliminary hearing; you may choose the trial itself, or some time in between. Just remember not to have the rally on the day nobody comes!

Chapter 17

LOBBY THE LAWMAKERS

"Greater than the tread of mighty armies, or the barriers of isolation, is the irresistable force of an idea whose hour has come."

Victor Hugo

Our freedom will not be won, or even long perpetuated, in the courts. To go to the courts except out of necessity is a tragic waste of the Lord's money and the energy of His people. You are not a compromiser when you seek a legislative solution to the problem. The philosophy seems to be developing across the nation that negotiated settlement is a mark of weakness and the "neo," "pseudo," "jello" crowd are the only ones who work the legislature.

Brethren, I am here to tell you that our only hope is the state legislature. As we organize for legal defense we should be organizing simultaneously to get people registered to vote and put candidates in office. America is a nation under law. Laws are made and changed in the legislature. Any victory won in court in no wise negates the fact that the laws must be rewritten to accommodate the court decision. The choice is simple. Either go to the legislature to get an acceptable law on the books BEFORE you go to court, or AFTER you finish in court. Either way——like it or not——the General Assembly of your state is the place the laws under which you live will be written.

279

The old Secular Humanist slogan, "The church should not be involved in politics," must be fought tooth-and-nail to eliminate it from the minds of fundamentalists across this nation. "Politics" is not a green sludge found running through the gutters of the state captial. "Politics" is not some form of poisonous fungus which grows in the basements of the marble edifices in Washington. "Politics" is people! People governing other people. Often people manipulating other people. But, with all its faults and pitfalls, the political process is a system which relates specifically to what we seek to accomplish in the world. You are involved in politics at the present moment. During the last session of the Legislature in N.C. they dealt with abortion, ERA, sex education, liquor, marijuana laws, child care, divorce laws, etc. etc. etc. Any preacher not busily engaged in preaching against murder, liquor, immorality, destruction of the family unit, and drugs has not read his Bible lately. These were the major POLITICAL issues confronting our General Assembly in the last session.

Men, elected by the people, gathered in the state capital to debate and deal with the subjects discussed from our pulpits, and pass laws concerning these matters under which we must live as Christian citizens. Where do you find in the Bible that a Christian view of morality is to be confined to the pulpit? You see, we are discussing political issues in the pulpit almost every week that passes. What we have not been doing is focusing our political views and activities in such a way that we do any good. For Christians to sit around in a fundamental church and tell one another they do not believe in tax-funded abortion is the height of absurdity. We all knew that before we ever came. God says we are to take our message of truth and morality and godliness to the world. The people on Mars Hill need to be told what we believe, not the crowd gathered for fellowship and prayer at the home of Lydia the seller of purple. Moses much preferred his sheep on the backside of the desert to the court of Pharoah where he had to get involved in politics. Fundamental preachers have not changed since that day.

"They all with one consent began to make excuse" when faced with the need to go to the state capital. "Evangelist So-and-So is in my church for a week of meetings and I can't go." Bless your heart, the Lord sent Evangelist So-and-So to preach for you so you would be free to go to the Legislature! The time has come to honestly face some issues. Any man who must stay home to go soul winning, when he is needed in the state capital, is a hypocrite. If his true interest is witnessing, instead of building a personal local empire, he would admit that there are more lost people in the state capital than at home. Witnessing is not the problem. We can witness anywhere we find people on two legs. All too often the procrastinator refuses to let his own empire suffer, without knowing that soon his empire will crumble in the face of government encroachment.

GET OUT THE VOTE

Any Bible believer is aware of the responsibilities of Christian citizenship. Our problem is that we, as leaders, have not taken the initiative in explaining how this works in practice. It is a sin against God not to be a registered voter. It is a sin against God not to get out and vote on election day. Polls indicate that 60% of America's fundamentalists are not even registered to vote. Brethren, that is a result of poor leadership. We have not taught our people that to "render unto Caesar the things that be Caesar's" means upholding our freedom by participation in government. You could vitally influence the preservation

281

of our freedom by going to every Bible-believing pastor in your county and educating them on the need to get their people registered to vote. When election time rolls around, mention it in every service for two weeks prior to election day. Put up posters on the bulletin boards. Offer transportation to the polls. Use election day as a patriotic focal point, and preach on the role of the Christian citizen, as the day approaches.

Quite often the complaint is, "I don't know the candidates." "What good will it do me to vote if I have no idea where the various men stand?" This is a problem to be overcome by the state organization. Find volunteers to research the voting records of the candidates as well as attend public meetings to get the views of potential opponents. The state needs to be divided into sections with men assigned to compile this information. Print up a sheet, to be distributed to your people, showing them the views of the candidates. There is no need to call for a particular party affiliation or to endorse candidates from the pulpit. You are doing nothing more than supplying them with the necessary information to vote intelligently. A little sound preaching on the need to become an involved Christian citizen will produce volunteers from your church who would be excited about doing the legwork for you.

GET OUT THE CANDIDATES

One serious difficulty is the usual situation where we must vote for one of two liberal peas in a political pod. If your state is typical, the parties are in the hands of those who see that the choice is limited. However, it is also true that you have the potential to take over the politics of your state if you do it county by county, or precinct by precinct. If each conservative church in your area would send a delegation to those party meetings you would outnumber the liberals two-to-one. Be that as it may—in spite of the strength of the party in power, you may run your own candidates and elect them by sheer force of conservative numbers. In most states a man may get on the ticket without endorsement from the party machine. The state organization should be prepared to give advice to conservative candidates seeking office.

Be on the lookout at all times for fundamentalists, as well as other conservatives, to encourage to run for office. This is the only solution to our problem. We must get liberals out of the state house and conservatives in—at least in sufficient numbers to swing a vote. Laws are changed by Senators and Representatives, not by judges, and until we recognize this our emphasis is in the wrong place.

THE PROFESSIONAL LOBBYIST

In the chapter, *Organizing for Battle,* mention was made of the professional lobbyist, or "Executive Director", as he is called in some states. As soon as possible, the state organization needs a full time man in the state capital. Some states require that he register, if he is on a salary. Usually such registration is with the office of the Secretary of State. This man should be known by name and face to every member of the General Assembly. If he is functioning properly, he will be in the Legislature almost daily when it is in session. He should be monitoring all legislation to spot any bill of interest to our cause, and meeting regularly with legislators, to keep them aware of our presence.

In the "off season" he may travel and speak for the organization, recruit schools, assist in starting new schools;

but during the legislative session every other activity should be abandoned so that he may fulfill the only essential reason for having an Executive Director—protecting your liberty. The professional lobbyist must dress neatly, get along well with people, know the answers to pointed questions concerning our cause, and last, but by no means least, have an excellent rapport with the ever present media people who cover the Legislature. Any good Executive Director will know every one of them by name, what paper or station they serve, as well as their personal views concerning our cause. The professional lobbyist will either be the greatest asset or the greatest liability your state organization has, depending on his personal dedication and sacrifice to hit that Legislature every single day.

THE VOLUNTEER LOBBYIST

Many state organizations are too small to support a full time man. Should this be your situation I have some bad news for you. God's will is for somebody somewhere in your state to do the job. If somebody, somewhere, should be doing it that somebody may be you. It is possible to share this responsibility among several volunteers but there are disadvantages. For example, a vital factor is recognition. To swap around too often with too many people is to lose the personal friendships which may be built with individual Legislators. With the "swap around" method you also get some men volunteering out of a sense of obligation, rather than a compulsion from the Lord. Lobbying is not secular work. It is a spiritual endeavour in which the Spirit of God moves through the personality of men to turn hearts and minds to accomplish His purposes. The number of men needed may vary with the size of your Legislature. There is a difference between going to the General Assembly as a lobbyist, and going as a constituent. A lobbyist is one who is known to be the representative of a group. Much of his effectiveness depends on that knowledge. Most legislators will show absolutely no interest in your views unless you are 1——from their district; or 2——representing a group which has people in their district. For this reason the number of lobbyists working the General Assembly at any given time should be limited, and their efforts coordinated.

THE CONSTITUENT

While the lobbyist is a regular face in the Legislature, understood by all to be spokesman for a cause, the constituent is someone who has come from "back home" to visit a particular Senator or Representative. Politicians understand votes, and little else. However, it is possible to create in his mind the idea that you are one of his most politically active constituents. As a leader you should be known by face and name to every State Legislator from your district. You should make a personal visit to the capital to see them, at least twice, in every legislative session. You may call them at home on issues; send them a telegram now and then; write them a letter often enough that they know you have not forgotten them. They should be aware that you represent an unknown quantity of voters who are politically involved, and watching him personally, at all times, to see how he votes on issues.

The people in your churches and schools are also constituents. As many as possible should make a personal visit to the General Assembly at least once in the session. These visits are much more effective if they take a friend and go spontaneously rather than by busload from the church. If they go separately from week to week, he will conclude by the end of the session that millions of conservatives must exist in his home town. For all practical purposes he is right. We are not a majority, but if you follow the advice of this chapter we can make him or break him in any given election. Active liberals outnumber conservatives in this country, but not by a great majority. They have the same problem we do in terms of apathy and procrastination. The big difference lies in the fact that we have our back to the wall in many states. It is either get out the vote, or get on down to the jail and check in. With that form of motivation, if the legislators of North Carolina ever allow us to go to jail, we will produce a backlash which will unseat practically every member of the General Assembly in one fell swoop. Many, including the governor, do not yet believe this, but we do have the votes——and any hard line confrontation with us will be the catalyst to immediate realization of long term goals.

While we advocate fundamentalist principles and fundamentalists are a distinct minority——we are not alone. Our cause is religious liberty, parental rights, morality in government, and a great deal more, near and dear to the hearts of grass-roots America. We can, for example, under the right conditions, mobilize practically every person in North Carolina who voted for Jesse Helms for the U.S. Senate. He is a Republican in a Democratic wilderness, as far to the right as any major politician in this country. Given any assault on our freedom in North Carolina, we can generate that kind of support and turn enough votes to put a governor out of office.

What I suggest is not seeking to frighten legislators with straw men and fool them into thinking we have non-existent political clout. We have more clout than they ever dreamed possible. It simply must be organized and brought to bear on specific candidates and issues. It WILL be used to unseat the enemies of religious liberty, and the good gentlemen at the State House need to know so before it is too late.

Letter writing is a powerful force to be wielded by the constituency at large. Periodic rallies over major issues are an excellent means of demonstrating support. To hold an unseen rally in the capital city is a waste of time. To hold a rally on the Capitol steps, or in front of the Legislative Building, or at the Governor's Mansion, is a powerful weapon. We must face politicians with the reality of our convictions and dedication of our people. Our people have the dedication——they need to be headed in the right direction. That direction is the voting booth and the General Assembly of your state.

Chapter 18

PUT ON THE ARMOR

"Finally, my brethren, be strong in the Lord and in the power of His might. Put on the whole armour of God, that we may be able to stand against the wiles of the devil."
Ephesians 6:10-11

"Finally" is a word which signifies the end of the story. It does not imply that all has been said which could have been said. When the Apostle penned these words by inspiration of God, he was summarizing much more than the end of a brief epistle to a local church---he was summarizing his life.

The Apostle was here communicating to men and women who were about to enter a time of tremendous struggle. Paul had said that he fought wild beasts at Ephesus. The Ephesian church was about to embark upon an era when thousands upon thousands of Christians would be thrown to the lions for their faith. We face many lions, if the Lord has not come, in the next few years:
      ——The lion of government control,
      ——The lion of economic depression,
      ——The lion of spiritual declension,
      ——Satan, himself, as a roaring lion, walking about, seeking whom he may devour. Of course, our God is able to stop the mouths of lions. He did it for Daniel. Daniel refused to allow the edict of the king to prevent him from obeying God.

We must remember, however, that John the Baptist went to jail and was not delivered. Paul was not delivered in the latter years as he languished in prison. Indeed, this very epistle was written from a prison cell. These are words for all seasons——in victory or defeat; in freedom or bondage——*"Finally, my brethren, . . . put on . . . the armour that ye may be able to stand."* Verse 13 says again, *"And having done ALL——to stand!"*

God says clearly that it is His will for us to do all that we can. *"Having DONE ALL——to stand."* Unless we witness faithfully and seek to win the lost, we have not *"done all"* we can. Unless we get informed and get involved in the issues which confront the church in this hour, we have not *"done all"* we can.

Finally, my brethren, I want to suggest to you that we apparently have NOT done all that we can, because we have not been standing. With all our talk of "standing for the faith" we have failed to turn rhetoric into reality. Far from "standing" and holding our ground in America and the world, we have been losing ground for decades.

Since the Bolshevik Revolution in 1917, which began with 30 men, Communism has engulfed over 1/3 of the world's population. That is "world evangelization" which should put us to shame. Communism is nothing more, nor less, than another branch of the tree of Secular Humanism. They have gone into the world to preach their gospel to every creature, and they are winning the war. *The children of this world are in their generation wiser than the children of light.* Traditional fundamentalism is a failure. They are winning the world and we are losing America. Perhaps the time has come when we should stop making excuses for our failure and take a few lessons from the Secular Humanists. Secular Humanism is winning the world because they believe their faith should permeate every facet of human existence. A Secular Humanist is a Secular Humanist from the crown of his head to the soles of his feet. A Secular Humanist is a Secular Humanist 24 hours a day, 7 days a week. He would never think of allowing judges to erect a wall of separation between the religion of Humanism and the state. He will fight to the death to keep the religion of Humanism in education.

Secular Humanism is alive and prospering, and winning the world, for the simple reason that their faith demands nothing less than total involvement in the education of their children and the government of their society. The purposes of Humanism are accomplished unobtrusively as, daily, they live out their faith with sincerity and dedication. They demand a Secular Humanist environment in every way—Humanistic business practices, recreation, education, morality, government, friendships, family life, and all the rest.

The Old Testament prophets were the king-makers and the king-breakers of the nation. The early preachers of America were the voice of God in community views of government and education. It is time we stopped being "soul" winners and started being "life" winners. We must get children saved at an early age and then train them daily for 12 years, just as the Humanists do with their children. We must take the older "souls" we win at later stages in maturity, and win their "lives" to a Christian view of politics and education and Christian citizenship.

Some will no doubt disagree. My response is simple: "Show me your results!" Point to America, the greatest Christian nation, with more fundamentalists in one spot than the world has ever known. Tell me we are not losing America by leaps and bounds. I say it is time to humbly admit that historic fundamentalism is a failure. For too long we have given our children and our government to the Humanists while we busied ourselves with Sunday School and building a successful church. Sunday School is not enough. We must have Monday school and Tuesday school and Wednesday school, etc., etc. And the churches today which are building Christian soldiers are behind the principle of Christian schools 100%.

Twice in this passage in Ephesians 6 God says we may be able to stand in the evil day. We *may* be able—but that enablement is, in both cases, predicated on putting on the armor. There is no such thing as a "group" set of armor. Armor is for individuals. Yet, when many individuals put on the armor, the natural result is an army.

We have not been standing in the evil day because too many Christians want to come and sit down in church Sunday after Sunday to examine some fellow in the pulpit who has put on the armor. You never win battles at armor-examination classes. Battles are won when the class members put on the armor and go out to meet the enemy. Our enemy, of course, is not the government. We are the government.

> *"For we wrestle not against flesh and blood, but against principalities, against powers, against the rulers of the darkness of this world, against spiritual wickedness in high places."*
> *Ephesians 6:12*

Our enemies are not the bureaucrats, or the Humanists, or some political figure. Satan is the enemy;

and only the "armor of God," the Lord Jesus Christ, can give us victory. As pastors, Christian educators, and friends of liberty—we must escape the defeatest attitude that "one person could never make a difference." Our God is the God of the individual. We must tell those who will listen of the need to put on the Lord Jesus Christ as our armor—to be clothed with His wisdom and power as we set out to change the attitudes of our family, our church, our community, our county, and our state.

Political conservatism is fertile ground for witnessing. We DO NOT exchange evangelism for social change. We DO NOT substitute political activism for witnessing. Fundamentalism and the Biblical view of life and destiny have never enjoyed the public attention and examination they are receiving in North Carolina today. This is a result of putting on the whole armor of God and stepping out into the battlefield—into the mainstream of life—and forcing the public eye to examine people who believe God and stand for His truth.

Our central message is the "New Birth." But if we are to continue to enjoy the liberty to preach that message, we must have what Lincoln called *"a new birth of freedom, that government of the people, by the people, and for the people should not perish from the earth."* If you believe the Bible, you believe that one person CAN make a difference.

Why must it be for another time and another place that *"One shall chase a thousand and two shall put ten thousand to flight?"* The Lord Jesus Christ is our armor, and He is the same yesterday, today, and forever. You can begin by putting this book in the hands of another Christian soldier, and may the Lord bless you as you earnestly contend for the faith which was once delivered unto the saints.

293

APPENDIX

294

MEMORANDUM OF LAW
COMPETENCY TESTING IN THE 50 STATES
1979

State	Is Competency Testing A State Law?	Is Competency Testing Required of Christian Schools?	Notes
Alabama	No	No	
Alaska	No	No	
Arizona	No	No	
Arkansas	No	No	
California	Yes	No	Public schools only
Colorado	Yes	No	Public schools only
Connecticut	No	No	
Delaware	No	No	
Florida	Yes	No	Public schools only
Georgia	No	No	
Hawaii	No	No	
Idaho	No	No	
Illinois	No	No	
Indiana	No	No	
Iowa	No	No	
Kansas	No	No	
Kentucky	Yes	No	Public schools only
Louisiana	Yes	No	Public schools only
Maine	Yes	Yes	Abandoned this year for both public and private. Expected to be rescinded at the next session of Legislature.
Maryland	Yes	No	Public schools only
Massachusetts	Yes	No	Public schools only
Michigan	No	No	
Minnesota	No	No	
Mississippi	No	No	
Missouri	No	No	
Montana	No	No	
Nebraska	No	No	
Nevada	Yes	No	Public schools only
New Hampshire	No	No	
New Jersey	Yes	No	Public schools only
New Mexico	No	No	
New York	Yes	Yes	Christian schools have not given the test and no suit has been filed.
North Dakota	No	No	
North Carolina	Yes	No	Public schools only

State	Is Competency Testing A State Law?	Is Competency Testing Required of Christian Schools?	Notes
Ohio	No	No	
Oklahoma	No	No	
Oregon	No	No	
Pennsylvania	No	No	
Rhode Island	No	No	
South Carolina	Yes	No	Public schools only
South Dakota	No	No	
Tennessee	No	No	
Texas	No	No	
Utah	No	No	
Vermont	No	No	
Virginia	Yes	No	Public schools only
Washington	No	No	
West Virginia	No	No	
Wisconsin	No	No	
Wyoming	No	No	

State	Statute	*Requirements of State Certification of Teachers in Christian Schools?*
Alabama	Code of Ala. s 16-23-1 Code of Ala. s 16-23-2	Yes
	Instruction in private schools shall be by those holding certificates. Requirements are set by the State Board of Education (administrative regulations).	
Alaska	NO APPLICABLE STATUTORY REQUIREMENTS	
Arizona	NO APPLICABLE STATUTORY REQUIREMENTS	
Arkansas	NO APPLICABLE STATUTORY REQUIREMENTS	
California	NO APPLICABLE STATUTORY REQUIREMENTS	
Colorado	NO APPLICABLE STATUTORY REQUIREMENTS	
Connecticut	NO APPLICABLE STATUTORY REQUIREMENTS	
Delaware	NO APPLICABLE STATUTORY REQUIREMENTS	
District of Columbia	NO APPLICABLE STATUTORY REQUIREMENTS	
Florida	NO APPLICABLE STATUTORY REQUIREMENTS (Note: Chapter 247 of the Florida Statutes which established "minimum standards" for private schools, including certification of private school teachers, was repealed by Laws 1969, c. 69-106 s 32)	
Georgia	NO APPLICABLE STATUTORY REQUIREMENTS	
Hawaii	NO APPLICABLE STATUTORY REQUIREMENTS	
Idaho	NO APPLICABLE STATUTORY REQUIREMENTS	
Illinois	NO APPLICABLE STATUTORY REQUIREMENTS	
Indiana	NO APPLICABLE STATUTORY REQUIREMENTS	
Iowa	NO APPLICABLE STATUTORY REQUIREMENTS	

State	Statute	Requirements of State Certification of Teachers in Christian Schools?
Kansas	NO APPLICABLE STATUTORY REQUIREMENTS	
Kentucky	KRS 161.030	*Yes

Requires Bachelor's Degree from accredited university.
*On face of statute. State minimum standards (which
included teacher certification) held unconstitutional
in Kentucky v. Rudasill (78 SC 642 TG) 1979

Louisiana	NO APPLICABLE STATUTORY REQUIREMENTS	
Maine	20 MRSA §1751	A certification of teachers in non-public schools is required for schools that accept public funds for tuition.

Requires good moral character.
Elementary school teachers must have training in
physiology and hygiene with special emphasis on
effects of alcohol stimulants and narcotics on the
human system.
NOT APPLICABLE TO CHRISTIAN SCHOOLS
REJECTING PUBLIC FUNDS.

Maryland	NO APPLICABLE STATUTORY REQUIREMENTS	
Massachusetts	NO APPLICABLE STATUTORY REQUIREMENTS	
Michigan	MSA §15-1923	Yes

Same requirements as would qualify teachers to
instruct in public schools.

Minnesota	NO APPLICABLE STATUTORY REQUIREMENTS	
Mississippi	NO APPLICABLE STATUTORY REQUIREMENTS	
Missouri	NO APPLICABLE STATUTORY REQUIREMENTS	
Montana	NO APPLICABLE STATUTORY REQUIREMENTS	

State	Statute	Requirements of State Certification of Teachers in Christian Schools?
Nebraska	79 NEB. REV. STAT. § 1701	Yes
	Certification of teachers in non-public schools is the same as for public schools.	
Nevada	NO APPLICABLE STATUTORY REQUIREMENTS	
New Hampshire	NO APPLICABLE STATUTORY REQUIREMENTS	
New Jersey	NO APPLICABLE STATUTORY REQUIREMENTS	
New Mexico	NO APPLICABLE STATUTORY REQUIREMENTS	
New York	NO APPLICABLE STATUTORY REQUIREMENTS	
North Carolina	NO APPLICABLE STATUTORY REQUIREMENTS (Note: Article 32 of the N.C. Statutes which established "minimum standards" including teacher certification, was repealed by ratification of Senate Bill 383 in 1979 with regard to Christian schools.)	
North Dakota	NO APPLICABLE STATUTORY REQUIREMENTS	
Ohio	OHIO. REV. CODE ANN. 3301.071	*Yes
	*Requires Bachelor's Degree from accredited college or university on face of statute. State Minimum Standards (which included teacher certification) held unconstitutional in State of Ohio v. Whisner, 47 Ohio St. 2d 181.(1976).	
Oklahoma	NO APPLICABLE STATUTORY REQUIREMENTS	
Oregon	NO APPLICABLE STATUTORY REQUIREMENTS	
Pennsylvania	NO APPLICABLE STATUTORY REQUIREMENTS	
Rhode Island	NO APPLICABLE STATUTORY REQUIREMENTS	
South Carolina	NO APPLICABLE STATUTORY REQUIREMENTS	

State	Statute	Requirements of State Certification of Teachers in Christian Schools?
South Dakota	S.D. COMPILED LAWS § 13-4-2	Yes

"No person shall be permitted to teach in any non-public school any of the courses prescribed to be taught in the public schools unless such person shall hold a certificate entitling him to teach the same course in the public schools of this state."

State	Statute	
Tennessee	NO APPLICABLE STATUTORY REQUIREMENTS	
Texas	NO APPLICABLE STATUTORY REQUIREMENTS	
Utah	NO APPLICABLE STATUTORY REQUIREMENTS	
Vermont	NO APPLICABLE STATUTORY REQUIREMENTS	
Virginia	NO APPLICABLE STATUTORY REQUIREMENTS	
Washington	NO APPLICABLE STATUTORY REQUIREMENTS	
West Virginia	NO APPLICABLE STATUTORY REQUIREMENTS	
Wisconsin	NO APPLICABLE STATUTORY REQUIREMENTS	
Wyoming	NO APPLICABLE STATUTORY REQUIREMENTS	

YEAR	CASE AND CITE	SCHOOL	MAJOR POINTS CONCLUDED
1923	Meyer v. Nebraska (262 U.S. 390)	Lutheran	*Right of school to determine curriculum *Right of teacher to teach *Right of parents to hire him *Control of parents over education of child *Validity of compulsory attendance laws
1925	Pierce v. Society of Sisters (268 U.S. 510)	Roman Catholic	*Control of parents over education of child *Validity of compulsory attendance laws *Right to attend church schools *Power of state to reasonably regulate all schools *Power of state to inspect, supervise, and examine teachers and pupils
1930	Cochran v. Louisiana (281 U.S. 370)	All religious schools	*Power of state to provide free textbooks of a secular nature for the child's benefit
1934	Hamilton v. Regents (293 U.S. 245)	University of California	*Free Exercise clause applied to states through Fourteenth Amendment *No right to a religious exemption from a mandated course in a state university
1938	Johnson v. Deerfield (306 U.S. 621)	Public	*Upheld mandatory "flag salute" in public schools over religious objections
1940	Minersville v. Gobitis (310 U.S. 586)	Public	*Upheld mandatory "flag salute" in public schools over religious objections
1943	West Virginia v. Barnette (319 U.S. 583)	Public	*Reversed the two previous decisions and found the mandatory "flag salute" unconstitutional *Reaffirmed application of Free Exercise clause to the states through the Fourteenth Amendment

YEAR	CASE AND CITE	SCHOOL	MAJOR POINTS CONCLUDED
1947	Everson v. Board of Education (330 U.S. 1)	All religious schools	*Power of state to provide bus transportation for the child's benefit *Establishment Clause applied to states through Fourteenth Amendment *Mandated state neutrality toward religious schools because of the wall of separation between church and state *State power to impose secular educational requirements
1948	McCollum v. Board of Education (333 U.S. 203)	Public	*Reaffirmed application of Establishment Clause to the states through the Fourteenth Amendment *Reaffirmed wall of separation *Struck down religious "released time" instruction in public schools *Stated emphatically that public education must be secular education
1952	Doremus v. Board of Education (342 U.S. 429)	Public	*Right to hold daily Bible reading in public schools
1952	Zorach v. Clauson (343 U.S. 306)	Public	*Released time religious instruction upheld for public school students off campus *Reaffirmed neutrality doctrine and added the accomodation doctrine *Reaffirmed wall of separation
1962	Ingel v. Vitale (370 U.S. 421)	Public	*Struck down mandatory prayer *Reaffirmed neutrality doctrine *Reaffirmed wall of separation
1963	Abington v. Schempp Murray v. Curlett (374 U.S. 203)	Public	*Famous prayer and Bible reading case featuring Madalyn Murray O'Hair *Struck down required prayer and Bible reading *Reaffirmed neutrality doctrine *Reaffirmed wall of separation

YEAR	CASE AND CITE	SCHOOL	MAJOR POINTS CONCLUDED
1967	Garber v. Kansas (389 U.S. 51)	Amish	*Decision allowed to stand which denied right to home instruction and attendance at an Amish school
1968	Board of Education v. Allen (392 U.S. 326)	All religious schools	*Power of state to lend textbooks to children in church schools *Reaffirmed child benefit doctrine *Reaffirmed neutrality doctrine *Reaffirmed wall of separation *Interpreted Pierce as requiring attendance at school meeting state-imposed requirements as to quality and nature of curriculum *Power of state to require minimum hours of instruction, specify teacher training, and prescribe subjects *Reaffirmed rejection of home instruction *State has proper interest in how schools perform their secular educational function *Court does not agree that all teaching in a church school is religious
1968	Epperson v. Arkansas (393 U.S. 97)	Public	*Court struck down "anti-evolution" statute *Reaffirmed neutrality doctrine
1971	Lemon v. Kurtzman (403 U.S. 602) (Lemon I)	All religious schools	*State salary supplement to teachers unconstitutional *Reimbursement to school for teacher salaries, textbooks, and instructional materials unconstitutional *Excessive entanglement doctrine propounded *Applied tax case precedent to education to evolve a three-fold test: 1. Statute must have a secular legislative purpose 2. Primary effect must neither advance nor inhibit religion 3. Must not foster excessive government entanglement with religion

YEAR	CASE AND CITE	SCHOOL	MAJOR POINTS CONCLUDED
	(Lemon v. Kurtzman—Lemon I) Cont.		*Reaffirmed state power to maintain minimum standards *Established test of "pervasive sectarianism" (extent to which religion permeates a school) *Reaffirmed compulsory attendance laws *Established test of "divisive political potential," an expansion of the entanglement doctrine *Affirmed modified wall of separation

1971	Tilton v. Richardson (403 U.S. 672)	Church related colleges and universities	*Upheld federal construction grants for buildings used for secular purposes
			*Reaffirmed test of "political divisiveness"
			*Applied the three-fold test of "Lemon I"
			  1. Secular legislative purpose
			  2. Primary effect
			  3. Entanglement
			*Reaffirmed test of "pervasive sectarianism"
			*Held that elementary and secondary church schools are more likely to have a pervasive religious nature than schools of higher learning

1972	Brusca v. State Board of Education (405 U.S. 1050)	Public	*For a state to fund a free public school system and refuse to equally fund church schools does not violate free exercise rights
1972	Wisconsin v. Yoder (406 U.S. 205)	Amish	*Reaffirmed power of state to impose reasonable regulations *Reaffirmed parents' rights to provide equivalent education in a private school *State's interest is not totally free from a balancing process when it impinges other rights *Must be state interest of sufficient magnitude to override religious interests *Only state interests of the highest order not otherwise served may override free exercise *Belief and manner of life must be inseparable to be protectable *Religious activities are often subject to state regulation to promote health, safety, and general welfare

	(Wisconsin v. Yoder) Cont.		*An apparently neutral regulation is not neutral if it unduly burdens free exercise *Reaffirmed compulsory attendance laws generally in order to provide an informed electorate and self-reliant citizenry *Primary role of parents in upbringing of children is beyond debate
1972	Biklen v. Board of Education (406 U.S. 951)	Public	*Public school teacher may be required to take an oath of loyalty to the state and nation in spite of religious objections
1972	Essex v. Wolman (409 U.S. 808)	All religious schools	*Reaffirmed doctrine of entanglement *Parents of children in church schools may not receive tuition reimbursements from the state
1973	Lemon v. Kurtzman (411 U.S. 192) (Lemon II)	All religious schools	*Final resolution of Lemon I applicable to that case
1973	Norwood v. Harrison (413 U.S. 455)	All religious schools	*Reaffirmed provision of textbooks to children in church schools under the child benefit theory *Established that textbooks may not be supplied to church schools with racially discriminatory policies *Reaffirmed under Pierce and Yoder that state's role in the education of its citizens must yield to rights of parents to provide equivalent education in private schools of parents' choice *Constitution may compel toleration of private discrimination in some schools *Reaffirmed that religious schools pursue two goals—religious instruction and secular education

YEAR	CASE AND CITE	SCHOOL	MAJOR POINTS CONCLUDED
1973	Commission for Public Education v. Nyquist (413 U.S. 756)	All religious schools	*Reaffirmed modified wall of separation *Reaffirmed three-fold test of Lemon I: 1. Secular legislative purpose 2. Primary effect 3. Entanglement *Reaffirmed that church schools perform secular educational functions *State grants to repair and maintain church facilities for health and safety of children are unconstitutional *Tax benefit to parents of children in church schools is unconstitutional *State law interfering with parents' right to have child in a church school violates free exercise
1973	Levitt v. Committee for Public Education (413 U.S. 476)	All religious schools	*State reimbursement to church schools for cost of mandated testing and record-keeping held unconstitutional *Reaffirmed reasoning cf Lemon I and, in particular, the "primary effect" test
1973	Hunt v. McNair (413 U.S. 734)	Religious colleges	*Upheld state construction grants for buildings used for secular purposes *Reaffirmed three-fold test of Lemon I: 1. Secular legislative purpose 2. Primary effect 3. Entanglement *Reaffirmed test of "pervasive sectarianism" (extent to which religion permeates a school)
1973	Sloan v. Lemon (413 U.S. 825)	All church schools	*Tuition reimbursement to parents of children in church schools held unconstitutional *Reaffirmed reasoning of Lemon I
1974	Marburger v. Public Funds (417 U.S. 961)	All religious schools	*Court, without opinion, upheld lower court finding based on entanglement that state could not reimburse to parents the cost of secular textbooks, instructional materials, and supplies

YEAR	CASE AND CITE	SCHOOL	MAJOR POINTS CONCLUDED
1975	Meek v. Pittenger (421 U.S. 349)	All religious schools	*Reaffirmed three-fold test of Lemon I: 1. Secular legislative purpose 2. Primary effect 3. Entanglement *State may not provide "auxiliary services" to children in church schools by financial assistance to the schools *Services which may not be financed include counseling, testing and psychological services, speech and hearing therapy, teaching for handicapped or remedial or disadvantaged students *Reaffirmed child benefit doctrine to allow state to provide secular textbooks *Held direct loan of instructional material and equipment to be unconstitutional
1976	Roemer v. Maryland (426 U.S. 736)	Religious colleges	*Reaffirmed three-fold test of Lemon I: 1. Secular legislative purpose 2. Primary effect 3. Entanglement *Upheld an annual subsidy grant to church colleges if funds are used for secular purposes *State effort to supervise and control teaching of religion in supposedly secular classes would create entanglement violation *Reaffirmed "divisive political potential" doctrine which is an expansion of entanglement *Reaffirmed test of "pervasive sectarianism"
1977	Wolman v. Walter (Slip Opinion No. 76——496)	All religious schools	*Reaffirmed three-fold test of Lemon I: 1. Secular legislative purpose 2. Primary effect 3. Entanglement *Reaffirmed that state may provide secular textbooks to children in church schools *Reaffirmed that under compulsory attendance requirements, state may insure adequate secular education

YEAR	CASE AND CITE	SCHOOL	MAJOR POINTS CONCLUDED
	(Wolman v. Walter) Cont.		*State may provide health services to all children in church schools to include doctors, nursing, dental, optometric, as well as diagnostic speech and hearing services *Also under health services, state has authority to provide objective psychological testing methods to students in need of treatment *Children in church schools found to have needs may be given therapeutic services, guidance services, and remedial services by employees of the Board of Education or Board of Health, but these services must be administered off the premises of church school *Reaffirmed provision of instructional material to be unconstitutional *State expenditure of funds to provide field trips is unconstitutional
1977	New York v. Cathedral Academy (Slip Opinion No. 76—616)	Roman Catholic	*Final resolution of Levitt v. Committee for Public Education (413 U.S. 476) applicable to that case
1979	N.L.R.B. v. Catholic Bishop of Chicago (Slip Opinion No. 77—752)	Roman Catholic	*N.L.R.B. may not attempt to distinguish between schools which are "completely religious" and those which are "merely religiously associated" *N.L.R.B. may not arbitrate charges of unfair labor practices in church schools *Reaffirmed entanglement doctrine